Lynn Abr   merfield

The expansion of research into the history of women and gender since the
1970s has changed the face of history. Using the insights of feminist theory and
of historians of women, gender historians have explored the configuration in
the past of gender identities and relations between the sexes. They have also
investigated the history of sexuality and family relations, and analysed ideas and
ideals of masculinity and femininity. Yet gender history has not abandoned the
original, inspirational project of women's history: to recover and reveal the lived
experience of women in the past and the present.

The series Gender in History provides a forum for these developments. Its
historical coverage extends from the medieval to the modern periods, and
its geographical scope encompasses not only Europe and North America but
all corners of the globe. The series aims to investigate the social and cultural
constructions of gender in historical sources, as well as the gendering of
historical discourse itself. It embraces both detailed case studies of specific
regions or periods, and broader treatments of major themes. Gender in History
titles are designed to meet the needs of both scholars and students working in
this dynamic area of historical research.

The women's liberation movement in Scotland

Manchester University Press

Love, intimacy and power: marital relationships in Scotland, 1650–1850
Katie Barclay
(Winner of the 2012 Women's History Network Book Prize)

Modern women on trial: sexual transgression in the age of the flapper
Lucy Bland

Modern motherhood: women and family in England, c. 1945-2000
Angela Davis

Jewish women in Europe in the Middle Ages: a quiet revolution
Simha Goldin

The shadow of marriage: singleness in England, 1914–60
Katherine Holden

Women, dowries and agency: marriage in fifteenth-century Valencia
Dana Wessell Lightfoot

Women, travel and identity: Journeys by rail and sea, 1870–1940
Emma Robinson-Tomsett

Imagining Caribbean womanhood: race, nation and beauty contests, 1929–70
Rochelle Rowe

*Infidel feminism: secularism, religion and women's emancipation,
England 1830–1914*
Laura Schwartz

Being boys: working-class masculinities and leisure
Melanie Tebbutt

Queen and country: Same-sex desire in the British Armed Forces, 1939–45
Emma Vickers

*The 'perpetual fair': gender, disorder and urban amusement
in eighteenth-century London*
Anne Wohlcke

THE WOMEN'S LIBERATION MOVEMENT IN SCOTLAND

Sarah Browne

Manchester University Press

Published by Manchester University Press
Altrincham Street, Manchester M1 7JA, UK
www.manchesteruniversitypress.co.uk

British Library Cataloguing-in-Publication Data is available

ISBN 978 1 5261 1665 9 *paperback*

First published by Manchester University Press in hardback 2014

This edition first published 2017

Printed by Lightning Source

For my parents,
Janice and Jervis

Contents

List of tables

List of figures

Acknowledgements

First and foremost, I want to thank those who agreed to be interviewed. I learnt a lot from each interviewee – completing this research certainly 'raised my consciousness'. The interviews will be deposited in Glasgow Women's Library for future researchers to use. I would also like to thank Aileen Christianson, Nadine Harrison, Mary Henderson, Elspeth McLean, Paula Jennings, Fiona Mackay, Siân Reynolds and Norman Watson for giving me access to source material. This book began its life as a PhD thesis under the supervision of Callum Brown and Perry Willson at the University of Dundee. This was an incredibly supportive environment in which to explore my ideas. In particular I would like to thank Callum Brown and Jim Tomlinson for their willingness to discuss my ideas and for providing me with opportunities to teach, and I would also like to thank Billy Kenefick for sparking my interest in women's history. I will always be very grateful to the Carnegie Trust for the Universities of Scotland for funding my PhD studies as without this funding I would not have been able to complete doctoral research. Moreover, I am indebted to Esther Breitenbach for providing me with source material and contact information, reading a draft and, more importantly, for continually offering me encouragement and support. Of course, all errors remain my own.

While converting my thesis into a book I was employed as a Teaching Associate in History at the University of Nottingham. I am grateful to the students who asked interesting and informed questions and to Elizabeth Harvey who provided me with support during periods of doubt and encouraged me to believe that my research was making a valuable contribution. I have also appreciated the support of the postgraduate community at the University of Nottingham, especially my conversations with members of the Gender Studies reading group and my MA module on Gender and Sexuality. The staff at Manchester University Press, especially Emma Brennan, have also been incredibly helpful and supportive and their guidance has been appreciated throughout this process.

To piece together the story of the women's liberation movement in Scotland I travelled the length and breadth of Britain, from the University of Aberdeen archives to the Women's Library in London. I feel very lucky to have been given the opportunity to conduct research in the Women's Library before its move to the LSE. While it is great that the collection remains open, the closure of the Women's Library building is such a sad loss. Archive and library visits were made easier because of the helpful staff, and Carole McCallum at Glasgow Caledonian University archives deserves a special mention for being an enormous help. Thanks also to the Trustees of the National Library of Scotland for granting permission to use material from their collections, as well as Esther Breitenbach and Bill McLoughlin (formerly of D. C. Thomson) for granting permission for the use of images. I have attempted to locate all copyright holders of material used in this book but please contact me to let me know if material appears without copyright permission, as I would appreciate being able to acknowledge this in future publications.

Being a member of various women's and feminist groups provided me with support throughout this process. For this I would like to thank all those who were involved in Engender's 'Women Thinking Equality' and 'Inspiring Women', Dundee Women's Festival group, Nottingham Radical Readers and the Nottingham Feminist Action Network. My conversations with members of these groups have informed and influenced this book. Likewise my family and friends kept me going and remained patient when it was clear that all I wanted to talk about was 'the book'; in particular, Christine and Keith Matthews who have been a constant source of support throughout this process even when they had more important things to think about. The friendship and encouragement of Susanne Sklepek-Hatton (and Tilda) and Shivani Gupta has also made this whole process much easier. I also wish to thank my sister, Emma for reminding me that it would all be worth it in the end. In this regard the WLM was correct: sisterhood is powerful! My nephews Peter and Christopher also provided much needed distraction and reminded me that there are more important things in life than writing a book. Final thanks must go to my parents, Janice and Jervis, for not only encouraging me to question but also for supporting my interests in history and politics. It is not going too far to say that without their love and support this book would have never been written.

Note on the text

For extracts from oral history transcripts used in the following text: a dash (–) indicates a hesitation; an ellipsis (…) denotes a section of the transcript that has been omitted because it did not add to the quotation. Where transcripts are marked with * in the notes this indicates that a pseudonym has been used as the interviewee has requested anonymity.

List of abbreviations

CP	Communist Party
CR	Consciousness-raising
DWCA	Doctors for a Woman's Choice on Abortion
EIS	Educational Institute of Scotland
EOC	Equal Opportunities Commission
EPA	Equal Pay Act
IMG	International Marxist Group
IWY	International Women's Year
NAC	National Abortion Campaign
NHS	National Health Service
NUS	National Union of Students
RCC	Rape Crisis Centre
RTN	Reclaim the Night
SAC	Scottish Abortion Campaign
SCOW	Scottish Convention of Women
SDA	Sex Discrimination Act
SNP	Scottish National Party
SPUC	Society for the Protection of Unborn Children
STUC	Scottish Trades Union Congress
SWLJ	*Scottish Women's Liberation Journal*
TUC	Trades Union Congress
WA	Women's Aid
WAC	Women's Advisory Committee
WCA	Women Citizens' Association
WIRES	Women's Information and Referral Service
WLM	Women's liberation movement

Introduction

Germaine Greer had published *The Female Eunuch* in 1970 but none of us had read it. We were not sophisticated. We were northerners. We didn't live in a big city like Manchester, and feminism seemed not to have reached us.[1]

The women's liberation movement (WLM) has often been linked with the 'big city'. Jeanette Winterson's comment is, therefore, particularly revealing in terms of the dominant perception that women's liberation was a movement of the metropolis. Yet it is evident that there were active women's liberation groups throughout Britain during the 1970s: from Brighton in the south to the Shetland Islands in the far north, and everywhere in between.[2] By unravelling national 'British' accounts, we can see that women's liberation attracted a diverse range of women in an equally diverse range of locations throughout the British Isles. This book shows that the movement, far from being a solely metropolitan phenomenon, actually extended its reach beyond the 'big cities' of England and to communities throughout Scotland.

Indeed, it would seem that the WLM has experienced an identity crisis. On the one hand media portrayals have often relied upon stereotypes to characterise WLM campaigners: bra-burners, man-haters, marriage-wreckers and the most unoriginal of all – the short-haired, dungaree-wearing lesbian.[3] On the other hand, academic accounts have mainly been written by those who were feminist activists in the 1970s influenced by their experiences within the movement.[4] While these participant accounts are important and useful, it is clear that a broader historical perspective of the WLM is required. A historical perspective which interrogates the media portrayals and participant accounts leads to greater understanding of this important social movement in Britain during the post-1945 period. In providing the first book-length account of the WLM in Scotland this publication contributes to complicating our understanding of feminist politics in post-1945 Britain.

Along with the suffrage campaign, women's liberation activism is one of the most renowned aspects of women's political history. At first glance, therefore, it would appear that we are familiar with its story. Indeed, for many years a basic narrative has dominated most accounts: the WLM emerged in the late 1960s and proved to be an extremely influential and important social movement throughout the 1970s. Women's groups were established throughout America and Western Europe in the late 1960s and early 1970s. Frustrated by their limited opportunities and inspired by radical political discussions amongst students, the civil rights movement and the New Left, these women began to question the unique roots of their oppression. The movement combined personal issues with political discussions and helped to raise awareness about domestic violence, rape and abortion, amongst many other issues. Indeed the WLM was important in shaping and contributing to public discussions about women's role which led to the implementation of a raft of 'progressive' legislation throughout the 1970s, including in Britain the Equal Pay Act (1970), the Sex Discrimination Act (1975) and the Domestic Violence Act (1976).[5]

Beyond this basic narrative there is little detail about the British movement. In contrast to the American WLM, for example, research into the history of the movement in Britain has been surprisingly slow to emerge. Historians have tended to rely on those first-hand accounts which were written by prominent activists of the movement. These participant accounts, including important insights from Sheila Rowbotham, Michèle Roberts, Anna Coote and Beatrix Campbell, have revealed how the movement was established and developed.[6] But, as Lynne Segal has pointed out, while these publications are extremely valuable, 'these historians are well aware of the dangers of their proximity to their own research.'[7] Apart from these publications, and books by David Bouchier and Anna Coote and Beatrix Campbell, published in 1982 and 1983 respectively, there have been no other book-length historical studies published on the British WLM.[8] This is beginning to change as researchers (mainly born after the height of women's liberation activism) have started to collect oral histories of the movement and to search archives for women's liberation pamphlets, newsletters and booklets. This research has revealed the experiences of grass-roots activists and more importantly has led to a shift in focus away from prominent members of the movement.[9]

Yet it remains the case that research into the WLM in Britain is desperately needed. There are a number of possible reasons for this situation. An important factor may be that the 1970s themselves have only recently attracted the attention of historical researchers. Books by historians and commentators such as Howard Sounes, Andy Beckett and Dominic Sandbrook illustrate an increasing interest in the decade.[10] Beckett's account has been particularly helpful in providing a context to the 1970s, shifting some of the focus away from institutional politics, and highlighting the importance of social movements in shaping the political agenda and culture of the decade. He said:

> [For] many political people in Britain in the 1970s, the time was dominated not by Heath and Thatcher and Callaghan but by the rise

of environmentalism, or feminism, or the Gay Liberation Front, or Rock Against Racism, and other new forms of politics with their own rhythms and preoccupations, only sometimes connected to those of the House of Commons.'[11]

Indeed, it is important that future research into the WLM should be contextualised in order that its impact can be assessed.

Another possible reason why there has not been more written about the WLM from a historical perspective was the understandable reluctance of feminists, at the time, to share their memories and material with some interested academic researchers. For example, David Bouchier's book *The Feminist Challenge*, which was published in the 1980s, detailed the origins, campaigns and membership of the movement in the USA and Britain. However, while writing this book during the early 1980s he met intense resistance from the movement. The 'A Women's Place Collective' wrote a letter to the WLM newsletter *WIRES* in September 1981, seeking to notify women that they had received a letter from Bouchier which outlined his proposed research and asked feminists to allow him access to material so that he could write his book. The collective was outraged because Bouchier was a man and had been commissioned to write an 'outsider's history' of modern feminism. As the letter concluded, the collective felt this was 'another attempt to define and interpret our experiences for us'.[12] Some feminists were frightened that their experiences would be used to further academic careers and, quite understandably, they wanted someone from the movement to write their history.

By far the most prolific writer on the WLM in Britain has been Sheila Rowbotham. She has combined her academic background with her personal experiences as a women's liberation activist to provide insightful analyses of many of the major issues confronting the WLM. Of central importance to any understanding of the personal politics of the WLM is her memoir *Promise of a Dream*, which offers important background information into the movement's beginnings against the backdrop of her own personal growth as a feminist. The personal narratives of individual feminists are important when considering the development of this movement as its politics was infused with personal experience, as summed up by one slogan which claimed 'the personal is political'.

While these participant accounts have proved to be valuable, a number of important gaps remain. In order to fill these gaps and to challenge the portrayals of the WLM a new generation of researchers has emerged. They have begun to question the accepted narrative of feminist politics in the 1970s. This new research was initially led by Eve Setch, whose article on the London Women's Liberation Workshop questioned the accounts produced by people such as Bouchier, Rowbotham and Coote and Campbell. She argued that these writers were guilty of perpetuating a rather generic account of the explosion of the movement on to the political scene during the late 1960s and early 1970s, gathering momentum on university campuses, before fizzling out in the late 1970s and early 1980s as a result of irreconcilable differences primarily over radical and socialist feminism, and disagreements over the importance of sexualities to the feminist agenda. Setch has challenged this view, arguing that, far from division being a drawback for the movement at large, it actually helped it to flourish and develop, and that division had been at the heart of the movement since its very beginnings.[13] The evidence from Scotland, in many ways, complements Setch's view. Following on from Setch, Jeska Rees and Natalie Thomlinson have sought to understand the impact of radical and revolutionary feminism and race on the movement.[14] These accounts have done much to complicate accepted narratives of feminism in the 1970s.

This book adds to these findings by arguing that simplistic accounts of the rise and fall of feminist politics have been perpetuated by historians' use of the 'waves' of activism. The term 'first wave' is used to describe the time of the suffrage campaign of the late nineteenth and early twentieth centuries and 'second wave' for the activities of feminists involved in the WLM during the 1970s. Recently historians have begun to question the helpfulness of these labels but this discussion has tended to focus on their impact on our understanding of women's groups which were active during the period 1918–68. This has led to historians rightly arguing that the 'waves' model has led to the activities of these groups being overlooked because of their inability to fit into the definitions of the first or second wave of feminism.[15] It is argued here not only that this has limited the study of the women's movement in the period 1918–68 but that it has also led to a rather simplistic view of the development of feminism, and especially the WLM, in the 1970s and beyond. While Marian Sawer and Sandra Grey argued that the second wave label helped to create an understanding that 'there has always been and always will be a women's movement, it is just its strength and visibility that varies', it is argued here that it instead encourages a perception that feminists have only been active twice; once their aims had been achieved they ended their campaigns and feminism became moribund.[16] As we will see, by looking at case studies of women's liberation activism, the story of the movement is more complex than previously assumed, and the second wave label has failed to encompass adequately the continuities which existed between various women's groups active throughout the twentieth century, and also left-wing activists during the 1970s.[17] Indeed, this argument has recently emerged in research about the movement in an international context. In the USA, for example, Stephanie Gilmore illustrated that a grass-roots perspective encourages historians to question the ways in which the movement has been characterised, especially with regard to political ideologies and the usefulness of the second wave of feminism metaphor.[18]

Indeed, Jane Lewis has recognised that important links existed between the WLM and those promoting social reform in the 1960s. Whilst some work is beginning to emerge on this theme, there is a need for future researchers to undertake analysis of the connections between specific campaigns started before and during the 1970s.[19] From the literature which exists, it would seem that many of the issues women's groups focused on before the arrival of the WLM were often very similar to those which women's liberation activists campaigned on, albeit with more emphasis on direct action than the established women's groups, such as the Townswomen's Guilds and Women's Institutes, of the 1950s and 1960s. Given the links between the campaigns of the WLM and other women's groups and campaigns why, then, did the second wave label emerge? Many women's liberation activists proudly used the label, believing it linked them to the first wave of the suffrage campaigns, which had a stronger focus on direct action than the women's groups of the interwar period. Furthermore, women's liberation activists, on the whole, were unaware of the work being undertaken by other women's groups. Feminist activists of the 1970s believed that they were radically new and different. Reflecting on this issue, Ellen Galford, an activist in the Glasgow women's liberation group, recalled that 'we all thought, presumably being kids, that we had invented the wheel but in fact you sort of look back and the same debates were going on with the Pankhurst sisters and dear knows well before that'.[20] This sense of reinventing the wheel was evoked by another interviewee, Kath Davies. Davies was a member of the Scottish Convention of Women, which was instrumental in the 1970s in building coalitions between those aligned with the WLM and members of other women's groups such as the Soroptimists and Church of Scotland Woman's Guilds. Working with older women through this organisation, Kath realised:

> what they'd already been involved in – and some of them had been working for change in the pensions systems since the twenties – there was a lot of expertise, an enormous amount of knowledge [there] and you couldn't let that go and start reinventing the wheel. You know, in 1973 I think we thought not only had we just discovered the wheel but we were going to be the ones who would – just wheel [inequalities] away!'[21]

For those few activists who were aware of the work of others women's groups, they tended to dismiss their work as irrelevant to their own campaigns. In her review of the Scottish Convention of Women's conference in 1978, women's liberation activist Nina Woodcock felt that 'in a University lecture theatre full of middle aged, middle class women I found it impossible to say anything (they probably wouldn't have listened anyway)'.[22] The WLM's use of the second wave label was, therefore, a way not only to link their activism with the suffrage era and to illustrate that theirs was an ongoing struggle but also to distinguish their work from groups active during their mothers' generation.[23] Nevertheless, as this book will suggest, the second wave label, in terms of the way it is currently understood, is problematic for histories of the WLM.

Structure of the book

Using oral history and documentary sources, this book charts the history of the WLM in Scotland. The biographical notes in Appendix I provide information on the backgrounds of the women who were interviewed. This book has two central arguments. First it presses for a more representative historiography in which material from other places outside of the large women's liberation centres, such as London, are included. It is hoped that this will enable histories to challenge the dominant media portrayal that it was a London-based movement. Second, it is argued that it is important to look at case studies, as not only do they enrich our knowledge about women's liberation but they also challenge the way the British movement has been portrayed by both participants and historians. More representative historical accounts are essential if we are to map and understand the reach of feminist activism throughout the British Isles. References to the Scottish movement have been disinclined to look in depth at regional variations between groups. A major theme of this book is to draw out these variations and to look at how the wider community interacted with local women's liberation groups.[24]

As this is the first full-scale account of the WLM in Scotland this book has been structured chronologically but distinct themes are discussed in each chapter. The first chapter contextualises the subject, summarising recent research into the movement in the United Kingdom. As more research is being conducted we are beginning to map feminist groups active in the 1970s throughout the British Isles in order to assess the continuities and differences between regional centres. Building on this evidence, the second chapter looks at the roots of the movement by offering portrayals of the women who went on to form women's liberation groups in Scotland. Using oral history evidence, it looks at their early experiences in life in order to understand how they related their personal and private experiences to political developments, and how they have subsequently come to understand the roots of the movement. To date there has been little research on who were the rank-and-file members of the WLM and their motivations for becoming involved. Yet it is clear that only by considering their early experiences can there be a greater understanding of what the WLM stood for, how it emerged and how its membership shaped the arguments of the movement.[25] Chapter 3 develops this theme, analysing the phenomenon of 'consciousness-raising' (CR) and the part it had to play in the WLM's development. Crucial to this chapter is a consideration of how feminists of the 1970s viewed this process and how they defined it. It also illustrates that CR groups were incredibly effective in recruiting new women and also in introducing complex feminist theories.

The desire to campaign is the focus of Chapter 4 where the impact of the groups in a local context is considered. Where, when and why women's liberation groups emerged form central themes for this chapter. The local political and cultural context was important in shaping the specific targets and campaigns for individual groups. These local workshops came together at national conferences and also worked together on major national publications, such as journals and pamphlets. Chapter 5 looks at these interactions. It is shown here how wider debates and discussions ongoing in the WLM internationally were interpreted in the Scottish movement, and seeks to understand the development of women's liberation politics from the mid-1970s onwards. The remaining two chapters of this book focus on campaigns taken up by the WLM in Scotland: to defend abortion rights (Chapter 6) and to campaign against violence against women (Chapter 7). Previous accounts of the WLM in Britain have attempted to grapple with the issues of division, single-issue campaigns and fragmentation. For example, David Bouchier in his book *The Feminist Challenge* appears to portray the WLM as divided, sectarian and weak *and* also diverse, creative and full of energy before concluding that fragmentation led to a weakening of the movement.[26] The final two chapters of this book revise this view, indicating that the fragmentation of the movement actually led to diversification. In some ways this was a positive development as by diversifying the WLM was able to extend the reach of feminism into other organisations and groups. In doing so, feminists of the WLM in Scotland were important in ensuring the voices of women north of the border were heard not only in the WLM in Britain but also in wider society.

While interrogating accounts of women's liberation, this book, at a basic level, helps to challenge the neglect of many publications to include evidence of feminist activism north of the border during the 1960s and beyond. This neglect has led to an assumption, by historians such as J.D. Young, that 'the middle-class Women's Movement was once again very weak in Scotland by comparison with the movement in England'.[27] Critics of this view were quick to emerge. For example in 1990 Elspeth King argued that 'it is alarming that the Scottish Women's Liberation Movement – because it chose on principle not to deal with the sensation-seeking tabloid journalists eager for stories on bra-burning – can be dismissed by Dr Young as scarcely having existed'.[28] Yet, despite King's protest, there is still little detail about the WLM in Scotland within the public domain. An article published in the Glasgow-based newspaper *The Herald* in 2007, which looked at the recently published autobiographies of prominent feminist campaigners Lynne Segal and Michèle Roberts and also discussed the WLM in Britain, illustrates this point. The only mention of Scotland was that during the early 1970s Scottish Women's Aid opened refuges in Edinburgh and Glasgow. Anyone reading this article would understandably have agreed with Young and naturally assumed that feminism failed to take hold north of the border in the 1970s.[29]

This book challenges this view by shining a light on to an often overlooked, but extremely important, episode in the history of British politics. In offering the first book-length account of the WLM in Scotland it not only complicates existing narratives of feminism in this period but also hopes to stimulate new research into the movement. It has often been observed that the history of women's political action has been overlooked. Indeed Elspeth King's clarion call from over twenty years ago is, unfortunately, still relevant today:

> there is a clear message for all women who were or are involved in the movement: take your historical papers, correspondence, minute books, cuttings and relevant information and deposit them in a Scottish library or archive before it's too late. Take your T-shirts, your badges, jewellery and posters to your local museum and demand that they be preserved for posterity. Do not be written out of history.[30]

This book hopes to contribute to this process.

Notes

1 J. Winterson, *Why Be Happy When You Could Be Normal?* (London, 2012), p. 132.
2 Indeed Winterson's reflection probably has more to do with class as we will see that the WLM, as a predominantly middle-class movement, failed to reach out successfully to working-class women.
3 C. Rose, 'Opinion: The Liberation Look', *The Times*, 29 November 2009. Erin Pizzey also recalled that 'All the photographs in the newspapers showed feminist women

wearing dungarees or boiler suits with flat heavy boots', *This Way to the Revolution: A Memoir* (London, 2011), p. 22.

4 L. Abrams, *Oral History Theory* (London, 2010), p. 98.

5 For accounts of the WLM in a British context see multiple publications by Sheila Rowbotham but especially: *Women's Consciousness, Man's World* (Harmondsworth, 1973); *The Past Is Before Us: Feminism in Social Action since the 1960s* (London, 1989) and *A Century of Women: The History of Women in Britain and the United States* (London, 1999). Other accounts include D. Bouchier, *The Feminist Challenge: The Movement for Women's Liberation in Britain and the United States* (London, 1983), and A. Coote and B. Campbell, *Sweet Freedom: The Struggle for Women's Liberation* (London, 1982).

6 S. Rowbotham, *Promise of a Dream: Remembering the 1960s* (London, 2001), M. Roberts, *Paper Houses: A Memoir of the 70s and Beyond* (London, 2007), and Coote and Campbell, *Sweet Freedom*.

7 L. Segal, *Why Feminism? Gender, Psychology, Politics* (Cambridge, 1999), p. 10.

8 Bouchier, *The Feminist Challenge*, and Coote and Campbell, *Sweet Freedom*.

9 E. Setch, 'The Face of Metropolitan Feminism: The London Women's Liberation Workshop, 1969-79', *Twentieth Century British History*, 13:2 (2002), pp. 171-90, J. Rees, '"Are You a Lesbian?": Challenges in Recording and Analysing the Women's Liberation Movement in England', *History Workshop Journal*, 69 (Spring 2010), pp. 177-87; J. Rees, 'A Look Back at Anger: The Women's Liberation Movement in 1978', *Women's History Review*, 19:3 (2010), pp. 337-56, S. Browne, '"A Veritable Hotbed of Feminism": Women's Liberation in St Andrews, Scotland, c. 1968-c. 1979', *Twentieth Century British History*, 23:1 (2012), pp. 100-23, and N. Thomlinson, 'The Colour of Feminism: White Feminists and Race in the Women's Liberation Movement', *History*, 97:327 (2012), pp. 453-75. See also unpublished work: J. Rees, 'All the Rage: Revolutionary Feminism in England, 1977-1983' (unpublished PhD thesis, University of Western Australia, 2007) and E. Setch 'The Women's Liberation Movement in Britain, 1969-79: Organisation, Creativity and Debate' (unpublished PhD thesis, University of London, Royal Holloway, 2000).

10 H. Sounes, *1970s: The Sights, Sounds and Ideas of a Brilliant Decade* (London, 2007), A. Beckett, *When the Lights Went Out: Britain in the 1970s* (London, 2009), and D. Sandbrook, *State of Emergency: The Way We Were: Britain 1970-1974* (London, 2010).

11 Beckett, *When the Lights Went Out*, p. 5.

12 *WIRES*, September 1981, p. 10.

13 Setch, 'The Face of Metropolitan Feminism', p. 171.

14 Rees, '"A Look Back At Anger"', and Thomlinson, 'The Colour of Feminism'.

15 P. Summerfield, 'The Women's Movement in Britain from the 1860s to the 1980s' in T. Cosslett, A. Easton and P. Summerfield (eds), *Women, Power and Resistance: An Introduction to Women's Studies* (Buckingham, 1996), p. 228. There is a growing body of work which questions the use of waves in the interwar period, yet less so for the postwar period. For the interwar period see, for example, J. Alberti, *Beyond Suffrage: Feminists in War and Peace 1914-1928* (London, 1989), C. Beaumont, 'Citizens Not Feminists: The Boundary Negotiated Between Citizenship and Feminism by Mainstream Women's Organisations in England, 1928-1939', *Women's History Review*, 9:2 (2000), pp. 411-29, and D. Spender, *There's Always Been A Women's Movement This Century* (London, 1993). In a Scottish context important research has been conducted

by Valerie Wright, 'Women's Organisations and Feminism in Interwar Scotland' (unpublished PhD thesis, University of Glasgow, 2008).

16 M. Sawer and S. Grey, 'Introduction' in S. Grey and M. Sawer (eds), *Women's Movements: Flourishing or in Abeyance?* (London, 2008), p. 2.

17 N.A. Hewitt, 'Introduction' in N.A. Hewitt (ed.), *No Permanent Waves: Recasting Histories of U.S. Feminism* (New Brunswick, 2010), p. 4.

18 S. Gilmore, *Groundswell: Grassroots Feminism in Postwar America* (New York, 2013).

19 J. Lewis, 'From Equality to Liberation: Contextualising the Emergence of the Women's Liberation Movement', B. Moore-Gilbert and J. Seed (eds), *Cultural Revolution?: The Challenge of the Arts in the 1960s* (London, 1992). Also argued by D.S. Myer, 'Restating the Woman Question – Women's Movements and State Restructuring' in L.A. Banaszak, K. Beckwith and D. Rucht, *Women's Movements Facing the Reconfigured State* (Cambridge, 2003), p. 289. Some work has been completed on these links: S.F. Browne and J.D. Tomlinson, 'A Women's Town: Dundee Women on the Public Stage' in J. D. Tomlinson and C. A. Whatley (eds), *Jute No More: Transforming Dundee* (Dundee, 2011); and C. Beaumont, 'The Personal Is Political: Voluntary Women's Organisations and Political Campaigning in the Postwar Years', unpublished conference paper, 'Women in British Politics', University of Lincoln, 6–7 May 2011.

20 Transcript of interview with Ellen Galford (EG), 2 April 2007, p. 10.

21 Transcript of interview with Kath Davies (KD), 12 December 2006, p. 9.

22 *MsPrint*, no. 2, November 1978, p. 27. Women's liberation newsletters and journals often did not provide publication details, including dates or issue or volume numbers. This is reflected in apparent inconsistencies in my references to them.

23 *The Second Wave – A Magazine of New Feminism*, 2:2 (1972), p. 1.

24 This approach is explored in more depth in Browne, '"A Veritable Hotbed of Feminism"'.

25 Oral history interviews were also conducted by the 'Sisterhood and After: The Women's Liberation Oral History' Project group. For more information: www.sussex.ac.uk/clhlwr/research/sisterhoodafter.

26 Bouchier, *The Feminist Challenge*, p. 208 and p. 217.

27 J.D. Young, *Women and Popular Struggles: A History of Scottish and English Working Class Women 1500–1984* (Edinburgh, 1985), p. 183.

28 E. King, 'Review of J.D. Young's *Women and Popular Struggles*' in S. Henderson and A. Mackay (eds), *Grit and Diamonds: Women in Scotland Making History 1980–1990* (Edinburgh, 1990), p. ix.

29 *The Glasgow Herald*, 17 August 2007, p. 22.

30 King, 'Review', p. ix.

1

The women's liberation movement in context

Historians are beginning to reassess and challenge the public portrayals of the 1970s. Recent publications by Andy Beckett, Dominic Sandbrook and Black, Pemberton and Thane indicate an increasing interest in this decade.[1] As they have concluded, the years between the governments of Edward Heath and Margaret Thatcher have tended to be overshadowed in historical accounts by the colourful 1960s. In comparison the 1970s loom large in public memory as a depressing age when political conflict and economic recession never seemed far away.[2] But this does the 1970s a disservice. As Sandbrook has correctly identified, 'many of the things we associate with the 1960s only gathered momentum in the first half of the [1970s]'.[3] However, media portrayals of the decade still persist such as the lights going out, rubbish piling up in the streets and a three-day working week. These have all led to 'a pervasive sense of crisis and discontent' which has continued to be associated with the decade right up to the present day.[4] But scratch beneath these images and evidence would suggest that the decade was far more complicated than this. If the 1970s are viewed from the perspective of protestors and political activists then it was an exciting and productive period for alternative politics. Indeed Black and Pemberton in their attempt to reassess the 1970s have argued that those who were 'seen as troublemakers of the 1970s can be read in different ways – in a wider context, and their actions as creative, democratic, demotic acts'.[5] This was especially true for many young women. Often described like the start of a great love affair, the early 1970s were a time of discovery and intense excitement.[6]

However in reassessing the 1970s historians must be cautious about declaring that it was the *most* important decade in our understanding of post-1945 Britain. While many activists viewed the 1970s differently from how the decade has subsequently been described, for the vast majority of people involvement in left-wing politics and protest movements was not part of their daily routines. But it is evident that there must be more recognition that the 1970s were 'about moments of possibility as well as periods of entropy' and that, while many people may not have become politically active, they were still affected by the changes which political and social movements campaigned for.[7] Indeed, these 'moments of possibility' were not restricted to women. Political activism flourished during this period, with many individuals active in a variety of different groups at the same time. Of central importance to these groups was the emergence of New Left thinking. With the fragmentation of the Communist Party in the late 1950s there was a proliferation of left-wing groups which sought to challenge the inflexibility of Communist thought and practice. The New Left was also characterised by its focus on the personal aspects of politicisation. Major theorists included Herbert Marcuse and Louis Althusser and these theories were promoted in Britain through the *New Left Review* and New Left Books (now Verso).[8] Consequently, New Left thinking influenced many sections of society, including, for example, psychiatry, the student movement, anti-Vietnam protest groups and anti-racist activism.[9]

These groups provided an important context to the emerging WLM, creating a radical political milieu in which protest methods and ideas were exchanged, and action was taken in solidarity. Central to these discussions was a focus on the personal aspects of politics, such as sexuality. For example the Gay Liberation Front (GLF) emerged in Britain in the early 1970s. It challenged existing reformist organisations by demanding that society should change its understanding and treatment of homosexuals, rather than homosexuals changing their lifestyles to fit in with society.[10] In this regard it seemed to be quite successful because, as Robinson has noted, the GLF changed 'the public face of lesbian and gay politics in Britain.'[11] As the 1970s progressed, women's liberation groups often supported the protests of groups like the GLF.

Theorising liberation

An important constituent of this emerging radical political milieu was the WLM. Influenced by this turn towards personal politics it produced a number of important texts and theories and helped to transform, or at the very least influence, the agendas of other social movements and groups of the time, often forcing many male activists to acknowledge that women suffered from particular forms of oppression. A major trend in recent historical research has been to shift attention away from the published texts of the movement and towards the activities of the grass-roots.[12] While this is clearly an important development in determining the impact of the movement and in understanding its diversity, it is evident that the ideas contained within feminist publications of the late 1960s and 1970s were significant not only in stimulating the movement but in giving feminist activists a sense of identity and a set of ideas to organise campaigns around. For example, Betty Friedan's 1963 publication *The Feminine Mystique* is often seen as being important in stimulating the rise of the WLM not only in the USA but elsewhere too. Indeed, McQuiston has argued this publication 'took the lid off the isolation of those "happy housewives" and lit a spark of revolution'.[13] Exposing the myth that American women were happy to remain in the home, Friedan urged women to campaign for equal rights. There are clear problems with asserting that paid employment would liberate women but this book is widely recognised as one of the most influential books of the twentieth century as it led many women to acknowledge for the first time that they were leading lives which made them unhappy.[14] Labelled as Friedan's European counterpart, Germaine Greer's *The Female Eunuch* was also highly influential and was clearly 'the key feminist tract' in many countries in Western Europe.[15] Its influence was such that feminism in the 1970s often became synonymous with one name: Germaine Greer.[16] This is interesting given that Greer was never directly involved in the WLM. But this publication's focus on sexuality and the body was a radical departure from most writings on gender and was, therefore, extremely novel in both its content and its approach.[17]

Other influential feminist writers included Juliet Mitchell, Kate Millett and Shulamith Firestone. Like Greer, Firestone also focused on the body and the personal aspects of politics. She moved the parameters of the debate about the oppression of women to focus more specifically on the cultural exploitation of women. Her most notable and controversial passage was on the ability of science to free women from the role of childbearing.[18] What these publications illustrate is a growing interest in 'the body' and women's personal freedom. Indeed during this period we can observe a shift amongst feminist campaigners from the importance attached to the notion of equality towards favouring liberation. The concept of liberation echoed developments in New Left thinking and allowed feminist activists to widen the campaign against female oppression to include all aspects of women's lives. Campaigns would no longer focus solely on women's public roles as the WLM highlighted the discrimination women also faced in the home and in relationships, successfully blurring the division between the public and the private.

These texts not only inspired women to adopt a feminist identity; they also helped to form new theories about women and feminism. Indeed much more research is needed in order to understand the different ideas which emerged from the WLM and how these ideas shaped understandings of feminism during the 1970s and beyond. Until recently women's liberation theories have tended to be described in an overly simplistic fashion, carving the movement up into two camps: radical and socialist feminists. Many accounts describe how socialist feminists believed that the purpose of their politics was to challenge capitalism and to address class divisions, at the same time as challenging the oppression of women. In contrast radical feminists believed that class was not the central division in society, instead preferring to emphasise the division between men and women. They argued that the women's movement should not be aimed towards a class war but should be attempting to overthrow patriarchy.[19] Radical feminism had emerged at the British women's liberation conference in 1972 when a group presented a paper which took a 'pro-woman line reminiscent of Redstockings'.[20] Throughout the 1970s supporters of these theories appeared to be jostling for position, each trying to make sure that one or the other would determine movement politics. This was an ongoing conversation for many women's movements in the USA and Western Europe but it was particularly important in Britain because of the prominence of class.[21] There were other ideologies, including, for example, revolutionary feminism, which Rees has described as the 'younger cousin' of radical feminism, but which is often mistakenly understood as the same ideology as radical feminism. Instead, revolutionary feminism emerged in the later 1970s after a group of Leeds-based women presented a conference paper which argued for the movement to focus on 'men as the enemy'.[22] As will be illustrated in this book, these ideological differences were never entirely clear cut in Scotland. Yet, while acknowledging the problems with simplistic labels, it is clear that these theories were very important in producing an understanding of women's liberation. These theories may not have been adopted wholeheartedly by every woman in the movement but they formed an important focus for discussions and led to fruitful debates about what the aims of the WLM should be.

Practical examples of women's liberation

While these ideas were important the practical example of the WLM in the USA also encouraged the growth of a movement in Britain. It was in the USA that women's liberation first emerged. Different reasons have been offered for the rise of women's liberation in the USA. Factors such as increasing numbers of women attending universities, rising prosperity, a backlash against a stultifying femininity which was an integral part of 1950s American society, and, arguably most importantly, the rise of social and political movements, such as the Civil Rights movement, the Students Non-Violent Co-ordinating Committee (SNCC) and groups campaigning against American participation in the increasingly unpopular Vietnam War.[23]

Women's liberation also arose out of the contradiction identified by Friedan in *The Feminine Mystique*. As more women were encouraged to go to university they found that upon graduation they were not expected to get a job or to have any career aspirations but were instead still expected to get married and to raise a family.[24] Many young women looked at their mothers' lives and demanded more. Their expectations were raised at the very point when New Left thinking was arguing for a more egalitarian society and more opportunities for the younger generation. These internal and external forces led to small groups of women beginning to meet to discuss their frustrations. From these discussions political action emerged. It was these actions which catapulted women's liberation from being a discussion topic amongst a small group of politically engaged women to capturing, for a time, the attention of the media, government and wider society. For example in 1968 a group of feminists protested against the Miss America contest. They placed high-heels, bras and women's magazines, such as *Cosmopolitan*, into a 'freedom trash can'. Whether or not the contents of this trash can were set alight is unclear, but what is clear is that the damage had been done. The label 'bra-burners' became synonymous with women's liberation and the media found a shorthand way to ridicule and belittle feminist activists for many years to come.[25]

But it is evident that women's liberation made a real difference to gender relations in American society. A whole raft of legislation was passed (or at the very least its passing was accelerated) such as the Equal Rights Amendment (ERA) (1972). More importantly they helped to raise the expectations of many women and introduced the topic of sexism and female oppression on to the political agenda.[26] Perhaps the greatest legacy of the American movement, however, was that it inspired many more women in the West to start their own groups. Watching their American sisters with interest, many women, including women in Britain, decided to replicate their action and begin women's liberation movements within their own countries. While there were differences in emphases and character between these movements, the theoretical underpinnings of the WLM in the West was always strongly influenced by American writers and activists.

Mapping the movement in the British Isles

The movement in the United Kingdom, therefore, emerged partly as a response to the activities of feminists in the USA. More research is needed in order to map the different feminist groups active within Britain and Northern Ireland, and how they fit into a broader narrative about the growth of feminism and women's political participation in the UK in the postwar period. From existing accounts it is evident that women's liberation emerged in the UK slightly later than in the USA. As in the USA there were a number of internal and external forces which led to the rise of the WLM. But there were also other local examples which forced women to think about the ways in which they related to the wider political system. The first important local example was the strike by female machinists at the Ford Plant in Dagenham in 1968. This strike began because the machinists were angered that their work was not regarded as skilled and they were paid less than men. Characterised as an equal pay dispute, this strike caught the attention of the media. Despite women's long history of trade union activism, the press still operated under the illusion that women were reluctant to strike, and the sight of outspoken Ford machinists challenging management to award them equal pay was, therefore, extremely newsworthy.[27] While their strike was not entirely successful in the short term (their aims were, however, achieved later), it did radicalise women within trades unions and also provided an important inspiration to those who formed the WLM. Another important local example emerged from Hull. A group of women campaigned about safety issues for local fishermen. From this campaign they created the Hull Equal Rights Group in 1968.[28] This provided an important model for groups of women throughout Britain who wanted to focus on the issue of women's equal rights.

There was a pressing need for these groups to get together and share their conclusions. A conference was, therefore, organised, held at Ruskin College in Oxford in February 1970. The organising group anticipated a turnout of only around three hundred women but to their amazement more than twice that number attended.[29] This was a truly inspirational moment for those who wanted to create a WLM on a national scale. As the editorial in the journal *Socialist Woman* made clear, 'the attendance at the women's weekend at Oxford shows the potency and potential of the women's liberation movement'.[30] Divisions were evident at this conference, indicating that Setch was right to assert that the movement was never united.[31] Yet despite these differences in opinion there was a real sense that there was 'no going back now for women' and that the Ruskin conference had been 'a huge success'.[32] As Coote and Campbell observed, there was 'a great sense of exhilaration. The women knew they were in at the start of something big.'[33] Most significantly it was at this event that the initial four demands of the movement were formulated (see Appendix II). This not only established the political programme for the movement but also gave it an identity; a way to introduce what the movement stood for to those who were not involved.

While this broad narrative has been established, much less is known about how women's liberation affected specific locations throughout the British Isles. New research is emerging which has illustrated the uneven developments in feminist thought and action during this period. For example studies which have looked at feminist groups in Leeds, London, Wales and Northern Ireland are allowing us to gain more of an insight into the development of women's liberation thought and practice.[34] Of central importance to this new research has been a shift from focusing on the leadership and published accounts of the WLM towards inter- rogating sources produced by local groups and interviewing grass-roots activists. This is clearly an important development in widening the scope of women's liberation studies.

In order to establish a full account of feminism in the United Kingdom, research into the WLM outside England is desperately needed. Deirdre Beddoe, Myrtle Hill and Margaret Ward have provided impor- tant insights into feminist activism in Northern Ireland and Wales. As in Scotland the movement in these countries was shaped not only by international and national concerns but also by local developments. For example in Northern Ireland the group, Northern Ireland Women's Rights Movement (NIWRM) focused on employment rights and sex discrimi- nation, but unity was always difficult to achieve. This was because of the destructive impact of 'the Troubles' which called for loyalty based upon religious grounds rather than gender. This proved to be an extremely diffi- cult local political context for feminist groups to operate within.[35] In Wales too, there was a focus on the local context. While women in feminist groups in places like Cardiff, Swansea, Pontypridd and Lampeter read Friedan and Firestone, they also discussed Elaine Morgan's *The Descent of Woman*. Welsh-born, Morgan was a prominent feminist theorist and her local roots appeared to lead to a particular focus on her work within Wales.[36] Furthermore there was an appreciation that their lives differed significantly from those of women living in London and that often they felt as if they had more obstacles to overcome than many of their English sisters. As Beddoe recognised, 'the English experience is not a universal one and fails to take account of the major differences which determine life-choices and everyday existence of women in Wales, Scotland or Ireland'.[37]

The Scottish example is, therefore, only one of many case studies which must be researched in order to understand the diverse development and impact of the WLM in the British Isles. It will be shown that the Scottish movement, similar in many ways to other geographical examples, also differed in some significant ways. Such differences indicate that the British WLM, rather than being a homogeneous movement, was always subject to change. It evolved and developed and so did the women involved in it. Moreover a significant by-product of the movement was that it transformed the lives not only of those who were active within it but also of those who were never engaged in feminist activism. As Lent has argued:

> it may be that the greatest achievement of this new movement at this time was its hidden impact on women all over the country. These women may not have joined a local group or actively supported a campaign, but their outlook and relationships were transformed in small but significant ways.[38]

This change in women's lives is one of the most important and interesting stories of British society in the post-1945 period. It is imperative, therefore, that the WLM should be placed within its wider context in order to understand why it developed in the way it did but also to understand better the ways in which women's lives changed in contemporary Britain.

Notes

1 A. Beckett, *When the Lights Went Out: Britain in the 1970s* (London, 2009), D. Sandbrook, *State of Emergency: The Way We Were: Britain 1970–1974* (London, 2010), and *Seasons in the Sun: The Battle for Britain 1974–1979* (London, 2012), L. Black, H. Pemberton and P. Thane (eds), *Reassessing 1970s Britain* (Manchester, 2013).

2 Sandbrook, *State of Emergency*, p. 10, and Beckett, *When the Lights Went Out*, p. 1.

3 Sandbrook, *State of Emergency*, p. 10.

4 Ibid., p. 9.

5 L. Black and H. Pemberton, 'Introduction: The Benighted Decade? Reassessing the 1970s' in Black, Pemberton and Thane (eds), *Reassessing 1970s Britain*, p. 6.

6 S. Rowbotham, *The Past Is Before Us: Feminism in Social Action since the 1960s* (London, 1989), p. 17

7 Beckett, *When the Lights Went Out*, p. 5.

8 M. Donnelly, *1960s Britain: Culture, Society and Politics* (Harlow, 2005), p. 55, and Beckett, *When the Lights Went Out*, p. 309.

9 N. Crossley, *Contesting Psychiatry: Social Movements in Mental Health* (Abingdon, 2006), p. 99.

10 B. Dempsey, *Thon Wey: Aspects of Scottish Lesbian and Gay Activism 1968–1992* (n.d.), pp. 9–10. For a very good account of the emergence of gay politics in this period see L. Robinson, *Gay Men and the Left in Postwar Britain: How the Personal Got Political* (Manchester, 2007).

11 Robinson, *Gay Men and the Left*, p. 68.

12 E. Setch, 'The Face of Metropolitan Feminism: The London Women's Liberation Workshop, 1969–79', *Twentieth Century British History*, 13:2 (2002), pp. 171–90, J. Rees: '"Are You a Lesbian?": Challenges in Recording and Analysing the Women's Liberation Movement in England', *History Workshop Journal*, 69 (Spring 2010), pp. 177–87, J. Rees, 'A Look Back at Anger: The Women's Liberation Movement in 1978', *Women's History Review*, 19:3 (2010), pp. 337–56, and S.F. Browne, '"A Veritable Hotbed of Feminism": Women's Liberation in St Andrews, Scotland, c. 1968–c. 1979', *Twentieth Century British History*, 23:1 (2012), pp. 100–23.

13 L. McQuiston, *Suffragettes to She-Devils – Women's Liberation and Beyond* (London, 1997), p. 76.

14 Obituaries – Betty Friedan 'Feminist Author', *The Scotsman*, 22 February 2006.

15 A. Marwick, *The 1960s – Cultural Revolution in Britain, France, Italy and the United States c. 1958–c. 1974* (Oxford, 1998), p. 683, and A. Marwick, *British Society Since 1945* (London, 1990), p. 242.

16 J. Green, *All Dressed Up – The 1960s and the Counterculture* (London, 1998), p. 408.

17 M. Pugh, *Women and the Women's Movement in Britain 1914–1999* (Basingstoke, 2000), p. 323.

18 S. Firestone, *The Dialectic Of Sex: The Case for Feminist Revolution* (Frogmore, 1973), p. 193.

19 E. Breitenbach, '"Sisters are doing it for themselves": the Women's Movement in Scotland' in A. Brown and R. Parry (eds), *The Scottish Government Yearbook 1990* (Edinburgh, 1990), p. 212.

20 A. Coote and B. Campbell, *Sweet Freedom: The Struggle for Women's Liberation* (London, 1982) p. 29.

21 M. Threlfall, 'Conclusion' in M. Threlfall (eds), *Mapping the Women's Movement: Feminist Politics and Social Transformation in the North* (London, 1996), pp. 292–4, and E. Meehan, 'British Feminism from the 1960s to the 1980s' in H.L. Smith (ed.), *British Feminism in the Twentieth Century* (Aldershot, 1990), p. 193.

22 Rees, 'A Look Back at Anger', p. 342.

23 For accounts of the WLM in the USA see S.M. Evans, *Born for Liberty: A History of Women in America* (New York, 1989 and 1997 editions); C. Giardina, *Freedom for Women: Forging the Women's Liberation Movement, 1953–1970* (Gainesville, 2010), and J. Brenner, 'The Best of Times, The Worst of Times: Feminism in the United States' in M. Threlfall (ed), *Mapping the Women's Movement: Feminist Politics and Social Transformation in the North* (London, 1996).

24 A. Lent, *British Social Movements since 1945: Sex, Colour, Peace and Power* (Basingstoke, 2001), p. 61.

25 S. Rowbotham, *A Century of Women: The History of Women in Britain and the United States* (London, 1999), pp. 378–79. As Lynn Abrams has argued, a dominant representation of the WLM became 'angry man-hating "bra-burners", created in large part by the media', *Oral History Theory* (London, 2010), p. 98.

26 Evans, *Born for Liberty* (1989 edition), pp. 290–1.

27 Donnelly, *Sixties Britain*, p. 163. For an account of women and class struggle see A. Hughes, *Gender and Political Identities in Scotland, 1919–1939* (Edinburgh, 2010).

28 Sandbrook, *State of Emergency*, p. 373, and Lent, *British Social Movements since 1945*, pp. 64–5.

29 Coote and Campbell, *Sweet Freedom*, p. 21.

30 *Socialist Woman*, May–June 1970, p. 1.

31 Setch, 'The Face of Metropolitan Feminism', p. 171, pp. 189–90.

32 *Socialist Woman*, May–June 1970, pp. 203.

33 Coote and Campbell, *Sweet Freedom*, p. 21.

34 Research into the WLM continues – Bridget Lockyer has recently published an article on the movement's impact in Bradford: 'An Irregular Period?: Participation in the Bradford Women's Liberation Movement', *Women's History Review*, 22:4 (2013), pp. 643–57.

35 M. Hill and M. Ward, 'Conflicting Rights: The Struggle for Female Citizenship in Northern Ireland' in E. Breitenbach and P. Thane (eds), *Women and Citizenship in Britain and Ireland in the Twentieth Century: What Difference Did the Vote Make?* (London, 2010), pp. 123–4.

36 D. Beddoe, *Out of the Shadows – A History of Women in Twentieth Century Wales* (Cardiff, 2000), p. 160.

37 Beddoe, *Out of the Shadows*, p. 179. F. Mackay, 'The State of Women's Movements in Britain: Ambiguity, Complexity and Challenges from the Periphery' in S. Grey and M. Sawer (eds), *Women's Movements: Flourishing or in Abeyance?* (London, 2008), p. 18.

38 Lent, *British Social Movements*, p. 78.

2

The women of the movement

In many accounts of the WLM the membership is usually described in very general terms. Women's liberation activists were white, middle-class, university students or graduates and in their early twenties to mid-thirties.[1] While this general characterisation is not in doubt, oral history interviews conducted for this book pointed towards the involvement of both older and working-class women in the movement, and they also allowed a more in depth understanding of who supported the movement and their reasons why. Interviewing was also important in allowing me to question the chronology of the movement. Many of those who have written about the WLM tend to set the emergence of the movement within a very short historical context, citing the sexual revolution and the introduction of the Pill as key conditions. This is not to deny the importance of these historical developments. However, by looking at the roots of the WLM through some of the participants' life stories it is clear that their experiences both as girls and as women were important, and arguably the ideas and experiences which informed the movement developed over a longer period before emerging in the mid- to late-1960s.[2] Of course, how personal experiences related to a developing political consciousness was different for every woman, and not every interviewee was willing to discuss why she had got involved in the WLM. However, it was interesting to note that many of the women dated their interest in 'feminist' issues from their childhood. Indeed, from those that emphasised the personal nature of their politicisation interesting themes emerged about how early experiences shaped their future lives as campaigning feminists. This chapter maps some of these important experiences. Issues such as the mother/daughter relationship, relationships with men, early experiences of education, employment and interactions with the labour movement are discussed.

Oral history interviews: theory and practice

Before looking at these experiences it is important to consider the ways in which oral history interviews have been used in this book. Twenty-nine interviews were collected from women who were involved in the movement or associated with it through other organisations. These interviews were normally held in the woman's home as it was the most convenient venue for most interviewees, as well as being a space which would, it is hoped, encourage them to feel as comfortable as possible. Indeed, of central importance in the collection of my interviews was allowing women as much space and time as possible to form their thoughts. For this reason a loose structure was adopted as I avoided a set questionnaire and instead asked open questions which were based on the interviewees' responses. The only question I planned in advance was the opening one: 'What got you interested in issues surrounding women?' I decided upon this question as it was open and allowed women to begin the interview at whatever point they wanted to, with some women opting to discuss their childhoods and other women beginning by talking about the first time they came into contact with the WLM. I transcribed all the interviews and included every hesitation and false train of thought, and I have tried to avoid editing quotations too much in this book: see the 'Note on the text' at the beginning of this book for the way in which the extracts have been presented. During the ethics process I decided to offer my interviewees the option to request to view transcripts and before I published any extracts I always asked for permission and allowed them to see what I had written. This complicated and slowed down the writing and publication process but it has led to fruitful discussions with my interviewees as they have often questioned my interpretation or clarified their thoughts. At all times they have respected my right to form my own interpretation and I have, therefore, found this collaboration extremely helpful.

Oral history theory has significantly developed since it began to re-establish itself as a historical research method in Britain from the late 1950s onwards, and it has now moved beyond seeing interviews merely as a way to establish facts.[3] The early pioneers of oral history in Britain, including Paul Thompson, believed that interviews could be used as a way to inject those groups who had often been hidden by history into mainstream historical accounts.[4] Giving these groups a voice, therefore, became a central aim of the burgeoning field of oral history. While this is a laudable aim, many oral historians soon realised that this approach was problematic as it ignored the power imbalance between interviewer and interviewee, and it also became evident that it was not always easy to encourage historical accounts to become more representative.[5] Yet it is evident that using oral history is often still the only way to uncover histories of groups or the experiences of individuals who do not appear in 'traditional' source material. It is for this reason that the method of oral history has always been attractive to historians of women (including myself in the writing of this book), who are seeking to challenge the absence of women in mainstream historical accounts. Indeed, in my attempt to research the grass-roots perspective of the WLM, it would have proved almost impossible without conducting oral history interviews.

However, recent theoretical debates about memory, narrative and subjectivity have also shaped the way I approached interviewing. These theoretical innovations have encouraged oral historians to question how people structure their life stories, what 'silences' emerge and how the interviewer and wider culture shape the interview which is produced.[6] In particular the concept of 'composure' is useful when considering the history of the WLM. Composure occurs in two main ways: first, when an interviewee tries to compose their narrative or life story and, second, when respondents, seeking composure, attempt to fit their life stories into public histories. Penny Summerfield has shown that composure is particularly difficult for those groups who experience 'cultural silences' and as historians it is imperative that we 'understand not only the narrative offered, but also the meanings invested in it and their discursive origins.'[7] What interviewees omit and what 'silences' occur in their testimonies point towards an uneasiness or an inability to integrate their experiences into public discourses. Listening on this level encourages the interviewer to hear 'what women implied, suggested, and started to say but didn't. We need to interpret their pauses and when it happens, their unwilling-ness or inability to respond.'[8] While the WLM has been written about and arguably has not experienced 'cultural silence' as it has been discussed in the media and has been portrayed in film, these representations often do not adequately represent the ways in which the interviewees experienced the movement. Many of the women I interviewed seemed pleased that an opportunity had arisen for them to tell their story and to raise awareness about the WLM in Scotland. Including historical actors in research can, therefore, lead to 'a more intimate, direct, and different view' of historical events and processes.[9]

Yet it is evident that certain silences emerged during my interviews. On a practical level there was understandable unease about describing instances of graffiti, with the names of those involved in such actions intentionally omitted. Most silences of this nature were because of the interviewee's evolving identity; far from being young, single and carefree, many of my interviewees understandably felt uncomfortable given that they now had to think about their professional status or family.[10] Furthermore some interviewees became anxious when questioned about their personal development as feminists and I am sure some stories of abuse and abortion, for example, were not told because of my status as a stranger. Rather than pressing them on these issues, I preferred to use Anderson and Jack's approach of honouring the interviewee's 'integrity and privacy' and avoided intrusion into areas that 'the narrator has chosen to hold back'.[11]

There were factors which influenced the topics covered in the interview and, as with all sources, the context is important to consider. Just prior to the start of this research, Scottish Women's Aid and Rape Crisis Scotland had conducted oral history projects into the origins of these organisations in order to produce commemorative publications. Some of the women I interviewed had explored many of the same issues with interviewers from these projects (and in the case of the Scottish Women's Aid project I had been involved in this process as an interviewer) and, therefore, already had an idea of many of the topics I might want to cover. Moreover the majority of interviewing was conducted in 2007 when there was increasing interest in the forthcoming fortieth anniversary of 1968, and this may have influenced what was remembered by the interviewees, especially the centrality of student protest in their emerging interest in feminism and women's liberation.[12]

Moreover, the concept of intersubjectivity was an important consideration for me when conducting my interviews and during the process of reflection afterwards. When reviewing the interviews it became clear that my presence as the interviewer also shaped the narrative. These intersubjective relations were revealed during some of the interviews. For example, it was remarkable how many of the respondents assumed that I was a feminist without me, on many occasions, declaring my political views. In previous research on Women Citizens' Associations (WCA) (a group which emerged in the interwar period in Britain and was more like the Townswomen's Guilds than the feminist activism of the 1970s and generally regarded as more 'traditional') I interviewed one member, who was ninety years old and extremely reluctant to be labelled a feminist. During one recollection she said 'you're a young woman Sarah, you've been brought up nicely'.[13] Being brought up nicely obviously implied that I did not challenge her as the face of modern feminism. Yet, this identity seemed to shift when interviewing those connected with the WLM. For example, issues which interviewees wanted to talk to me about included asking me questions about what young feminists were currently campaigning on. Moreover, Anne Jackson saw me as a 'seed in the ground', attempting to interest people in the work of the WLM at a time when she felt feminism was unpopular.[14] It was interesting to observe that interviewees often assumed that we shared political views without me declaring my beliefs.

The second major way intersubjective relations were revealed was through the intergenerational dimension to the recordings. As I was younger than those being interviewed there were occasions when I appeared to be viewed as a daughter-figure. Susan Geiger has illustrated how, far from being a drawback, this can help to overcome being viewed as a stranger, and can help to accumulate more information.[15] This was certainly the case when conducting interviews for this book. For example, when Jan Macleod, an anti-rape campaigner in Glasgow, described a notorious rape case in the 1970s, she quipped that 'I'm not even going to ask you if you remember it! You probably weren't even born then!'[16] Because I was younger Jan explained this case in depth and arguably provided more information than she would have done had she been talking to someone closer to her in age. It is important for younger women to interview those involved in the WLM in order to elicit information about the movement's history. Although as an interviewer I am by no means neutral, my non-involvement in the WLM seemed to lead to fuller interviews.

Furthermore, interviewing activists some years after the height of women's liberation had given them an opportunity to reflect about the development of feminism and how this had affected their own lives. Indeed, there was a definite sense of a 'liberationist' narrative running throughout the interviews. Women often described the fervour and excitement surrounding the blossoming feminist culture in the 1970s. Indeed, some interviewees seemed to glorify the early days of the WLM. At times there was a feeling of sympathy towards me for living in a time when CR groups (in their original format) and the wider WLM did not exist.[17] This sentiment has tended to shape narratives. For example, Dean has argued that this 'melancholic longing for a return to a specifically "seventies" mode of feminist politics' pervades much of the literature on contemporary feminism.[18] However, while these factors shaped the interviews and it is important to be aware of them, the oral history dimension of this research, alongside documentary evidence, was a useful way to gain an insight into the emergence and development of the movement, and most importantly the ways in which the grass-roots historical actors viewed this process.

Student politics

Of central importance to understanding the growth of the WLM is the expansion of higher education. Many women felt universities, providing intellectual space to engage in discussions about democracy and discrimination, were important in giving them freedom to engage with feminist ideas. Prior to the 1960s universities had been the preserve of middle- and upper-class men. For example, only 25 per cent of undergraduates in 1961 came from families where the father had a manual occupation. The publication of the Robbins Report (1961) changed this situation. It not only highlighted the class bias evident in higher education but it also emphasised the need for women to return to work after having children.[19] This report led to a massive expansion of the sector as universities widened access. This greatly impacted on the demographics of the student body. For example, the number of women as full-time students at universities in Scotland increased by 57 per cent in the period 1960–70.[20]

Universities were also key sites of political protest during the 1960s. Indeed, when looking at many of the published accounts of the student movement of the 1960s it is clear why the WLM is often described as emerging out of a short historical context. The generation coming of age during the 1960s was emerging into a world which had witnessed anti-Vietnam war demonstrations, racial violence, the summer of 'free love' and student sit-ins. The central year in this narrative is 1968 – viewed by many as a momentous year with an explosion of mass protests throughout the USA and Europe.[21]

Angela Bartie has explored whether or not Scotland had a 1960s experience. She argued that many accounts focus on the media images of the 1960s: hippies, widespread protests and student rebellions – and that these 'are themes that do not sit easily next to images of Scotland in the 1960s', before concluding that the 1960s need to be understood in a more nuanced way. If historians move beyond relying on the media portrayal of the 1960s, she argues that it becomes evident that Scotland did have a '1960s' experience.[22] Indeed, the impact of the 'media 1960s' in Scotland was called into question by one interviewee, Aileen Christianson, who reflected on how far her experience as a student in Aberdeen fitted into this wider narrative. She said that, although miniskirts were being worn by women in London, they were viewed as deeply exotic garments by women in Aberdeen, who, probably rather sensibly given the inclement weather conditions, were 'more into big duffel coats, big jumpers, long hair and great big bags'.[23]

Student protest was an important part of this '1960s' experience in Scotland as young people began to question the organisation of courses, departments and the running of universities more generally. Indeed, it is evident that the ideas of '68 had a profound long-term impact on the women who would form the liberation movement in Scotland. Speakers at Scottish universities throughout the period included French student leader Daniel Cohn-Bendit, Anti-Vietnam War campaigner and editor of *Black Dwarf* Tariq Ali and Labour Member of Parliament Tony Benn.[24] The ideas from such speakers were influential in shaping demands for student campaigns in Scotland, which attempted to win students more of a say in the running of universities. This resulted in demands to have student representation on more senate committees, student participation in departmental policy decisions and freedom of speech, morality and dress.[25] Leaders in the campaign for reform of the representation system in Scotland were students at the Universities of Dundee and Edinburgh. In 1969, for example, the President of the Student Representative Council at Dundee, Ben Anderson, demanded that students should become full representatives on Senate and Court. He argued, 'let the Court and the Senate cast aside the shackles of tradition and outmoded ideas. Students have a useful role to play. They have their rights as individuals to have a say in their government.'[26]

Underpinning these campaigns was a sense of competitiveness as groups of students tried to make their university the first in Scotland to improve the representation system. Some students were frightened that their university might be left behind in terms of reform.[27] These student demands resulted in sit-ins and encouraged the rise on Scottish campuses of left-wing groups like Militant, International Socialists and International Marxists.[28] The emergence of left-wing politics on campuses throughout Scotland was important and often led to calls to overcome general student apathy as there were fears that Scottish students were not as radical as their European and American counterparts.[29]

These demands for fairer representation led to a focus in Scottish student politics on the role of the rector. The rector represented the interests of students on university boards, such as Senate and Court. By far the most significant event in confrontations over the role of the rector in student politics in Scotland was the 'Muggeridge Affair' at the University of Edinburgh. Malcolm Muggeridge, a journalist and commentator, had been elected in 1966 to the role of rector at Edinburgh University. Some students became frustrated by his lack of attendance at important meetings and felt he was not taking his role of student representative seriously enough.[30] Further inflaming the situation, a year before he was due to retire from the post, he delivered a speech at St Giles Cathedral in Edinburgh in which he made clear his opposition to the decision to make the contraceptive Pill available at the Students' Union. This sparked widespread debate over how far Muggeridge should have been allowed to voice his own opinions or whether he should have expressed the views of the students, whom he had been elected to represent. The University of Edinburgh's student newspaper, *The Student*, began a relentless campaign to force Muggeridge's resignation. The Students' Council also passed a motion which declared that it was the right of the student health service to supply the Pill. Previously Muggeridge had argued that if he ever disagreed with the views of the Students' Council he would resign. Noting this promise, *The Student* requested, 'We ask you, our Rector, do you agree with the Students' Council motion? – or will you resign?'[31] Muggeridge resigned in January 1968.

This resignation caused widespread controversy amongst students across Scotland. The student newspaper at Glasgow agreed with Muggeridge's stance on contraception and was aghast at how he, whom it had described as 'distinguished', had been treated. Its ire was focused on *The Student's* editor, Anna Coote. Coote, who would go on to be an extremely influential figure in the WLM in Britain, had been one of the student leaders in the campaign to oust Muggeridge. *The Glasgow University Guardian* accused her of gutter politics and labelled her a harlot.[32] Aberdeen University's student newspaper, *Gaudie*, was somewhat more guarded in its criticism, preferring to point out that Muggeridge was a distinguished and well-respected rector and had not deserved the treatment he had received.[33] More significantly, the 'Muggeridge affair' sparked demands for elected student rectors. The University of Edinburgh led the way in this regard and elected a student, Jonathan Wills, to the post of Rector in 1972, followed a year later by the future Prime Minister Gordon Brown, indicating an area in which student protest was successful.[34]

The other major event for students in Scotland in the 1960s and 1970s was the Queen's visit to Stirling University in 1972. Angered by the cost of supplying security for the visit, some students occupied the MacRobert Centre. Heading this protest was Linda Quinn, the editor of Stirling's student newspaper, *Brig*. This protest received widespread press coverage, even making the front page of *The Times*, as it was reported that between four and five hundred students had jostled the Queen. The press also printed a picture of a student drinking from a bottle of wine in front of the Queen.[35] *The Times* printed almost thirty articles about this protest in 1972, mainly because it contributed to media panics about the unruly behaviour of students and their increasingly anti-authoritarian views. The general public's anger and opposition to this protest reflected these media views. Many voiced opposition to the protest, complaining that students did not have the right to question the cost of the Queen's visit, given that they were supported by grants from the government. Some of the letters were less restrained and, like Anna Coote in Edinburgh, Linda Quinn became the focus for people's anger. For example one letter began:

> Dear Miss Quinn … You and the rest of your bloody students are a disgrace to this country … [why should the monarchy be abolished] just because a silly little bitch like you does not believe in it?[36]

An inquiry was set up at Stirling University to punish those who had led and participated in the protest. This inquiry was perceived by some students as a witch-hunt. Their opposition to the singling out of individual students fed into wider concerns and campaigns focused on changing the way universities were run.[37]

Women's involvement in student politics

Evidently women were taking the lead in many of the major events of student politics in Scotland in the 1960s and 1970s. Inspired by Quinn and Coote, many women were becoming involved in political activism for the first time. Given that most WLM members were students or graduates, the context of higher education and more specifically student politics was important in heightening their political awareness and in giving them the confidence to act upon their beliefs. Many of the women witnessed their first sit-ins and engaged in discussions about equality and fairness for the first time. As Bouchier has argued, 'women caught up in this exciting political atmosphere, began to organise quietly around the equality issue'.[38] Sandie Wyles, of Aberdeen women's liberation group, grew up in Stirling and remembered that women like Linda Quinn had seemed like deities:

> they were the people that were in charge. They were the ones running that show and we were just like wee lassies. We just thought 'oh this is fantastic' and they took us – under their wing completely. Treated us with a lot of respect.[39]

She believed that because of the controversy surrounding the Queen's visit there was a 'political feeling' in Stirling, which encouraged her to think about certain issues she might not otherwise have considered.[40] Likewise, Esther Breitenbach, founder member of Dundee women's liberation group, recalled how as a teenager her initial interest in feminism had been sparked by events like the Muggeridge affair.[41] On their arrival at university the women who would go on to form the WLM in Scotland found that, although some university students in Scotland engaged in increasingly radical political action in the 1960s, they still had to confront sexist views about women. Throughout the late 1960s and 1970s every student newspaper in Scotland printed pictures of female students thought to be particularly attractive. *The Glasgow University Guardian* printed pictures under the title 'another dolly from our files' and Aberdeen's *Gaudie* bestowed the title 'King's Kutie' (named after one of the colleges at this university).[42] Even societies and clubs thought to be more sympathetic to women's issues had female mascots and beauty competitions. For example, in 1969, the Labour Club at Strathclyde University picked a female student as their 'Labour Girl' and released a picture of her wearing a miniskirt, resting rather whimsically on a pile of boulders on a beach.[43] Some male students seemed to reflect rather than challenge gender stereotypes apparent in wider society.

Universities, at times, maintained a very macho culture. Strip shows were popular events on many university campuses. In 1970 a 'gentleman's evening' was held at Aberdeen University in which 'cultural films' were shown. As *Gaudie* reported, the night was attended by eight hundred men and was 'largely devoted to the frolics of nubile young ladies prancing round in the buff'.[44] Although the numbers of women had increased on campus, opinions about their role in university life would take longer to change. Emblematic of this view was an article published in Strathclyde University's student newspaper, *The Strathclyde Telegraph*, by Jim Hutchison titled 'Down women!' Hutchison argued that, although women were now becoming a power to be reckoned with, he was still 'unconvinced that the female sex is as capable as its male superior in holding high office', believing they were too sweet natured to be effective leaders.[45]

By far the most sexist aspect of student life in this period was the Charities' Queen contest. This was run by students in order to raise money for local charities, and the queen was selected to act as the public representative of this fund-raising. Viewed by many as merely a beauty competition, these contests attracted widespread attention from those who accused the organisers of blatant sexism.[46] On arrival at university, therefore, the women who would become active feminists of the 1970s found that student life had not changed as much as many would have hoped. As Rowbotham has summed up, 'at the same time our beliefs and activism meant that we were caught in an uncomfortable gap between the manifold aspects of "femininity" – our personal destiny – and a public discourse about democracy and equality'.[47]

Indeed, some women were not just passive observers of the events of the 1960s but had been involved in political action prior to attending university. Ellen Galford recalled growing up in New York and stuffing envelopes for the Congress of Racial Equality.[48] Aged sixteen, Aileen Christianson had attended a Campaign for Nuclear Disarmament (CND) march and Esther Breitenbach was a member of the same organisation as a teenager.[49] Women also recalled the music they listened to, including radical folk artists like Pete Seeger and the Kingston Trio and protest singers Woody Guthrie and Bob Dylan.[50] These future feminists immersed themselves in the politics and culture of the time. For instance, Margaret Elphinstone remembered being fourteen and cycling to Glastonbury when she came across 'longhaired, sandaled, necklaced people. And I remember looking across and thinking I wanted to be like. I want that'.[51]

Moreover the events at universities in the 1960s also encouraged some women to become active in student politics. For example Sheila Gilmore who studied at the University of Kent during 1967–70 became involved in politics because 'it was quite a peak time for the student movement' as her generation had been 'onlookers at May '68 in France'.[52] Some women took the conventional route into university politics by running for student office. For instance, Pauline Robinson, while she was a student at the City of Leicester College, was elected President. She also became the National Union of Students' representative and had to attend many conferences in the 1960s in Leeds, which she described as a 'hotbed' of communism.[53]

Pauline also became politicised through participation in anti-apartheid demonstrations. The issue of apartheid in South Africa was particularly effective in uniting students behind a common cause. Stories about university investments in South African companies were published in student newspapers, with *The Student* particularly keen to highlight Edinburgh's role in this.[54] Pauline recalled a boycott of South African fruit at her college and she reflected that 'campaigning against apartheid began a long life … of boycotting and proselytising about injustice'.[55] Aileen Christianson, whilst a research assistant at Edinburgh University, participated in the 'Stop the 1970s' tour by attending a demonstration in 1969 attempting to stop the South African rugby tour from going ahead.[56] In 1969 there were protests in Aberdeen surrounding the plans to allow a tour of the South African rugby team.[57] Fiona Forsyth, who was in her first year of a sociology degree at Aberdeen University in 1969, recalled that this particular protest had a profound effect on her politicisation.[58]

By far the biggest issue to confront students of the late 1960s was the Vietnam War.[59] A wave of opposition to American involvement in the Vietnam War swept across Western Europe, and Scotland was no different. Anti-Vietnam War protests were held on many Scottish university campuses, with twenty students holding an all-night vigil at the

Market Cross in St Andrews. Protests were also held at the Universities of Glasgow, Dundee and Aberdeen.[60] The University of Edinburgh listed the Vietnam Solidarity Campaign as one of its societies, and students from Glasgow, Dundee and St Andrews travelled to London to join a mass protest against the war in November 1968.[61] Students at Aberdeen contributed to this wave of opposition by marching alongside the Aberdeen Committee for Peace in Vietnam and the American folk and protest singer Tom Paxton in October 1967.[62] The women who would go on to become feminists in the 1970s were not immune from this fervent opposition to the war.[63] There were also other issues that affected individual women in different ways. For example, the environmental agenda had a tremendous impact on Margaret Elphinstone, who went on to become one of the first members of Friends of the Earth.[64]

The Left

One major way women gained their political spurs prior to engaging with the WLM was through involvement in left-wing groups. The radicalisation of student politics and the growth of left-wing groups appeared to go hand in hand. This worried some within the wider community, with the local press in Aberdeen reflecting on what would happen if the university turned 'into a hotbed of left-wing revolt'. It was also reported that there were rumours of a wider Communist plot to gain control of universities in order to infiltrate national politics.[65] This is clearly an exaggeration of the impact of left-wing organisations on university campuses but it is evident that by the early 1970s many left-wing groups, through involvement in broad-based socialist societies, had achieved a higher profile. Most of the women who would go on to be active members of the WLM in Scotland were attracted initially to the politics of the left. This was not uncommon. Even in the USA, where it has been argued that class was of less importance to the growth of feminism, it is becoming clear that involvement in the labour movement provided a route into the WLM.[66] There are similar examples in the Scottish context. Anne Ward, who emigrated from the United States to Scotland and joined the Glasgow Women's Liberation group, was active first in trade union politics.[67] Sandie Wyles and Anne-Marie McGeoch first met at the Labour Party Young Socialists, where they recalled being the only two girls present.[68] Within these groups women became well versed in socialist theory and realised that men and women suffered equally under capitalism and should fight together for a more equal society. However, some women complained that they never found a true home amongst the socialist machismo of these groups. They began to realise that, even amongst those who espoused views which were supportive of gender equality, they were quite happy for women to be relegated to minute-taking and tea-making duties. They also realised that some socialist men, whilst seeing the merits of a gender struggle, felt it was an unnecessary distraction from the workers' revolt. It was clear that women would have to wait for equality until the class struggle was won.[69]

Indeed, the observation that women within political groups were always relegated to making the tea was to become a symbolic comment on the wider inequalities in left-wing politics. This macho culture forced many women to consider where their specific demands could fit into the workers' struggle. While at first feminists had assumed that left-wing groups would be a natural home, as Marxist theorists like Engels had considered the role of women within society, they soon found that many of the men who were identifiably socialist failed to put these theories into practice.[70] This was not a uniquely Scottish phenomenon. Sheila Rowbotham argued that women were treated as a side issue, always coming somewhere between 'youth' and 'any other business' on the agenda.[71] Conversely Paula Jennings of St Andrews Women's Liberation Group soon realised that, far from ignoring the position of women, those within left-wing politics were actually troubled by feminism. She recalled one encounter with the Socialist Alliance group:

> These men who marched around in big, big beards and Lenin caps and … they were very threatened by us. And I remember a group of them saying they wanted to just talk with us about what women's liberation was about. And I remember we were almost – into a corner of what was – the reading rooms in the old Union, while they fired aggressive questions at us … and I remember how inadequate I felt and how angry I felt … They were really threatened … by us. And I also noticed that they seemed to live and breathe socialism and yet, at least two of them had girlfriends who were in the Tory club. So, it was obvious, that to them women were just decorative.[72]

Anne Jackson began her political involvement in left-wing politics before moving on to join the women's liberation group in St Andrews. She described that she 'did – work among a lot of general lefty students, early 1970s, anti-Vietnam war, all that sort of stuff. It just felt like a general nice lefty melange'.[73] However, this 'nice lefty melange' was soon challenged as feminists began to question whether left-wing politics could fully meet their demands. Yet this is not to deny the importance of the left. Giardina's reappraisal of the role of the Old and New Left in the emergence of feminism in the USA has highlighted the positive aspects of this engagement. As she rightly points out, 'the treatment of women by male movement colleagues appears disproportionately sexist by today's standards, whereas in those pre-feminist years, bad as it was, it was often slightly better than the norm in wider society'.[74] Too often histories of the WLM tend to refer to the 'left' without problematising this label and questioning how far the left was united in its response to feminist ideas.[75]

Early experiences

While the changing political and social context taught future feminists the methods of political protest, it was really experiences within the family which provided them with the reasons for their anger. During my interviews many of the subsequent ideas of women's liberation were traced by interviewees to their childhoods. Exploring the life stories of individual feminists is clearly important given that it was a political movement which was infused with notions of personal experience. In exploring the personal aspects of politicisation women's liberation activists hoped to expand the definition of politics, hence the famous WLM slogan 'the personal is political'.

There has been some literature on the broader theme of relating the personal experiences of feminist campaigners in Western Europe and the USA to their political motivations for involvement in the WLM. However, this literature has tended to emerge from an American and sociological standpoint, with little input from historians. In the British context Liz Heron's *Truth, Dare or Promise – Girls Growing up in the Fifties*, published in 1985, was important in exploring the girlhoods of those who would reach adulthood in Britain during the 1960s. In seeking to find out what made this generation different, she argued, 'it's also true that differences began in our childhood, and were influenced not only by what was to come, but also by what had been'.[76] There have also been a number of autobiographies written by influential activists. Important in a British context have been Sheila Rowbotham and Michèle Roberts.[77] While such autobiographies provide valuable insights into individual lives, it is also helpful to look at the experiences of less prominent activists and to draw together common themes. This approach will lead to understanding, as Caine has argued, 'more about why particular women took up particular campaigns: what the campaigns meant to them and how they were related to a wider set of ideas and objectives'.[78] It is argued here that the ideas underpinning the WLM had a longer maturation than is often recognised, and early experiences as girls and young women were often significant in contributing to the flourishing of women's liberation politics in the late 1960s. This was recognised at the time as, through small CR groups and workshop discussion, women's liberation activists discussed their early personal lives as being very important in their later politicisation. Indeed, the WLM was the expression of a collective frustration felt by many young girls and women growing up during the late 1940s and 1950s.

A key theme that emerged during the interviews was generational conflict. However, not every woman rebelled against her family and upbringing, with some actually carrying on a family political tradition. Some women who went on to support the campaigns of the WLM in Scotland grew up in families which included members of the labour movement.[79] The kinds of discussions which emerged in these families had a deeply politicising impact on these young women. They subsequently became infused with ideas about equality and fairness. However, not all members of the WLM grew up in families who supported left-wing politics, with Chris Aldred of Aberdeen women's liberation group raised by parents of farming stock who always voted for the Conservative Party. Chris said that they 'were very tolerant. Particularly my mother who'd always been, I suppose, at root, even though my mother voted Conservative, her principles were ones of equality and tolerance.'[80] A family's particular political persuasion appeared to matter less, therefore, than the ideas of equality, fairness and tolerance, which were more important in shaping the political consciousness of women like Chris and drawing them to feminism in later life.

The family was also important in providing a window on to what the wider world would be like. Many of the interviewees recalled early realisations that girls were not equal to boys. This was especially true if they had grown up surrounded by brothers. Pauline Robinson of Dundee women's liberation group crystallised this feeling when she said, 'I'd been really politicised by being brought up in a minority of girls in a large family where the boys' conditions were different from ours and I'd always asked "why can the boys come home later than us?", "why do boys not have to do this?"'[81] Fiona Forsyth, who would go on to join Aberdeen women's liberation group in the early 1970s, also talked about this feeling of difference when she realised, as a teenager, that boys were allowed to hitch-hike around Europe but girls were not.[82] Margaret Elphinstone was particularly affected by this feeling of gender difference. A self-confessed tomboy, Margaret, who would later help to found the Shetland women's liberation group, recalled 'a turning point when I thought that I do not want to grow up and be a woman. This is awful.' This revelation had occurred during a trip to visit her aunt in Canada with her family, including her cousin, John. During this visit her aunt's neighbour offered to take John out fishing and Margaret recalled how upset she had been at being overlooked. She described thinking that she 'was the outdoor one ... And he took John on this fishing trip and I was "the girls", me and Janet ... And I was gutted.'[83] In a revealing passage of her transcript, Zoe Fairbairns effectively summarised the contradiction many girls faced and how this led, in her case, to exploring feminism:

> there did seem to be a contradiction between the fact that I and my sisters (we were three girls, no boys) were all encouraged, pushed to get as good an education as we could, and to have careers; but any adult woman who had a career was looked down upon ... there was no joined up thinking on this ... particularly after the war ... education was available to anyone with the right abilities ... but when it actually came to careers and adult life women did not face equal opportunities. Women were not encouraged or supported in having careers and in having freedom. And I was very, very aware of this even as a young child. It caused me a lot of anxiety and I didn't quite know what the future held. But because I wasn't aware of anybody else saying or thinking these things, I thought it was just a sort of personal problem that I had. So to discover at the age of twenty while I was half-way through university that there was something called the women's liberation movement which was aware of these problems and recognised them for what they were, which was a political problem, a problem of human rights and a problem of justice, was so liberating.[84]

Many women echoed this sentiment. Anne Jackson, a member of St Andrews women's liberation group said that, although her mother had encouraged her to become well-educated, she was meant to 'give it all up and marry and have children ... that was just a disjunction, that didn't make sense to me.'[85] Moreover while a majority of the women interviewed for this research pursued an arts-based education, others, such as Judy Ekins, were interested in science. During one visit to a technical drawing office with her father she realised she would like to become a tracer but on enquiring was told that 'oh we don't take women. Women can't be tracers, they can't be technical drawers.'[86] Even within education it was clear that gender stereotyping existed, preventing women from pursuing their passions.

By far the most important relationship for many future feminists was that between mother and daughter. It clearly gave some women a key reason for generational conflict as they, growing up in the 1950s and 1960s, sought to differentiate themselves from their mothers. As a theme, this has been explored by both sociologists and psychologists and indeed had an impact on the WLM as a developing discussion topic during the 1970s. A key text in this regard was Nancy Friday's *My Mother / My Self – The Daughter's Search for Identity*, published in 1977. Friday discovered that 'for as long as I can remember, I did not want the kind of life my mother felt she could show me' and rather guiltily admitted 'I began to make the terrible judgment that she was not the woman I wanted to be'.[87] In Cathy Kerr's review of Friday's book for the Scottish women's liberation publication *MsPrint* in 1979 she argued that mothers 'unconsciously try and prevent daughters from obtaining independence by teaching one lesson with their tongue and a totally different lesson by their body language and their lifestyle and thus confuse their dependants into immobility'.[88] It is not surprising then that Rowbotham has argued that 'one of the most passionate relationships in modern feminist writings is that between mothers and daughters'.[89]

When looking at their mothers the young feminists of the 1970s did not always see a happy and fulfilled woman but rather someone who was dissatisfied with her life owing to her dependent status. For example, one member of the Edinburgh women's liberation group said:

> I can remember as a nice little middle-class girl in the fifties, I thought, well I'll not get married because if you get married, you lose your name and you lose this, that and the other and you would become boring and probably looking at my poor mother.[90]

Indeed, this perception that you could not be a mother *and* have a job was an important factor in the development of a feminist consciousness. For example, St Andrews women's liberation member Judy Ekins described how her mother had been one of the first probation officers in Luton, where Judy grew up. She had been forced to resign from her job upon marriage as her husband felt it would be inappropriate for her to work. Her father justified this decision by arguing that it would reflect badly on him, owing to a perception within wider society that if a married woman was working it was because her husband was not earning enough to support her and the family. His decision led Judy to admit that she 'didn't want to be a wife and mother, I saw that my mother was not very happy as a wife and mother, having given up being a Probation Officer'.[91] Zoe Fairbairns also came from a typically middle-class family in which it was expected that a woman would relinquish her career upon marriage. As Zoe recalled, her dad was, therefore, 'in a position to forbid his wife to earn money … and to maintain her at home as his personal servant'. Indeed, Zoe's portrayal of her mother was an unhappy one as she remembered many occasions when she found her 'mother crying over the fact that she couldn't get all her housework done before it all started again'. Whilst this episode led Zoe to feel sympathetic towards her mother it also made her feel frightened of what her own future would hold.[92] For those from working-class backgrounds the roles of mothers and fathers were also very different. For example, Sandie Wyles of Aberdeen women's liberation group remembered her father going out to Labour Party meetings and her mother would always say 'Is that you away out again?' realising that she would have to forfeit her own social life in order to look after the children. Sandie also recalled that it was her mother who did more housework than her father.[93] At what point in their lives they began to question this division of domestic labour remains unclear.[94] However, their testimonies reveal that they drew a sharp contrast between their own aspirations and the reality of their mothers' lives.

The theme of motherly dissatisfaction has also been explored by Sheila Rowbotham. She said of her own mother that 'she exuded a sense of unstated possibilities and deeper meanings – somewhere over the rainbow'.[95] Penny Summerfield has explored the generation of women coming of age in the 1940s – an important generation in any under-standing of the WLM as these women would become the mothers of the feminist activists. In her book *Reconstructing Women's Wartime Lives* Summerfield argued that some of the interviewees were marked by an 'ambivalence and restlessness' because of having to return to marriage and motherhood after having worked in various jobs as part of the war effort. Confirming the recollections of women like Zoe Fairbairns and Judy Ekins, Summerfield described how women after the Second World War felt frustrated as they would have liked 'to have retained the more exciting and rewarding job opportunities which war made available'. Her account showed that, although opportunities were opening for girls, many of these had to be fought for in the face of resistance from authoritarian parents. In some cases both mothers and fathers opposed their daughters' desire to work. However, in the case of mothers their message was somewhat more contradictory as they used the war 'to make their own bids for freedom, while still blocking those of their daughters'. In offering this account Summerfield has argued that women's experi-ences in the Second World War had the effect 'of disrupting the pre-war discourse of the daughter'.[96] This depiction clearly illustrates that young women in the 1940s experienced more freedom but that these opportuni-ties were quickly withdrawn in the 1950s. Young women of this genera-tion were frustrated by this development and clearly felt the mundane routine of marriage and motherhood sharply contrasted with the enjoy-ment and variety of working life. It is no surprise, therefore, that Zoe and Judy recalled the importance of their mothers' frustration in terms of their own growing up. A determination not to lead a similar life to their mothers motivated these members of the WLM in Scotland as they attempted to move beyond purely fulfilling a domestic role in life.[97] It is clear, therefore, that the mother/daughter dynamic was an important one in shaping future demands of the WLM as they sought to extend the role of women in order to provide greater choices for women. This led to important political demands and campaigns such as the fight for a woman's right to financial and legal independence.

Moreover it is interesting to consider the relative silence in many of the women's transcripts on the role and impact of their fathers in their childhood. Perhaps this is because, as Lynn Abrams has suggested, 'families invariably mean mothers and children. This is true both in contemporary discourse and in modern historiography.'[98] Reflecting this dominant discourse, most interviewees tended to contrast the public roles of their working fathers with the private domestic sphere, which their mothers inhabited.[99] Consequently it is the role of mothers which was emphasised by interviewees as being crucial in their development as a feminist.

Experiences of generational conflict and change in family life and education therefore led to a direct questioning of the role of women in society. At the heart of this questioning was a desire to challenge their upbringing. The movement was all-encompassing as women immersed themselves in the politics of feminism. As Sheila Rowbotham has subsequently argued of the membership of the WLM in the early 1970s, 'we were like lovers at the onset of an affair, filled with energy. We looked out so surely.'[100] Their utopian vision clearly had roots in the discrimination and discontinuity that many women discovered during their childhoods. Feelings of inadequacy about themselves as girls and frustration that their ambitions might never be fulfilled spurred women on to attempt to re-create the world according to feminist ideals. Specifically, experiences in the family and at school illustrated the different ways in which girls and boys were treated. To many girls this gender stereotyping seemed to be incredibly unfair. The desire to lead a different life from their mothers and the fact that education did not always provide an escape route from domesticity meant that the WLM would go on to form very specific demands around a woman's right to financial and legal independence, equal education and equal opportunities. The new political ideologies and approaches of the 1960s gave such women a language to express these frustrations. Universities were often critical in the increasing politicisation of young women and in this regard experiences with left-wing politics were often very important.

Members of the WLM not only argued for women's liberation but also lived it. A sense of joy at discovering the WLM is evoked in many of the oral testimonies. Often alone and isolated in the way they viewed the world it was a relief for them to find like-minded women. In describing this feeling there is a definite sense of a liberationist narrative, in which the WLM often shaped the lives of the women involved in it. This enthusiastic activism is probably the reason why a relatively small group of women were able to gain such high visibility and later influence government policy. The period of the late 1960s was obviously ripe for political activism of many kinds. Yet there were also individual circumstances which drew each of these women to the politics of the WLM. Whether it was rebelling against their mother or continuing on a background of left-wing politics, the interviewees all had in common a sense of injustice and inequality. It is striking how many of the women who were involved in the WLM recall an absolute delight and joy at finding their true political home. No political group or campaign before the WLM had resonated as much with them and it was this fact that made them such enthusiastic converts and campaigners.

In order to understand how these women formed the movement and why specific demands and campaigns emerged it is important to look at these early experiences. In describing their journey towards feminism, it is evident that the emergence of the WLM happened over time, as women growing up in the 1950s and 1960s were grappling with the changing political and cultural landscape in Britain. Historians tend to like fixed points of time to date when a movement or group began, but the WLM was not 'traditional' in its approach. Its formation was much more organic and was a process rather than an event. Indeed, Wandor correctly identified that 'the women's liberation movement did not just rise, fully formed, from the waves' but instead stemmed 'from a combination of experiences'.[101]

Notes

1 J. Lewis, 'From Equality to Liberation: Contextualising the Emergence of the Women's Liberation Movement' in B. Moore-Gilbert and J. Seed (eds), *Cultural Revolution: The Challenge of the Arts in the 1960s* (London, 1992), p. 96, D. Bouchier, *The Feminist Challenge: The Movement for Women's Liberation in Britain and the United States* (London, 1983), pp. 50–1, and A. Coote and B. Campbell, *Sweet Freedom-The Struggle for Women's Liberation* (London, 1982), p. 15.

2 There has been lots of discussion of the short historical context including H. McLeod, *The Religious Crisis of the 1960s* (London, 2009), p. 175, and L. Segal, *Is the Future Female?: Troubled Thoughts on Contemporary Feminism* (London, 1987), p. 75. I have

discussed this theme in relation to women and religion in S.F. Browne, 'Women, Religion and the Turn to Feminism: Experiences of Women's Liberation Activists in Britain in the 1970s' in M. Gauverau and N. Christie (eds), *The 1960s and Beyond: Dechristianization as History in Britain, Canada, the United States and Western Europe* (Toronto, 2013). The long historical context is now being recognised: see A. Lent, *British Social Movements since 1945: Sex, Colour, Peace and Power* (Basingstoke, 2001), p. 7.

3   R. Perks and A. Thomson, 'Introduction' in R. Perks and A. Thomson (eds), *The Oral History Reader* (London, 1998), p. ix.

4   Perks and Thomson, 'Introduction', p. ix.

5   Joan Sangster, 'Telling our Stories: Feminist Debates and the Use of Oral History', *Women's History Review*, 3:1 (1994), p. 7, and L. Passerini, 'Work Ideology and Consensus under Italian Fascism' in R. Perks and A. Thomson (eds), *The Oral History Reader* (London, 1998), p. 53.

6   A. Green and K. Troup (eds), *The Houses of History: A Critical Reader in Twentieth-Century History and Theory* (Manchester, 1999), p. 232. See also Passerini, 'Work Ideology'.

7   P. Summerfield 'Culture and Composure: Creating Narratives of the Gendered Self in Oral History Interviews', *Cultural and Social History*, I (2004), p. 69, p. 67.

8   K. Anderson and D.C. Jack, 'Learning to Listen: Interview Techniques and Analyses' in S. Berger Gluck and D. Patai (eds), *Women's Words: The Feminist Practice of Oral History* (London, 1991), p. 17.

9   J. Sangster, 'Gendering Labour History Across Borders', *Labour History Review*, 75:2 (August 2010), p. 149.

10 A. Portelli, 'What Makes Oral History Different' in R. Perks and A. Thomson (eds), *The Oral History Reader* (London, 1998), p. 69.

11 Anderson and Jack, 'Learning to Listen', p. 25.

12 For example, some of the interviewees in conversation after the interview would mention that they had been listening to Radio Four's series on 1968 or had read about the year's events in *The Guardian*.

13 Transcript of interview with Caroline Florence (CF), 22 April 2006, p. 17.

14 Transcript of interview with Anne Jackson and Paula Jennings (AJ and PJ), 27 August 2007, p. 42.

15 S. Geiger, 'What's So Feminist About Doing Women's Oral History?' in C. Johnson-Odim and M. Strobel (eds), *Expanding the Boundaries of Women's History: Essays on Women in the Third World* (Bloomington, 1992), p. 312.

16 Transcript of interview with Jan Macleod (JM), 10 July 2007, p. 9.

17 Transcript of interview with Nadine Harrison (NH), 12 June 2007, p. 7; Transcript AJ and PJ, pp. 41–2.

18 J. Dean, *Rethinking Contemporary Feminist Politics* (Baskingstoke, 2000), p. 10.

19 S. Sharpe, *Just Like a Girl – How Girls Learn to Be Women – From the 1970s to the Nineties* (London, 1994), pp. 9–11.

20 C.G. Brown, 'Charting Everyday Experience' in L. Abrams and C.G. Brown (eds), *Everyday Life in Twentieth Century Scotland* (Edinburgh, 2010), p. 28, and C.G. Brown, A.J. McIvor and N. Rafeek, *The University Experience 1945–1975 – An Oral History of the University of Strathclyde* (Edinburgh, 2004), p. 146.

21 E. Hobsbawm, *Age of Extremes: The Short Twentieth Century, 1914–1994* (London, 1994), p. 300, pp. 444–6.

22 A. Bartie, 'Festival City: The Arts, Culture and Moral Conflict in Edinburgh 1947–1967' (unpublished PhD thesis, University of Dundee, 2006), p. 14.

23 Transcript of interview with Aileen Christianson (AC), 26 April 2007, p. 1.

24 *The Glasgow University Guardian*, 5 November 1968, p. 3; *AIEN*, 9 October 1968 (Courtesy of the University of St Andrews Library, StALF1119.A2), p. 1; *Annasach*, 18 October 1968 (University of Dundee Archive Services), p. 1.

25 As listed in *AIEN*, 2 October 1968, p. 3 (Courtesy of the University of St Andrews Library, StALF1119.A2).

26 *Annasach*, 17 January 1969, p. 1 (University of Dundee Archive Services).

27 See for example, *The Strathclyde Telegraph*, 22 October 1969, p. 1.

28 *The Student*, 29 April 1971, p. 4; *The Glasgow University Guardian*, 8 February 1968, p. 4; *Brig*, 28 November 1969, p. 1.

29 *The Glasgow University Guardian*, 13 May 1968, p. 1.

30 For a very good summary of this episode ten years later, see *The Student*, 9 November 1978, p. 4.

31 Ibid.

32 *The Glasgow University Guardian*, 29 January 1968, p. 4 and p. 1.

33 *Gaudie*, 24 January 1968, p. 1.

34 *The Strathclyde Telegraph*, 25 November 1971, p. 1.

35 *The Times*, 13 October 1972, p. 1.

36 *Brig*, 23 October 1972, p. 3.

37 *Brig*, 17 September 1973, p. 1; *The Times*, 14 October 1972, p. 1.

38 Bouchier, *The Feminist Challenge*, p. 3.

39 Transcript of interview with Sandie Wyles (SW) and Anne-Marie McGeoch (AMcG), 18 September 2007, p. 2

40 Transcript SW and AMcG, p. 4.

41 Transcript of interview with Esther Breitenbach (EB), 24 May 2007, p. 3.

42 *The Glasgow University Guardian*, 13 May 1968, p. 7.

43 *The Strathclyde Telegraph*, 9 October 1969, p. 8.

44 *Gaudie*, 4 March 1970, p. 10.

45 *The Strathclyde Telegraph*, 13 February 1968, p. 12.

46 Various articles on this topic, see for example, *Gaudie*, 14 February 1968, p. 7; *Brig*, 14 November 1969.

47 S. Rowbotham, *Promise of a Dream: Remembering the 1960s* (London, 2001), and M. Roberts, *Paper Houses: A Memoir of the '70s and Beyond* (London, 2007), p. xii.

48 Transcript of interview with Ellen Galford (EG), 2 April 2007, p. 1.

49 Transcript AC, p. 12; Transcript EB, p. 3.

50 Transcript EG, p. 3; Transcript of interview with Margaret Elphinstone (ME), 21 November 2007, p. 8.

51 Transcript ME, pp. 7–8.

52 Transcript of interview with Sheila Gilmore (SG), 28 June 2007, p. 1.

53 Transcript of interview with Pauline Robinson (PR*), 6 December 2006, p. 1.

54 *The Strathclyde Telegraph*, 6 December 1970, p. 2.

55 Transcript PR*, 6 December, p. 1.

56 Transcript AC, p. 2.

57 *Gaudie*, 3 December 1969, p. 1.

58 Transcript of interview with Fiona Forsyth (FF), 9 July 2008, p. 2.

59 Lent, *British Social Movement*, p. 50.

60 *AIEN*, 19 November 1969, p. 1 (Courtesy of the University of St Andrews Library, StALF1119.A2); *The Glasgow University Guardian*, 5 November 1968, p. 3; *Annasach*, 1 November 1968 (University of Dundee Archive Services), p. 1; *Gaudie*, 18 October 1967, p. 1.

61 *The Student*, 1 November 1968, p. 1; *Annasach*, 1 November 1968, p. 1 (University of Dundee Archive Services), *The Glasgow University Guardian*, 5 November 1968, p. 3.

62 *Gaudie*, 18 October 1967, p. 1.

63 Transcript of interview with Paula Jennings (PJ) and Anne Jackson (AJ), 27 August 2007, p. 6.

64 Transcript ME, p. 7.

65 *Gaudie*, 1 November 1967, p. 1; 9 October 1968, p. 3.

66 C. Giardina, *Freedom for Women: Forging the Women's Liberation Movement, 1953–1970* (Gainesville, 2010), p. 154.

67 Transcript of interview with Anne Ward (AW*), 28 August 2007, p. 1.

68 Transcript SW and AMcG, p. 1.

69 Ibid.

70 See for example F. Engels, *The Origins of the Family, Private Property and the State* (Moscow, 1968 edition).

71 Rowbotham, *Women's Consciousness, Man's World* (Harmonsworth, 1973), p. 19 and p. 35.

72 Transcript AJ and PJ, p. 4.

73 Ibid.

74 Giardina, *Freedom for Women*, p. 171.

75 Rowbotham and Segal have made this distinction. See for example, S. Rowbotham, *The Past Is Before Us: Feminism in Action since the 1960s* (London, 1990), p. 222, and L. Segal, 'Slow Change or No Change?: Feminism, Socialism and the Problem of Men', *Feminist Review*, 31 (Spring 1989), pp. 12–13.

76 L. Heron, *Truth, Dare or Promise – Girls Growing up in the Fifties* (London, 1985), p. 4. See also M. Wandor, *Once a Feminist: Stories of a Generation* (London, 1990), and J. McCrindle and S. Rowbotham, *Dutiful Daughters – Women Talk about Their Lives* (Harmondsworth, 1983).

77 Rowbotham, *Promise of a Dream*, and Roberts, *Paper Houses*.

78 B. Caine, 'Feminist Biography and Feminist History', *Women's History Review*, 3:2 (1994), p. 258.

79 Transcript AW*, p. 2; Transcript of interview with Margaret Adams (MA*), 3 May 2007, p. 1.

80 Transcript of interview with Chris Aldred (CA), 30 August 2007, p. 2.

81 Transcript PR*, 6 December 2006, p. 1.

82 Transcript FF, p. 1.

83 Transcript ME, p. 2.

84 Transcript of interview with Zoe Fairbairns (ZF), 5 June 2007, p. 1. Please note that Zoe changed some of the punctuation her quotes in consultation with me.

85 Transcript AJ and PJ, p. 2.

86 Transcript of interview with Judith Ekins (JE), 27 July 2007, p. 1.

87 N. Friday, *My Mother / My Self – The Daughter's Search for Identity* (Glasgow, 1977), p. 20.

88 *MsPrint*, 4, 1979, p. 19.

89 Rowbotham, *The Past Is Before Us*, p. 11.

90 Transcript AC, p. 1.

91 Transcript JE, p. 2.

92 Transcript ZF, p. 3. Although Zoe would make the distinction that while her home would have been regarded as 'middle-class' her mother was not, given that she relied financially on her husband to support her.

93 Transcript SW and AMcG, p. 2.

94 J. Sangster, 'Telling Our Stories', p. 10.

95 Rowbotham, *Promise of a Dream*, p. 3. See also C. Steedman, *Landscape for a Good Woman: A Story of Two Lives* (New Brunswick, 1987).

96 P. Summerfield, *Reconstructing Women's Wartime Lives: Discourse and Subjectivity in Oral Histories of the Second World War* (Manchester, 1998), p. 279, pp. 236–7, pp. 54–5 and p. 44.

97 Heron, *Truth, Dare or Promise*, p. 8.

98 L. Abrams, '"There was nobody like my daddy": Fathers, the Family and the Marginalisation of Men in Modern Scotland', *The Scottish Historical Review*, LXXVIII, 2:206 (1999), p. 221.

99 See for example, Transcript SW and AMcG, p. 2 and Transcript JE, p. 2.

100 Rowbotham, *The Past Is Before Us*, p. 17.

101 Wandor, *Once a Feminist*, p. 3.

3

Finding their anger in consciousness-raising

These early experiences became potent reasons to become a feminist activist only when shared with a small group of like-minded women. These small groups began to emerge in the late 1960s when women would meet to discuss the ways in which they felt oppressed by society. As in the USA and Europe, CR groups became the key entrée for most women who 'joined' the WLM in Scotland in the 1970s. Little is known about how these groups were organised and this chapter sheds light on to this process, describing the roots, locations and operation of individual CR groups throughout Scotland.[1] The purpose of these groups was to encourage participants to explore their life experiences and to transform these 'into a shared awareness' of women's oppression.[2] These sessions, therefore, acted as an initiation for new members.[3] From these personal discussions topics for political action emerged as women drew upon the life experiences described in Chapter 2. As Zoe Fairbairns of St Andrews women's liberation group summed up:

> then you suddenly begin to realise that what you thought was your own little neurosis was part of a whole political system ... that's the sort of experience that I'd call consciousness-raising: it was making the connection between something that was inside and felt very personal, and the wider world. And I think the slogan that 'the personal is political' ... was this great liberating idea. That nothing is too small to be important and that nothing is too big to be important.[4]

Women were recruited to individual CR groups through local and national women's liberation newsletters, such as *The Tayside Women's Liberation Newsletter* and *The Scottish Women's Liberation Journal*, where advertisements were placed by individual feminists eager to make contact with other women in the local area in order to start a group. The method of CR proved to be popular amongst supporters of the WLM, with groups beginning to spread throughout Scotland in the 1970s with, for example, at least four in Edinburgh by 1976 and groups in Dundee, Glasgow, Aberdeen and St Andrews also in existence.[5] In order to understand the development of the WLM in Scotland this and the next chapter will explore the stages in the movement's formation. First, the phenomenon of CR will be discussed by looking at the theory, how it operated and its impact on the movement. This is an important topic to consider when thinking about why 'personal' issues assumed such importance for women's liberation activists. Second, a brief history of local women's liberation workshops will be outlined in Chapter 4 in order to establish for the first time the variety of different feminist campaigns and activism evident throughout Scotland. By analysing the practice of CR and looking at the debates and discussions of local groups, the way the WLM developed and operated can be better understood. This will not only contribute to shifting the focus away from 'national' feminist politics to the local context, where women's liberation ideas were interpreted and put into practice, but it will also help us to question the ways in which the development and chronology of the movement have been described in existing accounts.

The theory of consciousness-raising

There has been some research into the origins and theory of CR and its role in the development of women's liberation politics in the USA and Europe. Commentators have provided a general overview of the theory behind CR, enhancing understanding of the phenomenon, but often have not provided examples of what the theory looked like in practice.[6] Nevertheless Coote and Campbell have set CR in a historical context, arguing that viewed from a historical perspective the idea of women meeting and talking about their life experiences was nothing new. What was refreshing about women's liberation discussions were the political conclusions the participants drew from their individual experiences.[7] Indeed, CR was not a new method, as many protest movements, such as the Civil Rights movement in the USA, had emphasised the importance of the role of its membership and their individual experiences in drawing together themes and ideas for a campaign agenda. However, the WLM was somewhat different in that it saw CR as a central part of its development and consequently it became a key strategy in the recruitment and retention of its membership.

The origins of CR as a feminist political method have been debated. Rowbotham has argued that it was directly inspired both by the practices of popular religious movements and the Civil Rights movement in the

USA in the 1960s. On the other hand, Evans has placed greater emphasis on the influence of student politics in the USA and on the process of 'speaking bitterness' in the Chinese Revolution of the 1960s.[8] What is clear is that the theory of CR was first developed in the 1960s by women's liberation activists involved in the New York radical feminist group called Redstockings.[9] Their emphasis on the personal was clearly expressed in their manifesto, which was published in 1969, when they argued:

> we regard our personal experience, and our feelings about that experience, as the basis for an analysis of our common situation. We cannot rely on existing ideologies as they are all products of male supremacist culture. We question every generalization and accept none that are not confirmed by our own experience ... The first requirement for raising class consciousness is honesty, in private and in public, with ourselves and other women.[10]

They saw CR as a way to disrupt existing political ideologies which had failed to include or had fundamentally misunderstood women. According to them CR would enable women to go back to the drawing-board and create new ideas and campaigns which were focused on women's lives and informed by their experiences. Having acknowledged this, the New York-based group developed CR as a way to introduce new women to the movement. An influential member of Redstockings was Kathie Sarachild, whose article on CR became an important part of the WLM's international development.[11] Sarachild explained that CR had emerged from a discussion in which one member of Redstockings observed, 'I think we have a lot more to do just in the area of raising our consciousness'.[12] This idea of 'raising our consciousness' became popular amongst the members of Redstockings and they began to explore issues related to their own lives. As Sarachild argued, 'we felt that all women would have to see the fight of women as their own, not as something just to help "other women," that they would have to see this truth about their own lives before they would fight in a radical way for anyone'.[13]

This theory was introduced into many women's liberation groups internationally, and Scotland was no different. Collecting oral histories helped to uncover in what ways this theory was understood by individual members. For example, Wendy Davies of Glasgow women's liberation group said:

> I think what was important [was] we knew we had to start with ourselves and work outwards ... what was important was that feminist theory started with the personal and then became political. We didn't start with the theory and say, okay how does that apply to me? We started

with ourselves and said what does this mean then? Is my experience a one-off, or is it actually replicated? And so I think those consciousness-raising groups ... were really important. It was cells, if you like, of [the] reconstruction of gender politics.[14]

Starting with themselves, as Davies described, was facilitated by the use of CR, which encouraged WLM activists to focus on the role of the membership and their life experiences in the development of their wider political agenda and theories of women's liberation. It made every participant feel as if she had a stake in the movement by encouraging her to immerse her whole life in its discussions. It gave women a sense of belonging; that it was their voices which mattered most. It, therefore, complemented the desire of many women in the WLM to be as non-hierarchical and decentralised as possible.

The practice of consciousness-raising

Despite many women's early enthusiasm for CR there was some opposition to its development and subsequent domination of the movement. As Sarachild explained, some women felt that the discussion of personal topics could not be clearly defined as political action.[15] Despite this opposition CR soon dominated the early development of the movement. It was hoped that CR groups would remain quite flexible. Inspired by theoretical discussions emerging from WLMs throughout Western Europe and America, most Scottish women's liberation meetings, including those focused on CR, attempted to avoid structure and were anti-hierarchical, preferring full participation by all instead of just a select committee. Committee posts, such as chairperson, secretary and treasurer, were abandoned in favour of collective responsibility. This decision was justified by international theorists, such as Jo Freeman, who argued in *The Tyranny of Structurelessness*, that:

> it was a natural reaction against the over-structured society in which most of us found ourselves, the inevitable control this gave others over our lives and the continual elitism of the left and similar groups among those who were supposedly fighting this over-structuredness.[16]

Supporters of structurelessness also argued that organising groups tended to benefit male committee members, whilst women were delegated the secondary tasks of taking the minutes and making the tea. In short, organisational structures stifled women. Women involved in the WLM wanted to create a new kind of political movement, one which was without rules and made women feel as comfortable as possible. Furthermore, by making women's voices and experiences central to the movement it would allow all women a chance to flourish and grow in confidence. Many women who participated in the Scottish WLM thrived under this new ethos. Chris Aldred of Aberdeen commented that:

> Well I thought that was great. I thought it was wonderful because one of the things that had really made me feel not at home in left-wing politics was the kind of structure and the resolutions and the – votes and everything. And I felt this kind of different approach was much more what I wanted to be doing.[17]

Of course, many feminists active in the movement eventually concluded that they could not completely abandon rules and structure. As CR became increasingly popular there were attempts to formalise the running of groups. Influential voices in this debate in an international context were radical feminists such as Sarachild who argued that instead 'new knowledge is the source of consciousness-raising's strength and power' and this had the potential to be stifled by the desire to organise.[18]

Despite this viewpoint CR became more organised in Scotland as women began to write articles on how their groups operated. These reflections, which appeared at times to be akin to 'how-to' guides, were circulated and published in various women's liberation newsletters.[19] These accounts of CR appeared to be quite influential as most groups were similar. A typical CR group consisted of a small number of women, normally no more than ten, who met on a regular weekly basis, usually in the home of a member of the group with each woman taking it in turn to play host. According to English-based feminist Sue Bruley the decision to rotate meetings was taken because 'everyone had to act out the hostess role and … even if things were a little cramped, it was important in building up a mental picture of each other that we become aware of the material conditions of our home environment.'[20]

Once the decision had been taken to start a CR group the first thing to do was to agree on some informal rules. These focused on how the meetings would operate and encouraged women to commit to regular attendance in order to create continuity to group discussions.[21] During CR meetings, women usually sat in a circle and discussed issues and experiences linked to an agreed theme. The theme was decided in advance and every woman was allowed to offer her own personal reflections on the chosen topic. No one was allowed to interrupt and every woman was given a chance to speak for however long she wished. Avoiding interruption, it was argued by St Andrews feminist activist Aspen, would help to 'build up an atmosphere of trust within the group, women must feel sure nothing they say will be used against them outside the group'.[22] The emphasis on 'constructing a biography' became a powerful tool for understanding many of the issues surrounding feminism of the 1970s.[23] As Frankie Raffles and Finella MacKenzie of St Andrews CR group argued, 'we think that consciousness-raising provides us with a truly radical weapon. From examining our personal lives we derive a political theory which we can translate into action.'[24]

The emotion of anger was an important one in the development of this process. It was a central dynamic of the movement, often contributing to the creation of campaigns and giving women the confidence to speak out and stand up for what they believed in. The importance of anger in feminist discussions was especially emphasised by revolutionary and radical feminists, who believed that it served the dual purpose of encouraging women to take action, and also, more importantly, in challenging gendered understandings of women and protest, especially the dominant view that women were passive and less likely to undertake direct action. CR served a useful function in locating this anger and giving women a forum in which they could express this emotion. It also encouraged women to move beyond just feeling emotions and instead to translate these feelings into action. Consequently, CR was seen as an ongoing process which was 'not simply a tool to raise one's consciousness to a pre-conceived level of "liberation" after which one emerges as a card carrying feminist in thought, word and deed' but played an important role in the continuing development of the movement.[25] The centrality of anger to CR discussions also meant that women's liberation theory and practice differed from other women's groups, placing more emphasis on liberation and the personal and emotional aspects of politicisation.

This method of feminist discussion, which led to political action being informed by a theory which was derived from the life experiences of activists, seemed to be very popular. CR groups were started in many towns and cities in Scotland and often outside the cities and the main centres of women's liberation, with groups being set up in places like St Andrews, Shetland and Falkirk.[26] A leading figure in the development of a CR group in Shetland was Margaret Elphinstone:

> I can remember very clearly the consciousness-raising sessions … in Lerwick. So, the meetings were always at … [at a member's] house. And sometimes the group was very big … .The consciousness-raising was very powerful. And I think these days nobody quite remembers how powerful it was because so much had never been said. It's rather like going back to one's childhood and teens, it's very difficult to realise the kind of mores we grew up among and how little we were ever told about

sexuality, how unmentionable sex was .... So those early consciousness-raising, I mean just talking about our growing up experiences was extraordinarily powerful.[27]

The open and frank discussions of issues which during their childhoods had been deemed off limits, came as instant relief. Wendy Davies of Glasgow women's liberation group echoed this sentiment when she said what 'we talked about would actually be seen as quite commonplace now. But it felt ... radical then to – talk about women's health for example.'[28] Many women interviewed for this research recalled the power of CR sessions with such words and phrases used to describe them as 'opened my eyes', 'worthwhile', 'powerful' and 'amazing'.[29] CR was discussed by twenty-three women out of a total of twenty-nine interviewed for this research, clearly indicating how integral it was to the movement as a whole.[30]

Discussions in CR sessions ranged from personal issues to feminist publications. As Chapter 1 illustrated, books were highly important to the development of the movement, disseminating feminist politics and ideas amongst the wider membership.[31] Extracts from books like Germaine Greer's *The Female Eunuch* and Juliet Mitchell's *Woman's Estate* were published in national and local women's liberation newsletters and they assumed almost biblical status in the propagation of women's liberation arguments. As Ruth Miller of Edinburgh women's liberation group remembered:

I was wanting to read just anything that I could ... Put into words the feelings that I was having – if anyone can put down in words why I, who am white and middle-class and educated, still feel that I'm not really a first class citizen in this society ... And, so reading all this stuff was really – helpful.[32]

CR groups became important tools in the discussion and analysis of these texts as women arrived at meetings bursting with new knowledge, eager to share their reflections on what they were reading. Of central importance in the developing feminist consciousness of the WLM in Scotland was Germaine Greer's *The Female Eunuch*. Interviewees recalled that this book clearly described, for the first time in their lives, many of the inchoate feelings they had experienced about their position as women in society.[33] Women who attended CR groups in Scotland like Aileen Christianson described it as a 'fantastic book' and Esther Breitenbach revealed that it had been 'inspirational at the time'. Sandie Wyles went even further, enthusing that *The Female Eunuch* had 'really blown' her away. She said, 'completely blown away. I stood – reading it and I was reading it and thought, "oh my God, can I afford to buy this?" And that,

that was really the start.'[34] Elizabeth Smith was particularly affected by Greer's writings and felt challenged by many of her arguments. She was working for a lawyer in a surveyors' firm when *The Female Eunuch* was published and because of reading books like Greer's she became acutely aware of the discrimination against women in the organisation in which she worked. As she recalled, *The Female Eunuch* had forced her to start asking pertinent questions about the place of women in wider society as she was able to 'see on the page in words' explanations for why the world of work operated in the manner it did. Smith was so inspired by Greer's writings that she actually began to photocopy pages from her book and place them on top of her manager's correspondence; when he opened his mail in the morning he was forced to first of all look at a page from *The Female Eunuch*.[35]

Aside from discussions of influential feminist texts, CR sessions also focused on the life experiences of those who participated in the group. Discussion topics ranged from love, jealousy and sex to work, relationships, and children.[36] For example, the question could be posed 'why are women suspicious of each other?' leading to participants sharing their thoughts on how this topic related to their own experiences. These could include what it had been like being educated in an all girls' school or how women had related to their sisters as children. From these very personal experiences a general discussion would then begin, as the group would try to draw out common themes enabling women to understand how their particular experiences of growing up fitted into women's wider subordination.[37]

Women often described having epiphanies in CR sessions when an issue was revealed to them for the first time or they were forced to think about a topic in a completely new way. Fiona Forsyth, who attended a CR group in Aberdeen during the early 1970s, remembered when one woman revealed she was a lesbian. Fiona recalled being 'really shocked' and that her 'head was literally spinning'. She admitted that it made her think about all of her previous relationships in a completely new way.[38] The topic of relationships and marriage in particular was consistently open for discussion. Pauline, who would later go on to join Dundee women's liberation group, talked of her experiences of a CR group in Tanzania. She particularly remembered one Canadian woman in the group and her story about the night before Christmas:

> she put – dough to make gingerbread men, it was some Western occasion ... and in the morning she thought I've got to make those gingerbread men. When she woke up, and she said she woke up really early, crept out of bed, and cut them all, then crept back into bed where

her husband was lying awake, saying 'isn't this wonderful? No children'. She was lying there rigid as anything and [said] 'yes, it's absolutely wonderful', thinking 'how am I going to get those gingerbread people cooked before the children come back? And not making him cross with me for just forgetting about all this stuff'. And I thought that for me was at the heart of the Women's Liberation Movement ... a man's demand versus your duty. Never mind your pleasure or anything else.[39]

The issue of marriage reinforcing a sense of a woman's duty and subsequently restricting her ambitions was explored in many CR groups throughout Scotland. Again, the comparison to their mothers was an important factor in explaining this focus on the role of marriage in women's oppression. In St Andrews Judy Ekins remembered that this was a major theme in discussions and was most readily reflected in their mothers' lives. She said:

and a lot of people talked about their childhood, how their conditioning had happened. You know, quite sort of subtly -. If they had brothers they could compare how they were brought up in comparison with their brothers. What they were allowed to do, what they weren't allowed to do. And also we talked a lot about our mothers. And because our mothers had – been alive during the Second World War and that for them, that had had a big influence, in that most of them worked – women worked in male jobs during the Second World War. They had a good time. They did things that men normally did. But after the war, they were conned ... women who had made this sacrifice but now you can go back and be fulfilled in the family. And they had – accepted this propaganda.[40]

Furthermore, the domestic setting of CR groups opened the doors not only to each other's past experiences but also to their present lives. Margaret Adams described going to one woman's house for a meeting in Dundee:

we turned up for the meeting, myself and my friend and – the woman – answered, it took her ages to answer the door. And she answered the door and she seemed to be quite upset. And she said 'oh we can't have it here, we can't have it here tonight' ... we just sort of abandoned it that day –. But I found out later that she was actually suffering from domestic abuse and – her husband was giving her a hiding [a beating] – before the meetings, so she obviously felt she couldn't let people into the house ... the house we went to have the meeting was a big house and she was a professional person and her husband was a professional person ... Brought it home [to me] that domestic violence happens in any class – it isn't just a working-class experience.[41]

The CR sessions also allowed women to get to know each other more intimately as they had to trust each other not to reveal secrets outside the group. On many occasions this led women to view each other in completely different ways. Margaret Elphinstone recalled one particular occasion when during a CR session a woman who seemed to have it all, an extremely good job and who was very confident and self-assured, began to tell her story:

> she just broke down, she said I don't think I'm a very nice person. And she began to cry. And it was an extraordinarily powerful meeting … it spoke to us all, I think, of how we felt and what it was like to be then and also the shock of coming from her of all people, that she would think she wasn't a very nice person. That is a moment I've never forgotten.[42]

Scottish CR sessions were by no means unique. Giardina found a similar pattern within the American movement. She described how 'to listen to ten or fifteen women telling the ways in which each worked toward a goal, and to see that even seemingly successful and beautiful, the seemingly happily married, felt they had failed brought home a message'.[43] CR groups created a common language and common view of the way women's liberation activists saw their place, as women, in the world.

Impact on the wider movement

This led to a sense of solidarity amongst the women. In the early days CR was warmly welcomed and widely adopted by women's liberation groups throughout the United Kingdom. As Bouchier has argued, the small group process of CR appealed to 'women on the basis of their full participation, rather than junior status in someone else's movement'.[44] It also made 'joining' the movement relatively easy as there were no forms to fill in or subscriptions to be paid and meetings were always held locally. This local aspect was an important development for the movement as it sought to be as decentralised as possible, rooting a group in its community in order to provide greater continuity to the movement.[45] It was also hoped that by being held in members' living rooms and kitchens meetings would make every woman feel instantly welcome and part of the movement, creating a particularly effective local and personal network.[46]

CR groups also provided an important space in which women could grow in confidence, offering a secure and positive environment where they felt safe to explore issues and voice their opinions without fear of censure. Larger political meetings, it was argued by advocates of CR, tended to silence less confident women, whereas small groups encouraged women to speak up and enabled them to be more assertive.[47] As one woman reflected at the time, 'I had found that experience rewarding, not only because it provided me with much needed emotional support, but also as an important means of developing my political understanding', whilst in contrast she found her central women's group, which was larger, 'rather intimidating'.[48] This was particularly important given the focus of women's liberation politics on the personal. Exploring personal issues required a more intimate and private environment, and CR groups provided this. For the first time, membership of a CR group also gave many women an identity independent of the men in their lives. By making women's voices central to CR, it recognised the importance of the experiences of individual women and encouraged them to view these experiences more seriously.

By revealing their thoughts, fears and ambitions women received in return a sense of belonging and the support of other women in the group through times of personal development and intense change. Sharing experiences also allowed other women to learn about individual women's lives. Margaret Adams of the Dundee group recalled learning a lot from discussions with foreign university students.[49] It was hoped that this context would enable a greater understanding of how much women had in common, irrespective of national and class boundaries.[50] The early experiences of CR groups occurred during an exciting period in the history of the WLM. Echoing the liberationist narrative outlined in the previous chapter, a sense of wonderment and discovery is evoked in oral testimonies, in which women felt part of a movement which was strong enough to create real, lasting change in society. For example, Paula Jennings said 'you felt you were part of a huge movement that was energising, exciting, [I] really believed that we could change the world'.[51] However, as CR groups became more popular, it was also critiqued as a feminist method. In order for CR to work, groups had to be closed off to new members.[52] This was because CR groups became unwieldy if more than about ten members attended. The principle of allowing all women a chance to speak for however long they wanted to meant that meetings were open-ended with no chairperson or central figure to declare when the meeting was officially finished. If there were too many women present it meant that meetings could last a long time or the rule about allowing all women a chance to speak would have had to be revised.[53] This would have contradicted the movement's desire to allow meetings to be guided by women's experiences instead of rules, and would have introduced a time limit on each woman's opportunity to speak. Procedures tended to differ in how to avoid CR groups becoming too large with, for example, one group in Edinburgh operating an invitation-only policy.[54]

Irrespective of this, it would have been difficult for new members to join an established CR group. The success of a CR group depended on a sense of trust and because women were sharing so much of themselves they quickly formed close relationships. This sense of mutual trust was difficult to extend to new members. Furthermore, meeting regularly in each other's homes led to a 'shorthand form of communication which seemed to give a group a terminology of its own'.[55] It would have been very difficult, therefore, for a new member to establish herself in a group of women who were already very familiar with each other. It would have meant explaining conversations that had occurred before the new member had joined. However what soon became apparent to all of the women involved was that after the first few months of open dialogue the same members found it difficult to offer new experiences for discussion. Once their life stories had been shared there was little new material left for discussion.[56] These closed groups also led to some women criticising the movement for appearing too cliquey, with some groups forming strong bonds and excluding those who joined the movement at a later stage. As one woman who attended the Scottish women's liberation conference in 1976 reflected, new women who attended their first events found conferences were attended by many 'unfamiliar faces'.[57] One woman recalled her first contact with the movement in which she had to face 'the jargon I didn't understand … the put-downs from more experienced members'.[58] The method of CR, which at one stage seemed such an effective way to recruit women, soon became a barrier to increasing the membership and subsequently hampered the development of the movement. Bouchier has described the inherent contradiction of CR: on the one hand it was an ideal way of bringing women in and introducing them to feminist theories, but, on the other, once groups became closed this prevented new women from joining.[59]

Critics of CR also emphasised the academic basis of some discussions and the barrier this could pose to those who did not enjoy reading those kinds of texts. Indeed, Isabelle Kerr found some of the reading quite hard going. She especially recalled reading Susan Brownmiller's *Against Our Will*: she remembered 'really ploughing through it', reflecting that 'for somebody who had never tackled feminist literature before – I found it such a slog'.[60] Esther Breitenbach explored the problematic nature of CR in an article for a conference document produced by the WLM in Scotland in 1976. She criticised the movement's emphasis on CR, which she believed did not have clear aims. Because women were allowed free will to discuss what they liked for however long they desired, Breitenbach argued that CR groups tended to be dominated by personalities and especially by women who were more articulate and expressed clearer thoughts and ideas, thus contradicting the principle of anti-hierarchy.[61] Furthermore, some women often felt that they did not have as much to share or discuss. Aileen Christianson, for example, felt her life experiences had been less dramatic in comparison to other women in the group:

> I think as far as I remember we met once a week and an awful lot of the first while got taken up with women talking about their individual experiences, one by one. And me and [another woman], who was a journalist ... we – it turned out had had this really douce West of Scotland upbringing in our various ways. My dad worked for the electricity board and her dad was a teacher or something and maybe her mum as well, I can't remember. – but some of the others had these really dramatic parents. [62]

While this did not impact negatively on Aileen's experience of CR, it is clear that, far from reassuring all women and making them more confident about the value of their experiences, CR could often encourage some women to feel as if their ideas were less worthy of discussion.

As the movement evolved, CR continued to form a part of movement activities but it became less central to women's liberation activism in the second half of the 1970s. One of the reasons for this was the conflict which emerged in some of the CR groups. Conflicts of personalities and interests created a less supportive environment for women to explore how feminism of the 1970s related to their everyday lives. Nadine, a member of one of the CR groups in Edinburgh, recalled that the reason why one of the groups 'started to fizzle [out]' was because of the 'group dynamics' in which there were a number of 'not very pleasant sessions' because of a variety of disagreements.[63] Anne Ward of a group in Glasgow also recalled how increasing conflict made it very difficult to sustain CR.[64] Many of the women who went through the process of CR emerged from these sessions as very different people. For example, Lorna Peters, who belonged to a group in Aberdeen, described the problems with CR:

> I think there was the whole tension with this whole consciousness-raising side of it. And the sort of inward look therapy that was a big bugbear with a group of us anyway ... I mean, there were big arguments about it. About whether – you had to sort yourself out or sort the world out. You can't sort the world out unless you were sorted out. – And people organised radical or feminist therapy two-day sessions and things like that. Oh God! Yeah, just lost the will to live at that point ... Your life changes, I suppose ... And I didn't have children. A lot of the women I knew were beginning to have children ... When I first was involved I was – in this kind of free-wheeling – I'm not having

relationships ... And then I did get involved, – and I in fact got married. And at which point, some of my feminist friends – were really disgusted with me that I was actually letting other women down.[65]

This resentment towards Lorna was not noted quietly but was voiced openly amongst the group. She recalled:

> some of my feminist friends ... wouldn't come to the wedding or anything like that. Although they knew my partner well and – it was heterosexist because you know lesbian women couldn't get married at that time. – I remember being sort of very hurt – but I, I could appreciate the argument and then we split up and I got involved with a woman – and that again sort of seemed to bring me into conflict with an awful lot of people.[66]

On the other hand, some women felt that raising their consciousness had a positive impact on their lives. For instance, Paula Jennings described how these discussions had encouraged her to experiment with how she looked:

> I used to be in full war paint everyday until I was thrown off the stage – protesting against the ... charities' queen contest. And from that day I stopped wearing make-up. Because it just seemed so clear to me that, that – we weren't being allowed to be who we were.[67]

Although CR sessions could prove highly emotive, with many women finding instant relief that they were not unique in their dissatisfaction, this emotion could also leave women feeling rather exposed and vulnerable. Women invested a lot emotionally in these small groups, which could often result in conflict when women felt they were not getting a good enough return on their investment. Ruth Miller described CR sessions as focusing on very 'painful discussions' which looked at the role of male children amongst many other issues. She believed:

> there had to be some kind of real hard-line stuff first of all to get through to then accepting all of us as human beings in society – But we had to really look at – how are we as women or young women or girls being – oppressed. And – we debated really difficult topics such as all men [are] potential rapists and those kind of things. And – the dilemmas some women were having: male children and how they were going to raise them and oh things that I don't think, I don't know, but I don't think they are debated in quite the same way now.[68]

Indeed, the inability of some groups to reconcile such divisions led to their demise. Aileen Christianson, a member of a CR group in Edinburgh, remembered how discussions focused on sexuality played a role in the ending of her group:

But then you would move on into talking about issues – but also talking about feelings, it was the whole point of consciousness-raising was raising your consciousness about being a woman and seeing the world in a feminist way ... It was all about women's liberation and so it was raising your consciousness so that you understood the way in which you as a woman were oppressed. So it was to do with individual consciousness-raising, done through talking in a group so it was supposed to be a comfortable, safe, area ... And it ended, the group ended, because – one of the women in it was the only lesbian and she got pissed off with being the only lesbian in the group, she's right, I mean she was quite right we had been going for about two years I think and it was time for it to stop.[69]

Conclusion

For many women involvement in a CR group was their first contact with the ideas and arguments of the WLM in Scotland. Although the theory behind CR was formed in the USA by the Redstockings group, the concept proved so popular that it crossed national boundaries and became a truly international phenomenon. It ushered in a new style of politics in which the emphasis was placed on women's personal experiences and in this regard was an effective way of making women feel as if they had a stake in the WLM, that it was theirs to shape and develop. This emphasis on the membership was particularly important in starting the movement as it provided personal and local networks through which women could quickly become acquainted with the wider issues of the movement and with other activists.

The local nature of CR groups rooted feminist politics in the wider community as women got to know each other in their own towns and cities. Holding meetings in each other's homes became an important way of pursuing the movement's aim of collectivism, making women share the responsibility of hosting CR meetings. It was also helpful for those women who had child-care responsibilities and, therefore, meant the movement was open to a more diverse range of women. The home was also a particularly useful context for pursuing the personal, helping women to open up and share their experiences in comfortable and intimate surroundings.

Initially CR groups proved very popular and were a powerful instrument in the development of the movement. Women recalled the absolute joy and relief of revealing an experience which they had thought was unique to their own lives, only to find that many other women had felt the same way. This bred a feeling of comradeship within a mutually supportive environment. However, this initial joy was soon replaced by a feeling of frustration as women began to see the limits of CR. The problems of the CR group provided the first real point of conflict for the movement acting as a precursor to what the wider WLM would face throughout the 1970s. The first major controversy was how to include all women's experiences in the campaigns and discussions of the WLM. There appeared to be an inability to reconcile the desire to include every individual woman's experiences with the realisation that in order to campaign for women's liberation, women's experiences would have to be universalised. Yet without CR many of the campaigns would never have come to fruition as the discussions generated in these groups helped to formulate new ideas and campaigns for the movement. CR discussions of early experiences of generational conflict and change, therefore, actually helped to set the agenda of women's liberation politics during the 1970s and beyond and this newly established agenda was then acted upon within local workshops. CR was, therefore, an essential part of the development of the politics of women's liberation.

Notes

1 J. Lewis, 'From Equality to Liberation: Contextualizing the Emergence of the Women's Liberation Movement' in B. Moore-Gilbert and J. Seed (eds), *Cultural Revolution? The Challenge of the Arts in the 1960s* (London, 1992), p. 112.

2 J. Mitchell, *Woman's Estate* (Harmondsworth, 1971), p. 61.

3 E. Breitenbach, '"Sisters are doing it for themselves": The Women's Movement in Scotland' in A. Brown and R. Parry (eds), *The Scottish Government Yearbook 1990* (Edinburgh, 1990), p. 209.

4 Transcript of interview with Zoe Fairbairns (ZF), 5 June 2007, p. 3.

5 *Edinburgh Women's Liberation Newsletter*, December 1976, p. 6.

6 See for example, D. Bouchier, *The Feminist Challenge: The Movement for Women's Liberation in Britain and the United States* (London, 1983), p. 87, S. Rowbotham, *The Past Is Before Us: Feminism in Social Action since the 1960s* (London, 1989), p. 6, A. Coote and B. Campbell, *Sweet Freedom: The Struggle for Women's Liberation* (London, 1982), p. 14.

7 Coote and Campbell, *Sweet Freedom*, p. 14.

8 Rowbotham, *The Past Is Before Us*, p. 6; S. Evans, *Personal Politics: The Roots of Women's Liberation in the Civil Rights Movement and the New Left* (New York, 1979), p. 214; A. Lent, *British Social Movements since 1945: Sex, Colour, Peace and Power* (Basingstoke, 2001), p. 63.

9 Bouchier, *The Feminist Challenge*, p. 87.

10 Redstockings, 'Manifesto' in R. Baxandall and L. Gordon (eds), *Dear Sisters: Dispatches from the Women's Liberation Movement* (New York, 2000), p. 91.

11 The Redstockings' manifesto was cited by two members of the WLM in Scotland as being extremely helpful in their understanding of CR. Transcript of interview with

Ruth Miller (RM*), 27 April 2007, p. 3; Transcript of interview with Paula Jennings (PJ), 15 October 2007, p. 9.

12 K. Sarachild, 'Consciousness-raising: A Radical Weapon' in Redstockings (ed.), *Feminist Revolution* (New York, 1975), p. 132.

13 Sarachild, 'Consciousness-raising', p. 132.

14 Transcript of interview with Wendy Davies (WD), 17 July 2007, p. 10.

15 Sarachild, 'Consciousness-raising', p. 132.

16 J. Freeman, *The Tyranny of Structurelessness* (New York, 1970) p. 2.

17 Transcript of interview with Chris Aldred (CA), 30 August 2007, p. 3.

18 Sarachild, 'Consciousness-raising', p. 135.

19 For examples of 'how-to' guides see *Tayside Women's Liberation Newsletter*, vol. 1, no. 8, May 1978, pp. 10–12, and *The Revolutionary and Radical Feminist Newsletter*, no. 2, March 1979, pp. 24–5.

20 S. Bruley, 'Women Awake: The Experience of Consciousness-raising' in Feminist Anthology Collective (eds), *No Turning Back: Writings from the Women's Liberation Movement 1975–1980* (London, 1981), p. 61.

21 Ibid., p. 61.

22 *The Revolutionary and Radical Feminist Newsletter*, no. 2, March, 1979, p. 24.

23 S. Rowbotham, *Promise of a Dream* (London, 2001), p. 6.

24 *Tayside Women's Liberation Newsletter*, vol. 1, no. 5, November 1977, p. 4.

25 *Edinburgh Women's Liberation Newsletter*, December 1976, p. 5.

26 A CR group was reported to exist in Falkirk in 1979, *Spare Rib*, April 1980, p. 25.

27 Transcript of interview with Margaret Elphinstone (ME), 21 November 2007, pp. 13–14.

28 Transcript WD, p. 11.

29 Transcript of interview with Margaret Adams (MA*), 3 May 2007, p. 3, Transcript of interview with Judy Ekins (JE), 27 July 2007, p. 15, Transcript ME, p. 13, Transcript RM*, p. 3.

30 Those women that did not discuss CR were not directly involved in the movement but associated with groups like the Pre-School Playgroup Association or Women Citizens' Association in the 1970s. See transcript of interview with Caroline Florence (CF), 31 March 2007, and Transcript of interview with Mary Henderson (MH), 14 June 2007.

31 A. Carter, *The Politics of Women's Rights* (London, 1988), p. 52; M. Pugh, *Women and the Women's Movement in Britain, 1914–1999* (Basingstoke, 2000), p. 323.

32 Transcript RM*, p. 13.

33 Carter, *The Politics*, p. 52; Pugh, *Women and the Women's Movement*, p. 323.

34 Transcript of interview with Aileen Christianson (AC), 26 April 2007, p. 3 (Aileen read *The Female Eunuch* before joining a CR group); Transcript of interview with Esther Breitenbach (EB), 24 May 2007, p. 4, and Transcript of interview with Sandie Wyles and Anne-Marie McGeoch (SW and AMcG), 18 September 2007, pp. 1–2.

35 Transcript of interview with Elizabeth Smith (ES*), 19 April 2007, p. 2.

36 Coote and Campbell, *Sweet Freedom*, p. 218 and Bruley, 'Women Awake', pp. 60–5.

37 *The Revolutionary and Radical Feminist Newsletter*, no. 2, March 1979, p. 24.

38 Transcript of interview with Fiona Forsyth (FF), 9 July 2008, p. 5.

39 Transcript of interview with Pauline Robinson (PR*), 6 December 2006, p. 4.

40 Transcript JE, pp. 15–16.

41 Transcript MA*, p. 4.

42 Transcript ME, p. 14.
43 C. Giardina, *Freedom for Women: Forging the Women's Liberation Movement 1953–1970* (Gainesville, 2010), p. 181.
44 Bouchier, *The Feminist Challenge*, p. 86; Evans, *Personal Politics*, p. 215.
45 Bouchier, *The Feminist Challenge*, p. 86.
46 'Organising Ourselves', published in *Shrew*, March 1971, as quoted in M. Wandor (ed.), *The Body Politic: Women's Liberation in Britain 1969–1972* (London, 1972), p. 105.
47 Wandor, *The Body Politic*, p. 103.
48 *Catcall – A Feminist Discussion Paper*, issue 3, July 1976, p. 16.
49 Transcript MA*, pp. 3–4.
50 *Catcall – A Feminist Discussion Paper*, issue 3, July 1976, p. 16.
51 Transcript of interview with Paula Jennings (PJ), 15 October 2007, p. 14.
52 This happened throughout Britain: E. Setch, 'The Face of Metropolitan Feminism: The London Women's Liberation Workshop, 1969–1979', *Twentieth Century British History*, 13:2 (2002), p. 178.
53 Wandor, *The Body Politic*, p. 104. E. Maitland (ed), *Woman to Woman: An Oral History of Rape Crisis in Scotland* (Glasgow, 2009), p. 104.
54 Transcript AC, p. 19.
55 Bruley, 'Women Awake', p. 61.
56 Bouchier, *The Feminist Challenge*, p. 219.
57 London School of Economics Archive (hereafter LSE) (MCINTOSH 1/15), *A Record of the Scottish Women's Liberation Conference, Glasgow, October 1976*, p. 27.
58 Ibid., p. 27.
59 Bouchier, *The Feminist Challenge*, p. 219.
60 Transcript of interview with Isabelle Kerr (IK), 21 August 2007, p. 6.
61 LSE (McINTOSH 1/15), *A Record of the Scottish Women's Liberation Conference, Glasgow, October 1976*, p. 23.
62 Transcript AC, p. 19.
63 Transcript NH, p. 2.
64 Transcript of interview with Anne Ward (AW*), 28 August 2007, p. 7.
65 Transcript of interview with Lorna Peters (LP*), 3 August 2007, pp. 12–13.
66 Transcript LP*, p. 13.
67 Transcript PJ, p. 9.
68 Transcript RM*, p. 3.
69 Transcript AC, pp. 19–20.

4

Women's liberation in the local context

This chapter offers a brief history of local women's liberation workshops in order to establish for the first time the variety of different campaigns and locations of feminist activism within Scotland. By analysing the practice of CR and looking at the debates and discussions of local groups, the way the WLM developed and operated can be better understood.[1] Workshops were focused on practical actions and were larger than CR groups, acting as a local forum to which individual CR groups were aligned. During the 1970s a number of women's liberation workshops and feminist groups were established throughout Scotland, from Shetland to the Borders and with large groups existing in almost every major university town. As Gelb has correctly identified, 'the major locus of activity [in the WLM] is the small local group'.[2] Much more must be done in order to look at women's liberation from the local and small-group perspective. In this way the complexities of feminism in the 1970s will be better understood. Moreover, as will become clear, the movement did not operate in isolation, but was shaped by the local communities from which it emerged. Looking at the movement from the perspective of the local context, therefore, allows us to understand the diverse range of ideas, identities and campaigns of the WLM in Britain. As the evidence from Scotland will show, approaches to women's liberation often 'varied regionally and between cities and smaller towns', and like any social movement the WLM was, therefore, much more complex than many accounts, which have focused on the national British context, have described.[3]

Little is known about the precise beginnings of the WLM in Scotland. Breitenbach argues that 'it is not possible to pinpoint the moment of birth of the first Scottish women's liberation groups'.[4] Nevertheless, as Table 4.1 shows, it has been possible to offer a rough estimate of the date of origin of the first women's liberation groups founded in Scotland in the early

1970s, based on information from oral testimony and local and national newletters. Establishing a clear chronological framework of the WLM's development in Scotland has proved difficult mainly because, as Chapter 2 established, the movement did not have a start date but rather emerged over time. Groups of women in towns and cities throughout Scotland were often more inspired by American and European feminist thinking than by the emergence of a women's group in a neighbouring town or city, thus making the idea of territorial expansion less useful. Nonetheless by the early 1970s there was a clear network of women's liberation workshops established. They met in a variety of different places and were attended by a range of women.

Table 4.1 Estimated start dates of local women's liberation workshops in Scotland in the 1970s

Location of workshop or group	Start date
Aberdeen	c.1970
Dundee	1972
Edinburgh	c.1970
Glasgow	c.1970
St Andrews	1970
Shetland	1972

Source: Various mentions of local groups in *The Scottish Women's Liberation Journal* and oral history interviews. See also E. Hunter, *Scottish Woman's Place: A Practical Guide and Critical Comment on Women's Rights in Scotland* (Edinburgh, 1978), p. 213.

Meeting places were diverse. For example, in Edinburgh, meetings were often held in the basement of a house on Royal Terrace owned by an American woman, Hildemarie Rutovitz. It was in the basement of this property that Edinburgh feminists planned, discussed and held feminist events. The Glasgow women's liberation workshop met in various places including Shelter's premises, the Iona Community House and individuals' homes.[5] Meeting places differed according to the requirements of the local membership. For example many of the members in Aberdeen were students and so they found it easier to meet in the Students' Union or in a nearby bookshop, Boomtown Books. This bookshop was an important focus for feminist activism in this city. Based in King Street, just near the university, it was owned by Alison McNaughton and it was latterly run by women's liberation group member Anne-Marie McGeoch. This bookshop was a workers' co-operative which stocked the latest in revolutionary theory and, therefore, provided a sympathetic environment in which to conduct meetings.[6] In contrast most meetings of the Shetland group were held in members' homes. One home in particular became a frequent meeting place because the owner lived in Lerwick which was fairly central and easy to access. This was an important consideration given that the group would have found it difficult to rotate meetings as many women lived in places that were quite isolated and hard to reach.[7] The local environment, therefore, often shaped the ways in which women's liberation meetings were conducted.

Membership

While it is evident that there were a range of women involved in the WLM, for some local groups many of the early activists were middle-class. As Fran Wasoff remembered of the Edinburgh group:

> It was quite a range but basically it was young, educated, middle class women – I remember being very struck – by the privilege of some – you know people who had been Oxbridge educated and they were the most articulate members of the group. Very few of the women were not college or university educated. I would say there were hardly any that were – over thirty. – You know so socially and economically it was a narrow stratum of society and one of the criticisms of the women's liberation movement in its early days is that it was a movement about the concerns of young, educated women. And you know that's exemplified by the relative interest in violence against women issues, abortion, employment issues and a relative neglect to motherhood issues 'cause very few people at the time were mothers.[8]

Yet there were exceptions to this. Glasgow seemed to be fairly diverse, with mothers and older people attending alongside the usual assortment of university students and graduates. However, there was still a connection between some women's liberation activists within the local group and the universities in Glasgow.[9] It would seem, therefore, that, while universities were important to the formation of the WLM, they were not crucial. Two examples from Scotland illustrate this point. First, research suggests that Stirling, which has a university, did not have a women's liberation group. This is surprising, especially since, as Chapter 2 illustrated, many students at Stirling were politicised by left-wing ideologies and the spirit of '68, and were at the cutting edge of student politics in Scotland in the late 1960s and early 1970s. Indeed, the lack of women's groups on campus was commented upon in one article in the student newspaper, *Brig*, where

Jane Kelly explained that this was because 'the cream of academic girl-hood is not interested'.[10] However, a more likely reason was that students from Stirling were drawn to large feminist groups in nearby Glasgow, with Glasgow women's liberation group advertised in *Brig* in 1974.[11] Second, there was a group on Shetland and yet the closest university was in Aberdeen. Yet it is evident that the group here was started by gradu-ates who had moved to Lerwick for work and family reasons.[12] Indeed, how far this group reflected the wider local community was called into question by a number of members who observed that the majority of the women involved were not native Shetlanders. This was to become a point of tension for the group. It was noted in *The Scottish Women's Liberation Journal* that 'most of us in the group are not local'.[13] Susan Playfair, who was from Shetland and moved to Edinburgh in the late 1970s to begin her studies, commented that the group in Shetland, although small and active, was divided because the women who took the lead in the group were 'slagged cos they're not Shetlanders'. She questioned this antago-nism, asking 'does it matter if they're doing the Islands good? Of course not!'[14] Margaret Elphinstone also reflected on this issue at length during her interview with me. She remembered that at one point there had only been one woman in the group who was from Shetland and that she under-standably 'got a bit cheesed off with being, as she said, "I feel like the token Shetlander", which felt like really bad to hear and we had a big discussion about it'.[15] This was not a uniquely Shetland experience as incomers were often very important in kick-starting a women's liberation group in both rural and urban areas.

Indeed in the later part of the period it is evident that there were a number of feminist groups emerging in local communities throughout Scotland. Feminists from Glasgow were influential in encouraging and supporting women in other areas, such as West and Central Scotland, to set up women's groups to campaign against violence against women and to defend abortion rights. Although these groups were not listed as women's liberation groups in the newsletters and journals, their creation was important in introducing aspects of the women's liberation agenda to new women in locations outside of the six main centres. For example, in 1978 six women in Cumbernauld and Kilsyth formed a women's group. The group consolidated its creation by organising a Reclaim the Night march in 1979. Women from Glasgow, Edinburgh, Fife, and Stirling joined them in order to support their efforts. Also in 1979 a Falkirk Area Women's Group was formed, building on the success of the Women's Aid (battered women) group which had existed since at least 1978. They began with six members and campaigned on the rights of women to access free and safe abortions.[16] Before setting up their own group, women in Falkirk had been urged to attend the women's liberation group in Glasgow.[17] In this way the Glasgow group was important in supporting the creation of new women's liberation groups and in extending the reach of women's liberation politics in Scotland, introducing it to women outside the main cities and university towns.

Discussion topics

Women's liberation workshops in Scotland undertook a variety of different campaigns but certain issues were emphasised by different local groups, indicating the importance of the membership and the local context in shaping women's liberation politics. In Glasgow there appeared to be a strong emphasis on the issue of health. This interest was consistent with the movement's emphasis on the personal. The body politic became an important theme in the discussions of many women's liberation groups as feminists stressed the empowering potential of self-help.[18] Women's health discussions in Britain were directly influenced by publications in the USA, particularly *Our Bodies, Ourselves*, published in 1971, which 'had pioneered accessible information on women's health'.[19] Women's health groups in the 1970s could also be found in Aberdeen and Edinburgh. Much like the American self-help groups, feminists in Scotland focused on encouraging women to know their own bodies and to participate in self-examination. It was argued that doctors had too much power because women knew so little about how their bodies worked.[20] In order to combat this power imbalance, women's health groups argued for 'self-examination of the cervix and vagina ... [in order to] recognise what is normal and healthy, the changes and variations that occur in relation to the menstrual cycle and between individuals – hopefully we can then recognise and do something about early signs of infection'.[21] Advice from health groups in the USA was published and distributed in newsletters that were read by Scottish-based feminists. The first session of a health group usually introduced women to the correct way to use a speculum. It was argued that self-examination could throw 'off the oppression of centuries' but that engaging in such an activity would take 'total commitment and sisterhood'.[22] The WLM has been accused of lacking a sense of humour but, as Wendy Davies of the Glasgow group revealed, discussions on women's health could take a comedic turn:

> I do remember lots of incidents with speculums [laughter]. Which amuses my friends. We used to sit around with speculums. Self-examination was very important ... The point of it was that we would

self-examine, so we all had plastic speculums that we had to buy at conferences. And mirrors and – usually somebody would demonstrate how to use it. And we'd all be very moved by it! [laughter] But I do remember being at a financial and legal independence meeting at [someone's] house and her daughter – charging through, she was about six at the time, with the speculum, going bang, bang, bang, bang, bang, you're all dead! [laughter][23]

This emphasis on health in Glasgow probably stemmed from the influence of Jill Rakusen. This is a good example of how individuals and the local context influenced the movement. An Englishwoman and a freelance journalist, Rakusen was well known throughout the WLM in Britain thanks to her work on the British version of the influential book *Our Bodies, Ourselves*.[24] This revised text was welcomed by the movement as much of the material in the original edition from the USA had been marketed for an American audience and, therefore, certain sections proved irrelevant to women in Britain. It covered issues such as sexuality, nutrition and birth control. The review of this book in *MsPrint* particularly welcomed the lack of a London bias as useful Scottish contacts and addresses had also been included, arguing that 'this is the best women's health book available in this country'.[25] Its impact cannot be overstated; as Rowbotham has described, Rakusen came up with the slogan 'power over our bodies, power over our lives' and this became very influential in the movement as a whole.[26] The fact Rakusen was well known in international feminist circles increased her influence over the group in Glasgow. Ellen Galford, a member of the same group, described Jill Rakusen:

Jill had enormous energy and knowledge and contacts, you know, she was involved in things in London and – there was this awful point where you sort of realised that people would come to a meeting ... and everybody would wait before Jill got there before things would start.[27]

While women's health was a priority in Glasgow, there was a focus on the availability of child-care facilities in Dundee, Edinburgh and Aberdeen in the early 1970s. One of the early actions of the Aberdeen group was to set up a playgroup near the university which members of the women's group staffed. This playgroup was run at a local church hall and women's liberation activists organised food and took it in turns to operate the rota. As Chris Aldred reflected, they thought this kind of activity 'was really important'.[28] An interest in this issue was further revealed by their discussion topics for their monthly meetings, which included the family and day-care facilities. The other major issue of importance to women in the Aberdeen group was abortion. Women's liberation activist Chris Durndell participated in a university-run debate in 1974. The motion was

'Abortion is a Woman's Birthright' and was defeated by 62 votes to 74, with 36 abstentions. In defending the motion, Chris Durndell argued that 'it was always the needs of society that dictated attitudes towards abortion.'[29] This debate was also an effective recruiter of new women to the cause of women's liberation, such as Lorna Peters. She recalled:

> I went to hear Chris at a debate on abortion ... and enjoyed it. And it was – huge, you know it was absolutely packed ... And she was speaking against a Professor ... who turned out was in SPUC [Society for the Protection of Unborn Children]. And I can't remember who the other speaker was, but he was a fantastic speaker. Very powerful. Very fluent and engaging and all that. And Chris was tiny as well, and she was just so brave and sort of took it on and she's a wonderful teacher. And it was just so amazing that somebody was saying something that actually engaged with – how I saw the world –. And I spoke to her afterwards and she told me about this meeting.[30]

The examples of Rakusen and Durndell illustrate that there were a number of inspirational women within the Scottish movement who could effectively articulate their ideas and in this way they helped to expand the movement and to shape the local politics of their liberation groups.

Activism

In order to highlight these campaigns women's liberation groups often participated in colourful protests. For example, in 1975, as part of the International Women's Day celebrations, the Edinburgh group organised a mock beauty contest in which Miss Fortune, Miss Treated, Miss Used, Miss Placed and Miss Conception were all entered as contestants.[31] However, not every instance of direct action was pre-planned, with some women in Edinburgh reacting to discussions and events in a more spontaneous manner indicating the intense commitment to women's liberation. During one Meadows Fair in Edinburgh in 1978 some women's liberation supporters noticed derogatory badges being sold at a neighbouring stall. The message on these badges was viewed by the women as insulting, as they felt they were promoting a light-hearted view of rape. Some women decided to take action and their protest was recorded in *The Edinburgh Women's Liberation Newsletter* where one of the participants described how they

> took that badge over to that man behind the stall and threw it down and said, 'I think this badge is disgusting! It's only fit for the rubbish bin!' And then I threw it at him. I'm really shaking still! She was. We hugged each other for reassurance. It's amazing how many inner taboos

we women have to break through before we can show our just anger at the men who oppress us … the struggle nearly always leaves us shaking. We went beneath a tree to talk about what we felt and what we wanted to do about the badges.[32]

Once they had conferred, they decided to design a poster to pin to the stall to alert everyone to the sexist and offensive badges. The police were called but the women were not to be deterred. They reported that they were

[a little] unsure about exactly how best to respond to the jeers and taunting questions from men (and women). As it was a spontaneous, not a planned confrontation we only had our 'instincts' to go by and, predictably, different women reacted in different ways. I was so pissed off by then that my 'instinct' was to shout back at the men with a fervour that surprised even me, sometimes even being provoked into revealing our strategy. For instance when taunted about my 'purity' and 'idealism' in 'wanting to change the world' by some of the men, I shouted back: 'Yeah, I'd like to change the world and I want to start with it by the castration of all men!'[33]

The emphasis on direct action continued throughout the 1970s with women in Edinburgh protesting about a number of issues. This included walking on stage during a performance at a local theatre because they had discovered that women workers at the theatre had been designated stereotypical jobs, such as cooking and cleaning.[34] Furthermore at the Remembrance Day parade in Edinburgh in 1979 some women from the group apparently arrived, dressed in black, and laid a wreath for all women who had been raped and murdered in wars. One member of the group, Sos, described how 'an anxious and bustling official asked us to remove it – we refused so he did it himself'.[35] In the same year they also injected egg shells with red paint and smashed them against advertising boards they felt were particularly offensive, including one for McEwan's beer which was described by the women as featuring a leering man who was drinking beer. The caption was reported to read, 'more satisfying body than page three'.[36]

Direct action was also undertaken elsewhere. In Aberdeen during International Women's Year (IWY) in 1975 the women's liberation group protested outside an event which was intended to celebrate women's groups in the city. It would appear that the IWY's celebrations in Aberdeen were met with a degree of apathy, with few events planned by September 1975.[37] In the local evening newspaper it was suggested that part of the reason for women's reluctance to get involved was IWY being associated with women's liberation. In an attempt to persuade women to become involved, the paper argued, 'it is a common misunderstanding that IWY is "just something to do with Women's Lib" but, in fact it is an opportunity for women to express themselves in the best way they know how'.[38] This indicates the uneasy relationship women's liberation groups often had with sections of the local community.

One event that was organised was a 'fayre' to celebrate women's groups in the city, which was held in the Music Hall in Aberdeen. This caused controversy amongst local women's liberation activists. Anne-Marie McGeoch and Sandie Wyles remembered they were not invited to participate, and Chris Aldred said the organisers had tried to stress that it was just an oversight, and in an embarrassed way invited the group to join in on the day of the event.[39] Irrespective of this, the women's liberation group was angered about not being included in the organisation of this event from its earliest stages. Groups like the Women's Rural Institute, Soroptimists and Housewives' Register were profiled. The Society for the Protection of Unborn Children (SPUC), an anti-abortion group and opponent of the WLM, was also present and this particularly angered activists who decided to stage a protest outside the Music Hall. To attract publicity they decided to dress up as Miss Conceived, Miss Taken, Miss Judged, Miss Used and Miss Laid, echoing the action undertaken by women in Edinburgh, suggesting that ideas for protests were shared by different groups. Chris Aldred vividly described the demonstration:

> There's ... Miss Judged, who is the graduate student ... Miss Conceived with a pillow stuffed up her jumper ... Miss Taken the bride ... Miss Used, the housewife. And I was there in my short shiny dress and my red high heels, borrowed, and a wig! – as Miss Laid. And we did it to draw attention to the fact that we hadn't been invited to take part in this women's day event.[40]

This led to some of their most successful publicity as they were profiled in the local press.[41]

A major focus for some campaigns was the refusal of certain pubs to serve women. In Dundee and Aberdeen the women's liberation groups protested about this ban on women. In October 1977 five women from the Dundee women's liberation group, supported by seven men, entered the Tay Bridge Bar in relays and tried to get served. They hoped to be able to collect evidence to present to the licensing board in order to prevent the pub from obtaining their Sunday licence. They found that the reaction to women in the bar was better than it had been in the early 1970s, when 'women setting foot in the place got bawled out immediately'. They appeared slightly disappointed that the policy of the bar was not to exclude women entirely but to ask them to take their drinks into the lounge. The women's group sent its evidence to the licensing board and cited the Sex Discrimination Act (1975). It was disappointed with the response which informed them that the licensing board could refuse an extension to a licence only on the grounds of public nuisance and any problems with sex discrimination should be referred to the Equal Opportunities Commission.[42] In Aberdeen, protest methods were similar. As Anne-Marie McGeoch described:

> So we would go and a whole bunch of us would try and get served ...
> So we'd have a picket outside and then call up the press and get photos.
> And ... that happened all the time. – We'd get thrown out of bars –
> because we were a bunch of rowdy women. Because – after a meeting
> ... we'd go across to the Northern Bar.[43]

At times, issues coalesced with the interests of the burgeoning gay rights movement in Aberdeen. In 1977 six men were asked to leave the Scotia Bar because five of them were gay.[44] The women's group in Aberdeen were quick to defend the rights of homosexuals. Sandie Wyles remembered that 'gay people were getting thrown out of bars so we were there and alongside us there was the libertarian socialists, the anarchists, the militant, you know everybody seemed to kind of come to support each other'.[45]

On Shetland the group took direct action against the opening of a strip club in Lerwick in 1978. The women's group picketed the club and also encouraged local people to sign a petition.[46] However, the women's liberation group found itself in an uneasy alliance with religious groups over this issue:

> And we went to demonstrate because we reckoned strip clubs were
> demeaning to women and when we got there we found the Christian
> Right alongside us. And, of course, it was all reported in *Shetland Times*,
> women's group with Christian fundamentalists or however, and you
> think, oh Jesus, this isn't – quite how we wanted to present ourselves.[47]

Indeed, the wider community in Shetland appeared quite apprehensive about the creation of a women's liberation group. An article in *The Scottish Women's Liberation Newsletter* in 1978 profiled the activities of the group in Shetland and it was noted that the group found it difficult to campaign in a small community given that everyone knew each other and any protests, therefore, were quite visible.[48] Margaret Elphinstone believed the community thought the group was 'weird'. She believed:

> [that there were] quite a few jokes. And I was working in the library and
> I think [one of my friends] I worked with in Shetland library – but he
> had a line in sort of very laconic, understated quiet little jokes, like 'oh,

see you out there on the street the other night' ... I also thought, yeah I don't want to defend this. I don't want to be controversial, I just want to be quiet. And also, being an incomer in a small community, part of you just wants to fade into the background.[49]

This clearly indicates that the local environment influenced the campaigns and protest methods that women's liberation groups adopted and that it was often easier to undertake direct action in large cities than it was in a smaller town where individual activists were more visible and open to scrutiny. Looking at the movement from this perspective is important in order to gain an understanding of the different opportunities open to and the limitations placed upon women's liberation groups throughout Britain, depending on the local community from which they emerged.

However, groups were often very similar in terms of their discussions and their operation. One of the most important issues for women's liberation groups in Scotland was child-care. In order to highlight the lack of child-care facilities the Shetland group gathered at Lerwick's market cross with placards demanding that the council provide more nurseries. It also directly lobbied the council through a letter-writing campaign.[50] Feminists in Edinburgh prepared a well-researched report for a working party, which had been appointed by the Edinburgh Corporation Education Department to look into the issue. Their report helped to shape the Education Department's policy towards nurseries.[51] It highlighted the lack of nursery facilities in Edinburgh, arguing that many women were discriminated against because of their inability to pay high nursery fees and also because of the limited opening hours of nurseries. One passage in the report made the case for a greater recognition of mothers as human beings, contending that:

> Women claim the right, as people, to fail to meet some ideal standard of motherhood, just because they are physically mothers, and to judge for themselves how their skills may best be deployed. The best interests of the children will not be served by confining them with a miserably frustrated mother, but by enabling both mother and child to be fulfilled and happy persons.[52]

In the report the group put forward plans for 'a radical proposal – a model nursery centre for Edinburgh'. They proposed that opening hours should be extended and if necessary a special sleeping room should be provided so that children could sleep over or rest during the day. They also demanded that there should be a Home Responsibility Allowance paid to women to enable them to pay nursery fees. These arguments were justified with statistics and the group appeared to be aware that in order to be taken seriously this had to be a well-researched report.[53] This was the kind of work which went unnoticed by many in the local community as the direct action protests gained more widespread publicity, but it clearly illustrates that women's liberation groups in Scotland had a range of campaigning techniques at their disposal.

Women's centres

In the later 1970s some local women's liberation workshops, and especially those in Edinburgh and Glasgow, became concerned by the lack of working-class women in their ranks, and this problem became a subject 'both of much soul-searching and much argument'.[54] They aimed to undertake outreach work by setting up women's centres and establishing women's studies courses. The idea of a women's centre was a major development for the Scottish movement, indicating a new commitment to the cause of women's liberation. The centres acted as sources of information, storing pamphlets and books and they also held workshops, for example, on abortion, relaxation and health. The idea of women's centres was popular and by 1981 a National (British) Women's Centre Conference was held. The first women's liberation groups to set up centres were in London from 1972 onwards.[55]

Drawing on this inspiration, Glasgow opened the first women's centre in Scotland in 1976 at 57 Miller Street. Through research grant money from the Equal Opportunities Commission and job creation schemes they were able to employ two paid workers.[56] The idea behind a women's centre was that it would enable women who were not involved in the movement to drop in and find out about women's liberation. They would be able to fit a visit in around their routines, rather than being forced to rearrange work and domestic commitments to attend meetings. As Glasgow women's liberation group argued at the time, these centres should act as 'a resource centre. A place where we have information, skills, knowledge, that can be used, not just by women in the movement but by all women at whatever point they're at'.[57] Centres were also important in establishing women-only spaces in towns and cities throughout Britain. The Glasgow group also opened a women's centre out of necessity as some groups had grown so large that it was no longer feasible to hold meetings in each other's homes.[58] Esther Breitenbach, a worker at the women's centre, revealed that many of their early aspirations were not realised:

> I think people thought having a centre would make a big difference and – you would get people dropping in and that – would be a way in which the movement would grow. But – it was up a close [tenement

stair] ... and it wasn't very big and it was a bit gloomy and – you'd have to know about it, you wouldn't just be walking by and say oh this looks attractive. So in a way ... it was never going to be a welcoming drop-in centre.[59]

Nevertheless, this example encouraged feminists in Edinburgh and they established their own centre at 101 Fountainbridge in 1977. Within these premises there was one front room with space for up to twenty women, a space for filing cabinets and a small back room with a cooker, a sink and a toilet. Rent for the facility was £8 a week and, as the *Edinburgh Women's Liberation Newsletter* recorded, this financial responsibility meant that 'the Edinburgh women's movement has moved to a new stage of commitment'.[60] Problems soon emerged in both Glasgow and Edinburgh women's centres as it became clear that the rules which had been applied to workshop meetings would not always work in the environment of the women's centre. As Ellen Galford remembered of the centre in Glasgow:

> there were huge issues around 'but wait, what if we say its women only? what about women who have children?' ... Someone said what about working-class women who – are going to be put off by all these middle-class separatist things, 'cause the word separatism was emerging, you know? And they won't want to come and people said 'yeah but what if a woman has been battered and she comes to us, you know, as a victim of male violence or rape and, you know, the first thing she sees is some guy sitting there reading a newsletter?' You know we need a safe space for women and then you have, as you say, but I'm going to feel restricted, I can't bring my partner here or my boyfriend here or my husband or whatever ... There was enough funding for two part-time workers doing a job share. And one of them, if not both, were heterosexual and one said but I want to feel I can have my boyfriend or whatever – come and pick me up here at lunch time or something ... I don't want to feel he has to stand at the door. And you know you'd get these huge rammies [fights].[61]

One of the workers was Wendy Davies. She was employed alongside Cathy Thomson at Glasgow Women's Centre in its early days. As an employee, Davies had to organise the rota, undertake general caretaking tasks and participate in outreach work. An important part of her job was to try to build links with community workers in peripheral housing estates in Glasgow, such as Drumchapel and Easterhouse. However, she admitted that this outreach work was not entirely successful.[62] Centre workers also came under fire from women within the movement who felt that paying feminist activists to run a centre conflicted with the movement's aims. The most vocal critics of this development were Paula Jennings and Maureen Watson who wrote to *Spare Rib* in 1977. Their letter, titled 'Selling Out?' argued that the only reason Davies and Thomson were employed was that Glasgow women's liberation group had secured money from the job creation scheme, which was just a part of the wider political system the WLM should be trying to dismantle. In securing this money, they argued 'it either means our activities are no threat whatsoever or else it is an attempt to subvert the Movement'.[63] Davies was not immune to this criticism and she was relieved when her contract at the Women's Centre came to an end:

> I was scunnered [fed up] with – what I felt was an inability and an unwillingness to take the next steps to make decisions and talk to the press and … to actually really get out there. And I felt it was far too navel-gazing and that there was a whole lot of work to be done.[64]

Despite this, the women's centre in Glasgow continued until the late 1980s. The centre in Edinburgh lasted until the 1990s, having moved from its original position in Fountainbridge to more central premises on Broughton Street.[65] In this way it can be seen that the WLM's legacy in Scotland lasted into at least the 1990s.

Women's studies

Another way women's liberation groups undertook outreach work was through education. Women's Studies courses sought to introduce students to subjects like Psychology, Sociology, History and English, but with an emphasis on women's experiences. They hoped to correct the inbuilt gender bias apparent in many courses offered at institutes of Higher and Further Education. Women's Studies courses also proved popular in England, Canada and the USA. According to Bouchier, by the end of the 1970s there were at least thirty degree-level Women's Studies programmes being offered at various universities and polytechnics in Britain. Moreover, in the USA, where the idea proved especially popular, 350 programmes were on offer and a National Women's Studies Association was also established.[66]

In Britain, Women's Studies was seen by some within the movement as the academic arm of the WLM, introducing women who were not necessarily active feminists to the ideas and issues of the women's movement.[67] In 1974 a group of women in Edinburgh, influenced by these examples, began their own course.[68] Esther Breitenbach was an early teacher on these courses. She said:

I was involved in some adult education work, [and] women's studies – [where] we taught a course at the Extra Mural department at the university. – And that had been something that somebody had set up a couple of years before and it was kind of team-taught by a group of people.[69]

The idea of team-taught Women's Studies courses reflected the non-hierarchical attitude of the WLM as women saw themselves as facilitators rather than teachers, encouraging all women to discover feminism and women's history for themselves. These courses became important spaces in the development of feminist theories and also directly challenged the organisation and teaching of courses offered at universities and colleges.

Glasgow women's group also offered Women's Studies courses during the 1970s. This Women's Studies group was formed in about 1978 and it actively encouraged those on the course to give papers and to participate in discussions of a range of texts.[70] The idea for Women's Studies courses in Glasgow had emerged from the local women's liberation group. In Aberdeen too there was an emphasis on women's education, with the establishment of Women's Studies courses in 1974. These looked at the topics of 'women in society' and 'women's rights' and were provided by the Extra-Mural Department at the University and also the Workers' Educational Association (WEA). These courses aimed to attract working-class women to feminism, seeking the 'elusive women from the housing schemes and working class women rather than the well-read feminists from suburbia'.[71] How successful this aim was remains unclear as little is known about what kind of women attended such courses, but it does illustrate the continuous soul-searching which some women in the WLM undertook with regard to how the movement could attract a more diverse range of women to the cause of liberation.

In Aberdeen these classes developed into a ten-week programme with course leaders Chris Aldred, a member of the local women's liberation group and course tutor for the WEA, and Margaret Marshall, leader of the WEA in the North East of Scotland, undertaking most of the organisation. This can be seen as part of an international turn towards focusing on the education of women workers, with women's groups setting up similar courses in Norway and Italy in the 1970s.[72] In this way the movement in Scotland, while shaped by the local environment, also reflected much wider international trends

Conclusion

Chapters 3 and 4 have shown how the WLM emerged and developed in Scotland. There were two stages in the movement's formation. First, CR groups proved to be a very popular and powerful instrument in the development of the movement. Building on these ideas, practical campaigns were then created within local women's liberation workshops. In looking at the WLM from the local perspective it is evident that women's liberation workshops in Scotland placed emphasis on different issues depending on what their membership was interested in. For example in Glasgow there was a strong emphasis on women's health and in Edinburgh they prioritised child-care. It can be broadly argued, therefore, that these different campaign emphases demonstrate that the movement was always partly fragmented and focused on different issues at different times. Furthermore, this fragmentation existed because the local context was important in the formation of the WLM, as it shaped the ideas, identity and campaigns of individual women's liberation groups.

It is evident that, as the WLM developed, groups became anxious about the unrepresentative nature of their membership. Solutions to this problem varied depending upon location. Some groups tried to tackle this problem by organising Women's Studies courses while others established women's centres. These both became key strategies in introducing people to feminist ideas and also helped women from local groups to begin networking with each other. Indeed, from the early 1970s onwards it appears that there was a desire amongst feminists to meet up with other like-minded women out with their local community. In order to do this, activists began to organise conferences and newsletters to create a feminist network in Scotland, making the cause of women's liberation more visible to the general public.

Notes

1 S. Browne, '"A Veritable Hotbed of Feminism": Women's Liberation in St Andrews, Scotland, c. 1968–c. 1979', *Twentieth Century British History*, 23:1 (2012), pp. 100–23; J. Rees, 'A Look Back at Anger: The Women's Liberation Movement in 1978', *Women's History Review*, 19:3 (2010), 19 (3), pp. 337–56; E. Setch, 'The Face of Metropolitan Feminism: The London Women's Liberation Workshop, 1969–1979', *Twentieth Century British History*, 13:2 (2002), pp. 171–90.

2 J. Gelb, 'Feminism in Britain: Politics without Power?' in D. Dahlerup (ed.), *The New Women's Movement: Feminism and Political Power in Europe and the USA* (London, 1986), pp. 107–8.

3 S. Rowbotham, *Women in Movement: Feminism and Social Action* (London, 1992), p. 265. See also A. Basu (ed.), *The Challenge of Local Feminisms: Women's Movements in Global Perspective* (Oxford, 1995).

4   E. Breitenbach, '"Sisters are doing it for themselves": The Women's Movement in Scotland' in A. Brown and R. Parry (eds), *The Scottish Government Yearbook 1990* (Edinburgh, 1990), p. 210.

5   Transcript of interview with Fran Wasoff (FW), 20 February 2007, p. 1.

6   Transcript of interview with Lorna Peters (LP*), 4 September 2007, p. 12.

7   *Scottish Women's Liberation Journal*, issue 3, November 1977, p. 13; Transcript of interview with Margaret Elphinstone (ME), 21 November 2007, pp. 12–13.

8   Transcript FW, p. 6.

9   Transcript of interview with Jan McLeod (JM), 10 July 2007, p. 1; Transcript of interview with Anne Ward (AW*), 28 August 2007, p. 4.

10 *Brig*, December 1977, p. 12.

11 *Brig*, 3 October 1974, p. 9.

12 Transcript ME, pp. 12–13.

13 *Scottish Women's Liberation Journal*, issue 3, November 1977, p. 13.

14 *Spare Rib*, September 1978, p. 11.

15 Transcript ME, p. 21.

16 E. Hunter, *Scottish Woman's Place: A Practical Guide and Critical Comment on Women's Rights in Scotland* (Edinburgh, 1978), p. 213, and *Spare Rib*, April 1980, p. 25.

17 For example see letter in *Spare Rib*, December 1975, by Fiona of Falkirk.

18 L. Segal, *Is the Future Female?: Troubled Thoughts on Contemporary Feminism* (London, 1987), p. 82.

19 S. Rowbotham, *The Past Is Before Us: Feminism in Social Action since the 1960s* (London, 1989), p. 75.

20 *St Andrews Lesbian Feminist Newsletter*, issue 2, December 1977, p. 10.

21 *Edinburgh Women's Liberation Newsletter*, August 1976, p. 5.

22 *Socialist Woman*, May–June 1973, p. 10.

23 Transcript of interview with Wendy Davies (WD), 17 July 2007, p. 9.

24 Transcript of interview with Ellen Galford (EG), 2 April 2007, p. 7.

25 *MsPrint*, no. 4, 1979, p. 18.

26 Rowbotham, *The Past Is Before Us*, p. 61.

27 Transcript EG, p. 7.

28 Transcript of interview with Chris Aldred (CA), 30 August 2007, p. 6.

29 *Gaudie*, 18 January 1974, p. 1.

30 Transcript LP*, p. 1.

31 *The Student*, 7 March 1974, p. 5.

32 *Edinburgh Women's Liberation Newsletter*, July 1978, p. 7.

33 Ibid., p. 9.

34 *Edinburgh Women's Liberation Newsletter*, July 1976, pp. 2–3.

35 *Spare Rib*, April 1980, p. 14.

36 Ibid.

37 *Gaudie*, 12 November 1975, p. 3.

38 Ibid.

39 Transcript of interview with Sandie Wyles (SW) and Anne-Marie McGeoch (AMcG), 18 September 2007, p. 26; Transcript CA, p. 33.

40 Transcript CA, p. 33.

41 Transcript CA, p. 33, and Transcript SW and AMcG, p. 27.

42 *Tayside Women's Liberation Newsletter*, October 1977, pp. 5–6, Transcript EMcL, p. 10.

43 Transcript SW and AMcG, p. 28.
44 *Outcome*, Summer 1978, p. 8.
45 Ibid.
46 Transcript ME, p. 13; *Spare Rib*, September 1978, p. 11.
47 Transcript ME, p. 13.
48 *Scottish Women's Liberation Journal*, issue 3, November 1977, p. 13.
49 Transcript ME, p. 18.
50 Transcript ME, p. 13.
51 Edinburgh Women's Liberation Group, *Nursery Report* (Edinburgh, undated but probably c.1974), p. xi.
52 Ibid., p. 3.
53 Ibid., p. 9.
54 Breitenbach, "'Sisters are doing it for themselves'", p. 213.
55 D. Bouchier, *The Feminist Challenge: The Movement for Women's Liberation in Britain and the United States* (London, 1983), p. 179.
56 Breitenbach, "'Sisters are doing it for themselves'", p. 213.
57 *Edinburgh Women's Liberation Newsletter*, March 1977, p. 2.
58 Breitenbach, "'Sisters are doing it for themselves'", p. 212.
59 Transcript EB, p. 11.
60 *Edinburgh Women's Liberation Newsletter*, October 1976, p. 3.
61 Transcript EG, p. 9.
62 Transcript WD, p. 17.
63 *Spare Rib*, March 1977, pp. 4–5.
64 Transcript WD, p. 18.
65 Breitenbach, "'Sisters are doing it for themselves'", p. 213.
66 Bouchier, *The Feminist Challenge*, p. 145–6.
67 *Catcall*, issue 4, September/October 1976, p. 16.
68 *MsPrint*, no. 4, 1979, p. 23.
69 Transcript EB, pp. 13–14.
70 *MsPrint*, no. 4, 1979, p. 23.
71 *Spare Rib*, June 1980, p. 24.
72 Rowbotham, *Women in Movement*, p. 280.

5

Building a network

While an emerging network of local women's liberation groups made the movement more visible to the general public, it served the additional function of encouraging discussion and debate amongst feminist activists about a range of issues facing women's liberation movements throughout the world. Indeed, discussions within the Scottish WLM did not significantly differ from those occurring in groups elsewhere in Britain, although different issues were often emphasised at different times. However, they did form one part of a wider discussion ongoing in the WLM in Britain about how to take the movement forward including a focus on structure, feminist ideologies and sexualities. This chapter analyses these debates in order to consider how feminists in Scotland interpreted international discussions of feminist theory. It first of all describes the forums where debates occurred before focusing on the debates themselves. In doing so it shows that, while debates were quite similar in the Scottish movement to elsewhere in the UK, there were additional issues, which have not received as much attention in the literature, which were important to activists north of the border, including organisation and recruitment, and the sourthern domination of the movement. This chapter demonstrates that discussions were often more complicated than they have been portrayed.

Forums for Debate

The movement in Scotland primarily debated various issues at conferences and through newsletters. The first Scottish conference was held in Glasgow in 1972. It was reported in the University of Edinburgh's student newspaper that this conference had attracted 'delegates from all over Scotland [who] emphasised the need for an effective central co-ordinating group as a potential mobilising body.'[1] As can be seen from Table 5.1, from

1972 onwards conferences became annual events and were held twice-yearly in 1976 and 1977. By rotating conferences around different locations women showed that they wanted the movement to be geographically representative. The British WLM also organised similar events. They were also held in various places, on a rotation basis, but the furthest north they travelled was to Edinburgh in 1974. This was to become a matter of some irritation for women active in the Scottish movement, especially in the north of the country, and almost certainly contributed to the organisation of separate conferences north of the border.

Table 5.1 Dates and venues of British and Scottish women's liberation conferences in the 1970s

Date	British conference	Scottish conference
1970 (February)	Oxford[1]	—
1970 (June)	Sheffield	—
1971	Skegness	—
1972	(I) Manchester	
	(II) London	Glasgow
1973	Bristol	Edinburgh
1974	Edinburgh[2]	Edinburgh
1975	Manchester	Aberdeen
1976	Newcastle	(I) St Andrews
		(II) Partick, Glasgow
1977	London	(I) Aberdeen
		(II) St Andrews
1978	Birmingham[3]	Edinburgh

Notes: 1 First four demands adopted at this conference.
2 Fifth and sixth demands adopted at this conference.
3 Seventh demand adopted at this conference.

Conferences had a dual aim: first, to gather together all feminists active in the Scottish WLM and, second, to introduce new individuals to the movement. As Breitenbach recalled, there 'was no structure of representation or delegation, and the conferences were open to any woman to attend'.[2] The movement's sensitivity to women living outside of the central belt was illustrated with the creation of fare pools. These established the notion that all women should share equally in the burden of travel costs. It did this by asking those who had travelled a relatively short distance to pay a subsidy in order to give those women who lived further away extra money to help cover their higher travel costs.[3] This was an important part of the collective ethos of the WLM.

Conferences were organised by a small group in the host city or town. A group of women active in the local women's liberation workshop would form a planning committee.[4] Ellen Galford explained how one planning committee was organised:

> Frankie and Paula came – representing Tayside women's liberation– and there must have been a couple of people from Edinburgh who came over to the Glasgow group and we all had a – planning group about the workshops, the logistics and all that kind of thing … but the actual – heavy duty housekeeping side of running the show for that weekend would have just been Glasgow women.[5]

Given the limited budget, conferences offered extremely basic facilities. They were advertised through many of the movement's newsletters and journals. For example, an advert for the St Andrews conference in 1976 appeared in *WIRES*, where women were informed all they had to pay was '£2.00 to cover meals and (floor) accommodation (bring sleeping bag)'.[6] Despite the basic facilities, these events were very popular, attracting around 150 women, and Nina Woodcock reported that there were three thousand women at the British WLM conference in 1978.[7] The planning committee was allocated a limited budget with which to provide food and refreshments. At the end of a conference, a float was passed on to the next planning committee in order to enable them to run next year's event. As Ellen Galford recalled, the limited budget meant that 'everybody would come and sleep in vast discomfort on floors and draughty church halls or people's unheated spare box rooms and – the sleeping bag was the main tool of political activism'.[8] After the final plenary session the conference delegates voted on where the next conference should be held. Chris Aldred provided an effective insight into how conferences ran:

> there was usually discussion about – what the demands of the movement should be. And about the way we should be organising or affiliate to other organisations or allow other organisations to affiliate to us. But the main bit of the conferences would have been workshops led by women who volunteered themselves to lead … You know so … it's a huge bit of event management being done. But – it was done by women's groups who I often think fell apart afterwards with the strain of doing it. Because people would get landed with quite a lot of work. You know and somebody who's willing to do it, would end up taking all the responsibility and then she would crack or walk off in the sulk or whatever at the end of it.[9]

Indeed, from the mid- to late 1970s onwards, the heavy workload involved in planning and organising conferences encouraged some women to call for better organisation in order to ease the burden for planning committees. Conferences retained an experimental feel throughout the period as planning groups tried out different ways of organising the events.[10] For example, at the Scottish women's liberation conference in St Andrews in 1977 women were divided into randomly selected small groups of ten, remaining in these groups for the whole weekend. Once they were allocated a group they were given three topics to discuss: separatism, the socialist current and women and violence.[11] This new structure seemed to prove popular and was replicated at the British women's liberation conference in Birmingham the following year.[12] Most women found early conferences to be very positive experiences, with Ellen Galford recalling that they were especially helpful in the facilitation of networking. She said:

> in those days at the feminist conferences you'd book a community centre or you'd get some sort of big church hall and everybody would come and sleep there. People would come from all over. I remember we had this freezing cold church hall somewhere in Partick in Glasgow … I was involved in the catering. We were working the miracle of the loaves and the fishes for hundreds of people because we had, like, one hotplate with one burner on it … so the Glasgow feminist dykes and the Edinburgh feminist dykes all got to know each other, and started a social life. You began to network.[13]

Indeed, Ellen Galford was not alone in recalling the positive early experiences of attending women's liberation conferences, with many women describing similar sentiments, including Ruth Miller, who emphasised that:

> they were absolutely brilliant in that – I felt we had lots of good debate around quite important issues and really strong opinions and strong views being put forward … a lot of people were writing some good things around that time so they were very heady and also – the social side of it was just wonderful. We had amazing discos in the evening and just good fun together and there – was just a really strong feeling of sisterhood like we were all in it together and we were all going to make big changes and yeah, it was – a really good feeling of togetherness.[14]

Another key way to network was through the pages of newsletters and journals which were produced and distributed by small collectives active in both Scotland and Britain. In the early 1970s feminists in Scotland predominantly read literature that had been produced in the

USA and England.[15] Important in this regard was *Spare Rib*. Launched in England in July 1972 to compete with mainstream women's magazines, this publication proved so popular that its first issue sold out.[16] Filling a niche in the market, the editorial collective aimed to 'put women's liberation on the news-stands'. They also hoped that *Spare Rib* would become the public face of the WLM in Britain, introducing people outside the movement to the issues and ideas that were being actively debated by feminists throughout Britain. As Bouchier has argued, *Spare Rib* offered 'the broadest and least sectarian image of British feminism, and the most accessible to uncommitted women who may pick up the magazine at their local newsagent'.[17]

WIRES was another important publication. It disseminated information about conferences, events and feminist groups. At the 1975 British conference in Manchester the movement agreed to create a Women's Information and Referral Service (WIRES). It aimed to act as a central facility for feminist news and publications. This service also produced a newsletter under the same name and it was run by a collective of women in places such as York and Leeds, with the Referral Service rotated around different locations every two years. Acting like feminist listings, *WIRES* detailed where future conferences were to be held and what groups were being set up. While *Spare Rib* acted as the public face of women's liberation in Britain, *WIRES* was instead the 'internal newsletter' of the movement.[18]

There was an abundance of feminist newsletters produced in Britain in the 1970s, written and produced from a variety of different political perspectives. Feminists in Scotland read a wide range of these newsletters, which were mainly English-based. These included *Women's Report*, *Women's Voice* and *Shrew*. Women active in the movement in Scotland also wrote letters to and articles for the various journals and newsletters, contributing regularly to the pages of publications such as *Catcall*. This was a non-sectarian journal aimed at encouraging the open discussion of theory, emphasising that 'personal opinions and experiences will be welcome; personal abuse will not'.[19]

However, by the mid-1970s feminists in Scotland craved information that was of particular relevance to the legal, political and cultural context north of the border. Publishing in Scotland did not get under way until the later 1970s. Indeed, it has been noted by Esther Breitenbach that women north of the border were slow to produce their own newsletters.[20] Bouchier has described how in the British context there was no lack of publishing outlets available for feminists and their ideas.[21] In stark contrast, women's groups and individual feminists north of the border found that Scottish publishers were reluctant to produce books and pamphlets which focused on the ideas emanating from the movement, arguably indicating a less welcoming environment in which to discuss and practise feminist politics.[22]

Publishing is an important element of any group or movement, enabling it to publicise and propagandise, becoming 'an instrument in the battle of ideas'.[23] Like Esther Breitenbach, Maggie Havergal, a member of the Aberdeen women's liberation group, described the emergence of Scottish feminist publications from 1975 onwards as 'a trickle'.[24] However, local groups throughout the 1970s had always published their own newsletters, acting as information bulletins for members. They were also particularly helpful in the circulation of important issues of a local, national and international nature. These local newsletters included Edinburgh, Aberdeen, Glasgow and a joint venture by St Andrews and Dundee, *The Tayside Women's Liberation Newsletter*. Read not only by women within the group, these were also distributed to women located in other parts of Britain. Another important newsletter in Scotland was *Nessie*, published with a radical/revolutionary feminist perspective. Started in 1979, it was supposed to be read by women only, as the editorial collective urged its readers to 'take good care of NESSIE: don't leave her lying around, and if you live with a man/men, keep her somewhere safe'.[25] By the later 1970s there was a proliferation of small-scale publishing ventures like *Nessie* which focused on a particular aspect of feminist thinking or on a specific campaign.

From 1977 onwards the movement began producing the *Scottish Women's Liberation Journal* (*SWLJ*), which became *MsPrint* in 1978. In the first issue the editorial collective argued that:

> the journal will also provide a forum for discussion for women in Scotland. A vehicle for debate on various controversial issues is badly needed. It is simply impractical to attempt to conduct discussions through already existing journals based in London.[26]

The *Journal* was very important in conceptualising feminist issues and themes for a Scottish audience. It also signalled to the rest of the movement in Britain that women active in Scotland wanted their own newsletters and spaces to discuss issues which were important to them. Most articles were written from a Scottish perspective, emphasising the country's distinct historical, legal and political heritage, including articles on 'Women, the British Economy and Scottish Politics' and 'Women in Rural Scotland'.[27] The idea for the *SWLJ* emerged from discussions at the Scottish women's liberation conference in Glasgow in 1976.[28] It was eventually launched at the Aberdeen conference in 1977. The journal was run by an editorial collective of between nine and eleven women from all around Scotland. Esther Breitenbach, a founder member of the *Journal* collective, recalled that 'we used to meet in different places and then – it was printed by Aberdeen People's Press so we used to meet up in Aberdeen to do – the layout'.[29] The collective was open to any woman in the movement in Scotland and its general aim was to be 'a feminist, non-sectarian journal, and … open to all shades of political opinion contained within the women's movement'.[30] It also created area contacts for the journal. These contacts organised the journal's distribution in their area and also registered feedback from women active in the movement. They also helped 'the pages … reflect the opinions and concerns of women in all parts of Scotland, and not just the more dominant population centres of Edinburgh and Glasgow', again indicating the Scottish movement's concern to be geographically representative. Like other newsletters, the *SWLJ* was financed through subscription and by selling as many copies as possible. The journal's finances were precarious and owing to a lack of money, there was a long gap between the publication of issues two and three.[31] Nonetheless, it proved to be a well-read journal, with the first issue selling out. Sales figures gradually increased throughout the period with nine hundred copies of one issue in 1978 being sold.[32] As the editorial collective contended in 1977, these sales figures proved 'that there is a need for such a publication'.[33] Clearly, there was a network of women's liberation groups within Scotland and Britain, which was discussing, debating and swapping ideas through newsletters and conference discussions. Indeed, debating feminist ideas and theories was at the very heart of the movement.

Radical and socialist feminism

One of the most hotly contested debates which filled the pages of various newsletters and dominated many conference discussions was the validity of radical feminism as opposed to socialist feminism and vice versa.[34] The tension between the radical and socialist feminist positions, which at first was overlooked in deference to the ideal of 'sisterhood', has been portrayed as impossible to resolve. This debate has dominated many accounts of the WLM, as commentators have sought to explain why there was a loss of enthusiasm amongst feminist activists for British women's liberation conferences in the second half of the 1970s. As Coote and Campbell have argued, 'since the early 1970s, many feminists within the women's liberation movement have identified themselves as "radical feminist" or as "socialist feminist" and the gap between the two has seemed increasingly wide and unbridgeable'.[35] Indeed, Lovenduski and Randall believed this was the 'most damaging of all' the debates in terms of its impact on the development of the movement.[36]

The first two issues of the *SWLJ* analysed both feminist positions. Finella McKenzie in her article on 'Feminism and Socialism' argued that socialist feminism was inadequate because it tried to fit feminist 'activities into the existing leftist analysis and framework of priorities – in which women never go first'.[37] Conversely, socialist feminists believed that radical feminism oversimplified women's subordination, placing too much emphasis on men as the enemy rather than the system of male supremacy. This was an important distinction for socialist feminists who felt that by designating men the ultimate enemy it actually led to accusations that the movement was full of man-haters and, therefore, not representative of the views of many women outside the WLM.[38]

Disagreements over ideological issues could become nasty, with women trading insults and personally attacking one another, indicating the passion and commitment involved in women's liberation activism. One woman admitted that it had taken her three months to formulate an adequate response to critics of radical feminism, given that her 'first draft was pure anger, spilling all over you'.[39] As Anne Jackson recalled, these personal attacks could lead to splits and for her it contributed to a growing disillusionment with the movement:

> the painful meetings, the confrontations. Friendships splitting up. Relationships splitting up. Small cliques splitting up from other small cliques. Movement splitting up. And I do remember, it might have been about the Edinburgh Women's Liberation Conference, being somewhere on the outskirts of Edinburgh and just a huge row erupting about something and just thinking, I think I've had enough of this. I think I've had enough. And I didn't abandon feminism but I certainly started to pull back from that point. You know, just why do we have to, why? I always satirise myself, but actually my gut feeling is still, why can't we all just love each other? You know, and it is a source of great grief –. I mean I actually feel that the patriarchal culture has got a lot to do with why the women's liberation movement didn't succeed. And why it was suppressed. But I wish we had not, I wish we had managed to stay more with the arms linked going forward together rather than the arms linked pulling each other back or fighting with each other.[40]

Increasingly, women began to organise conferences that were focused on either socialist or radical feminism. A radical theory conference was held in Edinburgh in July 1977, which two hundred women attended. This was followed in May 1978 by a Scottish socialist feminist conference, which was held in Glasgow.[41] These conferences were not without controversy. One woman reported that she left the radical feminist theory conference in 1979 feeling 'heavied [sic], guilt-tripped and alienated, thinking sisterhood is so powerful it can kill'.[42] Furthermore, at the same conference one woman was angered to find a pile of Revolutionary Communist magazines. She felt that whoever had put the publication on display had sold radical feminists 'out to the enemy'.[43] These separate conferences changed the movement's focus to specific issues and ideas, as women were bombarded with invitations to a variety of different events. Indeed, socialist feminist groups were set up in Scotland in Aberdeen and Glasgow and a newsletter, Scarlet Women, was produced from 1977 onwards.[44]

This was also clearly illustrated in the running of the SWLJ. Although in theory the journal aimed to be open and non-sectarian, in practice the collective found this impossible, leading to a split in 1978. The split that occurred within the collective focused on ideological differences, between socialist and radical feminism. Members of the collective, including Esther Breitenbach and Geri Smyth, both sympathetic to the socialist feminist agenda, issued a statement a few days before a scheduled editorial meeting. They argued that:

> the women's movement is not homogeneous and contains not only varying but conflicting views ... we wish to direct the Journal towards women in the labour movement, towards the problems women face at work, and to their activity in the trade unions ... we are opposed to the publication of purely personal accounts of women's experiences which do not develop theory.[45]

This created an outcry in the women's movement. Many women felt that the statement had not been released with sufficient time for other members of the collective to reply. By issuing a statement, Breitenbach and Smyth were accused of elevating themselves to the position of 'stars'. Alison Buckley, a member of the SWLJ collective, summed up her feelings:

> In this case it's Esther's collective, and I've often felt that Esther seems to have more say than other women, not just because she has been on the collective longer and might have more information because of experience than other women ... It strikes me that the four women believe it is their publication, that they are the editors and the content must be up to the 'standards' both literary and political, e.g. the desire for 'artists' and 'writers' to contribute to the Journal, thus negating 'ordinary' women's creativity.[46]

The disagreement focused on whether or not the SWLJ should include more 'cultural' content, such as poetry and short stories, or whether it should move in the direction of concentrating on Scottish politics, looking at the specific political culture in which the WLM was operating. Most radical feminists were opposed to focusing too narrowly on Scottish politics. Kathryn McIndoe of St Andrews women's liberation group angrily replied to the socialist feminist statement, arguing that:

> To feminists who do not build their theories on what they read, overhear, or are told by their male Trot party leaders, poetry and accounts of personal experience are not mere frivolous limp-wristed exercises in obscure 'aesthetics' as seems to be implied.[47]

Indeed, many radical feminists hinted at plots to suppress information. In presenting their side of the argument, half of the old editorial collective produced a one-off journal entitled *Whatever Happened to the Scottish Women's Liberation Journal?* They described how they found

> an unwillingness to discuss political differences but also complete refusal to work together on the collective ... We consider in retrospect that we made a tactical blunder. What we should have done was to say: 'we want to continue producing a broad-based Scottish Women's Liberation Journal. You piss off and produce a separate journal'.[48]

They argued that the cause of the disagreement was not whether more poetry and short stories should be included but rather due to political differences. The split, therefore, had massive implications for the women's movement as whole.[49] Or, as Breitenbach has stressed, 'the divisions within the women's movement were reproduced within the collective running of the Journal'.[50] The socialist feminist faction of the collective went on to produce *MsPrint*, which became one of the central publications of the women's movement in Scotland in the late 1970s and through to the 1980s. This was no longer based on an open editorial collective, and members who wished to participate had to be sponsored by someone before being formally admitted.[51] It clearly shows a shift towards more editorial control.

Yet, despite this emerging division, some women in the WLM in Scotland remained more pragmatic about their political positioning. For instance, Lorna Mitchell, a member of Edinburgh women's liberation group, argued that 'I'm a cultural/radical/socialist feminist ... I don't claim I do very much, but I'm doing a bit and I don't judge the bits other people are doing by unrealistic criteria'.[52] This sentiment can also be found in the *Tayside Women's Liberation Newsletter* where it was argued that guilt was used as a weapon of power by both sides: 'radical feminists guilt-trip socialist feminists for "collaborating with the enemy". Socialist feminists guilt trip radical feminists for "putting new women off the movement"'.[53] Caution must be applied when using rigid binary concepts to describe the arguments and beliefs of women who in practice were often complex and contradictory. As Rowbotham has effectively argued, 'real women are a complicated and argumentative lot. Instead of presenting "women" as an abstract category, it is better to see "women" as people, who within particular historical situations are continually making choices about how they see and align themselves'.[54] Focusing on the split between radical and socialist feminism in historical narratives of the WLM in Britain, therefore, does not entirely describe the diverse range of opinions and viewpoints contained within the movement. For example, when describing her views, Ruth Miller admitted to me that she was 'pretty much socialist feminist ... but – I'm not sure, and I'm looking at this and what does this mean and you know some things maybe feel really uncomfortable and so, yes it wasn't always a comfortable place to be'.[55]

Sexualities and separatism

Another issue which caused intense debate and has subsequently become a focus in some accounts of the movement is sexualities and separatism.[56] From this debate there have emerged significant stereotypes which have remained within accounts of the period. As Whelehan has noted, 'it is still commonplace to associate radical politics with lesbian feminists, even though this scarcely seems to be the case'.[57] A good example of this is Bouchier, who argued that 'by 1976 the lines seemed to be drawn between heterosexual feminists (mainly socialists) and the lesbian feminists (mainly radicals)'.[58] In reality there was more crossover than this, with socialist feminists found within the ranks of lesbian groups and radical feminists deciding to remain in heterosexual relationships.

However, an increasing focus on sexualities in the discussions of feminist activists did create conflict. For example, in one article in the *Edinburgh Women's Liberation Newsletter* Linda McFarlane argued that the numbers of those attending group meetings were dwindling owing to the insistence of some lesbian women of meeting only with other lesbians. Her observation was criticised, as one woman argued: 'I would not come to many of the meetings you create as in no way can I identify with them. In the same way that you do not come to lesbian meetings ... Why ask Dykes to stop your loneliness/isolation when you are part of a socially acceptable majority?'[59] Indeed, there were a small number of women within the Scottish movement who adopted a separatist identity. In practice this meant dissociating themselves from men and creating a separate culture in which only women existed. Some separatists also remained suspicious about those feminists who chose to continue to share their lives with men and accused them of 'collaborating with the enemy'.[60] However, as Breitenbach has argued, 'it is true that some lesbian feminist women took a separatist position and argued that all feminists should become lesbians as political choice ... By no means all lesbians took this view'.[61] Partly owing to the adverse publicity given to the separatist position, most, if not all, lesbians, irrespective of whether or not they agreed with separatism, began to feel somewhat ostracised by other women in the movement. Ellen Galford recalled that lesbians 'probably seemed to be more scary than scared to some people. Even some of us were totally nice, sociable, cream puff, hated arguments, hated fights, didn't want to fight with anybody, wanted to be everybody's friend.'[62]

Of course, the issues of politics and sexuality, at times, intertwined. Some women discovered their lesbianism through feminism, as the movement 'facilitated intimacy between women'.[63] Pauline Robinson, who left her marriage on discovering her sexuality, wondered

> how much of that is driven, was driven by our passion for women and feminism. I know that I discovered my lesbianism through feminism and I know that I probably would never ever make a relationship with a man again but I would like to think of a world like [the novel] *Woman on the Edge of Times*, where it actually didn't matter what gender you were but while we have a patriarchy it bloody does matter what gender you are. And I can't help but – see sex with men, which it always seems to have to be penetrative, as being anything but a weapon and an act of invasion.[64]

Paula Jennings also questioned how much of an influence the WLM had in determining her sexuality. On considering whether her sexuality would have changed had she not joined the WLM she asked:

> But who knows? Who knows? If there had been no supportive context I don't know. Because it wasn't something that was clear in my mind and I certainly had really pretty good relationships with men. So, it wouldn't have been as clear as it was for, for some women.[65]

But far from women like Pauline and Paula intentionally separating themselves from the rest of the movement and deciding to exclude heterosexual women, they instead wanted to socialise with other lesbians who understood the challenges they faced. Events like lesbian discos were held in cities like Edinburgh and Dundee in order to facilitate the creation of a network for communication and interaction.[66] In this regard, therefore, it can be seen that women were beginning to opt for smaller women's liberation forums in order to meet and socialise with women who were facing similar issues.

Yet this is not to overlook the fact that the separatist position caused tension in feminist circles in Scotland, especially in Glasgow. As 'Lyser' noted in her review of the St Andrews women's liberation conference in 1977, 'separatism is a tactic which caused a lot of hassles in Scotland'.[67] There was some confusion over how sexuality could be a political choice; that, in order to be regarded as a 'true' feminist you also had to assume the lesbian separatist position. Esther Breitenbach remembered the discussions on this issue:

> there were tensions around sexuality and political lesbianism and the idea that [it] – was a choice that people could make or should make on a political basis. – I think a lot of women were uncomfortable with that – you know you can debate how – to what extent one can choose one's sexuality ... and a lot of that was really quite fraught and difficult and you know – fed into political divisions. I – would say some of the personal difficulties might have been presented as being political oppositions but were really to do with difficult personal relationships.[68]

Some activists felt separatism was an untenable position given that 'men are all around us. There's no likelihood of them withering away'.[69] In Glasgow the presence of Australian and English separatists certainly challenged the members of the women's centre, as Ellen Galford witnessed:

> There were also some Australian women in Glasgow who were ... very intense separatists and they tended to come in and slightly bust things up ... they played on and created sort of tensions but particularly this – woman from London who herself came from an extremely privileged background ... she had all these sons who were all in boarding school – but she was very kind of holier than thou. But she also – could be charming but so manipulative that she created ructions in both cities – she just had ways of playing people against each other and it drove a lot of people really apart from each other ... People no longer felt sort of comfortable, people kind of went off, maybe groups broke up and did their own thing. I wouldn't say by any means the separatists destroyed things, they raised interesting issues, there were interesting things to talk about, they were important questions that were asked but I think what you get is in any movement, whether it's a religious community or a political movement, when people are really trying to lay their lives on the line and really change things about themselves and about society, people are kind of living on the edge so there were always those who were manipulative and power-trippy and will come in and take it over.[70]

Separatists also caused outrage when they refused to work with heterosexual women. Fiona Forsyth, in one edition of the *SWLJ*, complained about a group of separatists who had attended a conference but refused to work with the rest of the delegates, rather preferring to conduct discussions amongst themselves. They had apparently justified this decision because they felt they would not find common ground with women who still related to men.[71] On the other hand some separatists felt marginalised by the wider movement which they felt did not fully understand their beliefs. One separatist believed that separatism had fallen out of favour within feminist circles and had become 'affectionately enshrined in everyone's memories along with the miniskirt, hippie headbands and fishnet stockings.'[72]

Tensions around these issues erupted in the movement in Scotland in 1978. This was made public in Jessica Barrett's interview with Elspeth King, which appeared in *The Evening News* in 1979. King, who was the curator at Glasgow People's Palace and had attended meetings at Glasgow Women's Centre, had just published a pamphlet on the women's suffrage movement in Scotland. In this interview, King argued that the WLM 'should take a leaf out of the book of the Suffragettes and exploit sexual attractiveness and femininity'. King later stated that the women's movement in Scotland had now 'become synonymous with lesbianism and separatism and it is serving to disturb rather than create confidence in many happily married women'.[73] King's views were met with widespread disbelief in the WLM in Scotland. In response to her critics she argued in a letter to *MsPrint*:

> The daughter of a domestic worker and a miner, I would have had my backside kicked had I dared wear dungarees, crepe soled boots, cropped my hair and lived on Social Security. This, however, was the predominant pattern at the Women's Centre in Miller Street ... I personally do not mind how people dress or express their sexuality. On the other hand, my conservative exterior and lightly painted face unleashed aggression bordering on hatred from the dungaree brigade.[74]

She later argued that 'currently, with so many women being stabbed in the back, Sisterhood is Pathetic. In fact, it stinks.'[75] Clearly her arguments had as much to do with class as sexuality but it was her perceived attack on lesbianism which caused the greatest controversy. The *MsPrint* collective replied to King, arguing that 'to attack the Women's Liberation Movement on the account of the presence of lesbian women in it, is to reinforce and foster the prejudice against lesbianism and homosexuality'.[76] King left the women's centre in Glasgow but her comments had crystallised the tension surrounding sexual identities.

What King had highlighted was that some women active in the movement could be very judgemental as they formed idealised versions of what a 'true' feminist should be like. They would then be quick to point out the flaws and weaknesses of any woman who they believed failed to measure up. These idealised versions were summed up by one women's liberation activist in *The Tayside Women's Liberation Newsletter* of October 1977 for an article, titled 'The Inadequate Feminist'. She described how there were three kinds of women active in the movement. First, the 'alpha woman' who were described as writing 'fiery words, shatterproof articles, she is articulate'. The second group were depicted as 'beta' women who 'cannot quite make it – because of some horrific conditioned defect e.g. shyness, fear, lack of assertion …' Finally, the remaining women formed 'the rabble', as they were 'shrivelled with fear, inadequacy, rejection, resentment, helplessness, and self-effacement'.[77] This description of a hierarchy was somewhat crude in practice but it effectively illustrated the ways in which feminists often judged each other. Guilt was an important emotion in shaping the group dynamics of the WLM as well as the ways in which individual activists perceived one another. The weight of expectation often immobilised some women, fearful of expressing opinions in case they were criticised or attacked. Sandie Wyles recalled experiences at conferences:

> the groups would usually split into women with children, straight women, gay women and then this lesbian-feminist and then lesbian separatist. So there was starting off with all these wee cliques and women would whisper to each other and you would think is that me they're talking about? Oh she's got long hair, oh she's not a lesbian. What is she coming here for? I got that a lot because I had long hair at that time and, oh she's not really a lesbian. Oh come on, you know, who do you think you're kidding? And you would hear it at the back of you … so you just had to kinda keep going because you knew fine if you turned round they would probably punch you one. They were really, really heavy and aggressive. And quite angry. Very angry. I think they had lots of personal issues in their lives that probably needed to be resolved somewhere but they all kinda unfortunately came to these conferences! I remember going to the St Andrews one, which was a real kind of touch-paper one. Where the room kind of split and again these dykes with the action packs, that came to visit … there was a box at the – door of St Andrews University for the janitor. A just nice working class guy, oh come in girls. We're not girls. Oh sorry, right, well if you need any help, you know I'm here and I'll just keep my head down! And this girl had put a big poster on the back of his box, do not feed the animal, do not feed the animals or something. And they thought this was hilarious. And that stayed up for a lot of the conference. And then somebody spotted it and said that's terrible, imagine if that was your dad … They said well he's a man, isn't he? And like I don't care if he was your dad, he's a man. And you know we don't want anything to do with him. So the politics – became very, very polarised.[78]

As women immersed their whole lives in the political campaigns of the WLM they became sensitive to any slight or criticism. This was especially true for women who chose to come out as lesbians in this period as they found the movement somewhat contradictory. On the one hand, it provided lesbians with a supportive environment, enabling them to express their sexuality. On the other hand, however, lesbians could also find themselves open to criticism for being exclusive and socialising only with other lesbians in the movement. These criticisms became more acute with the emergence of the separatist ideology which directly challenged the WLM, forcing it to assess how women should relate to men. Women who chose to remain in relationships with men often felt judged by lesbian separatists and in turn separatists believed they were misunderstood.

Structure and recruitment

When considering why women stopped engaging with conferences as a format for feminist discussion, there is a tendency in the literature to focus on feminist splits according to political ideologies and the 'negative' role of sexualities in discussions, at the expense of considering other reasons which also contributed to this general trend. While we have seen that these two issues were discussed in newsletters and at conferences, and have subsequently dominated discussions in the literature, there were other concerns which also contributed to the ways in which the movement developed in the second half of the 1970s.[79] Adopting a 'national' approach to studies of women's liberation can arguably lead to debates and discussions being overlooked. One of the most important debates from the mid-1970s onwards was how to organise a movement which, at least in theory, was opposed to hierarchy and structure and, more importantly, how far this approach helped to recruit new women. By the end of the 1970s meetings were not running as smoothly as they had done in the earlier part of the period. As the October 1976 edition of the *Edinburgh Women's Liberation Newsletter* reported, 'representation of other areas of Scotland besides Glasgow at planning meetings has not been high, and when there are several women from other areas, as at the first planning meetings, that tends to be a result of their activity as individuals, and not necessarily as a result of contact with any large group of women.'[80]

This loss of enthusiasm for conferences was reflected in the declining numbers of those who attended both the British and Scottish women's liberation conferences. A clear turning point for WLM conferences in Britain was in 1974. Held at James Gillespie's High School in Edinburgh, this event also acted as the Scottish movement's annual conference. Over nine hundred women attended this conference, where deep divisions over the issue of sexuality emerged, culminating in the adoption of the sixth demand which focused on lesbianism.[81] Esther Breitenbach, who attended this event, observed that 'the euphoria of the first wave of sisterhood was wearing off, and in its place was to come increasingly bitter division', marking a new stage for the WLM.[82] At times, it appeared as if familiarity bred contempt. Instead of conferences providing the space for people to meet and converse, they instead produced friction and dissent. Esther Breitenbach said, that in the early days conferences inculcated 'a really good feeling – and felt celebratory and kind of empowering' but by the late 1970s numbers 'were tailing off'.[83] At the annual Scottish women's liberation conference in St Andrews in 1977, for example, instead of the anticipated two hundred women, only ninety turned up.[84] Initially conferences had encouraged openness and collective responsibility, but, as Setch has illustrated, because conferences acted as the movement's public forum they tended to magnify fragmentation.[85]

However, there were other issues besides sexualities which emerged during this conference which also contributed to a loss of enthusiasm for large conferences and should be considered when analysing activists' experiences of women's liberation conferences in the late 1970s. These issues tended to be linked to poor organisation and a lack of provision for those attending the conferences. A major issue for some women at the British conference in 1974 was the poor provision of child-care, where 'at the final plenary session some mothers voiced complaints about the child-care arrangements, there was a restless stir and murmurs about handling that at another time ... the men who ran the crèche were treated with hostility by some people'.[86] The controversial nature of this conference led to rumours that local groups, such as Dundee, had disbanded as a 'direct result of the Edinburgh conference'. Women in Dundee felt the planning committee had been disorganised, failing to provide adequate crèche facilities.[87] Their objection is not surprising given that, as Chapter 4 outlined, there was a strong emphasis on the issue of child-care in the Dundee group.

Women attending conferences in Scotland in the late 1970s frequently voiced their concerns about the organisation of conferences. At a conference held in Inch Community Centre in Edinburgh in 1978 only sixty women attended. Unfortunately a rock group had also booked the centre for band practice. Owing to the noise many women felt unable to continue and the conference was abandoned. One commentator in *MsPrint* argued that 'decisions taken were totally undemocratic in that they were arrived at without sufficient time and care being given to make sure that the issues were thoroughly worked through'.[88] Underpinning these frustrations was a questioning of how far the WLM could develop while still adhering to the ideals of structurelessness and collectivism. A lack of structure, which had initially been a popular idea for many in the movement, attracting women who had become disenchanted with the rigid organisation of left-wing groups, now appeared to make some feel as if they were being prevented from fully participating in movement discussions.[89] As Chapter 3 outlined, the publication central to this discussion was Jo Freeman's *The Tyranny of Structurelessness*, published in the USA in 1970. Effectively crystallising the feelings of many women who had become disillusioned with a lack of organisation, Jo Freeman argued that whilst anti-hierarchy was a good idea in principle, in practice it created tensions; or as she concluded 'contrary to what we would like to believe, there is no such thing as a "structureless" group'.[90]

However, Setch has convincingly argued that one of the major myths about the WLM is that 'because it rejected traditional structures, it was structureless'. Instead, she writes that the movement in Britain was 'always structured, however loosely, and that this structure was developing and constantly under scrutiny'.[91] An example of this structure was the seven demands (see Appendix II), which guided and influenced the campaigning agenda of local groups throughout Britain. Zoe Fairbairns has argued that these demands served 'a useful purpose by providing a minimum programme, a rallying point, a loose but sustaining structure for an otherwise unstructured movement'.[92] Nonetheless, while Setch is correct to question how far the WLM was structureless, it is evident that there was a chaotic core to the movement with many activities and meetings run completely on whim, without organisation. A growing exasperation with a lack of structure was evident in a letter published in the *Edinburgh Women's Liberation Newsletter* in 1975. It described how the women's group in Edinburgh had received requests for speakers from various local groups who were keen to find out more about the movement. It was noted that, because there was no speaker's panel, these invitations were

> getting lost or remaining unanswered; we had one the other week that I was given – I kept asking people and not really having time to organise it, and I later learnt that 250 people had attended the meeting where we were supposed to be speaking.[93]

In the same year, Paula Jennings and Frankie Raffles warned that whilst 'we basically agree with structurelessness we feel there should be more attempts to tackle its bad points, some of which are: it allows for individuals to dominate groups and for groups to dominate the movement.[94]

There are many examples of the problems associated with this lack of structure. For example, Zoe Fairbairns described:

> There was always that sort of sense of apology that anything that even looked remotely like leadership ... [For example] the leftie groups in St Andrews organised a thing called Liberation Week ... it was going to be a week of events of various kinds of left-wing politics. [Someone] – said we ought – to do some sort of street theatre about sexist behaviour in the streets and particularly harassment of women in the streets. And so we went around wolf-whistling men and making – sexist-type remarks to them in the streets. Whether that was a good idea or whether that was a bad idea, I don't know, but we did [it] ... of course the press got on to it and just loved it – because it was funny – and it [gave them a reason to avoid] having to write about more serious things which may have been a reason why it was a mistake. But anyway suddenly there we were in the press – and of course the press always needs to have a named spokesperson to attribute quotations to. We put out a press release in the name of the group, we didn't put a name on it. And at some point somebody, some journalist rang up ... and said, 'look can we put a name on this?' and [someone] gave my name without even my knowledge. And suddenly I was being quoted as the spokesperson for the group ... I was quite happy to be associated with what we were doing. I'd done it too and I thought it was right ... but I didn't like the fact that it looked as if I was taking a leadership role. So I sort of went around apologising to people and say[ing] 'oh no I – didn't say that and I don't know who said I was the spokesperson' ... We ought to have got together with the group and decided who was going to be the spokesperson with that person's agreement ... but that's the sort of misunderstanding that happens ... [if you] kid yourself that there are no leaders and no spokespeople, a vacuum will develop into which somebody will fall ... so that was a bit of a problem.[95]

Trying to avoid being identified as a leader was a common experience for many feminists active in women's movements in Europe and the USA and was discussed by Freeman.[96] But an opposition to leadership often meant that public messages became confused and those who were thrust into the limelight had to resist taunts that they were becoming a 'star' of the movement, something to which the ideology of the WLM was completely opposed. It also impeded the organisation of conferences, with Paula Jennings recalling the harsh treatment meted out to organisers. She described how some conference planning groups were treated:

> [they] would be just shot down in flames at the end of the conference.

They had spent a whole year, planning these –, I mean and doing it unpaid in their spare time. Huge conferences. And I remember, I think it was the last conference that anybody organised, the planning committee sitting up on the stage in tears.[97]

Such treatment would have undoubtedly had an impact on the willing-ness of activists to volunteer to organise conferences.

Aside from these organisational problems, the anti-structural attitude also meant that workshop meetings became overly complicated. Much like the experience of CR, workshop meetings could become quite protracted, as every woman was encouraged to speak and no one was allowed to interrupt. As Ruth Miller recalled:

> it meant no-one took responsibility ultimately and so we'd have a meeting of the whole group that would last a whole day … I have worked in a more collective way and it's a great way to work when it works … [but what] we didn't understand was that working collectively could still be individuals working to their strengths … and I think we were just a bit too naive and thought working collectively meant everybody did everything and or everybody had a say in everything all the time and it took so long to – make decisions – so we did some things really badly but we also did some things really well. But I – wouldn't want to work collectively again it was just – too much. [98]

Far from collectivism encouraging freedom of expression it could, at times, lead to many issues reaching stalemate, resulting in a paralysis of the movement.

In order to overcome dwindling numbers many feminists tweaked the structure of conferences, hoping to attract new activists. As was discussed earlier in this chapter, women attending the St Andrews and Edinburgh conferences in 1977 and 1978 were split into groups of ten for the first time, indicating a desire to return to the small group structure that had dominated the earlier part of the period. They were also limited to three subjects for discussion. As Fiona Forsyth, a member of the Aberdeen group, wrote at the time, 'women's liberation is about the links between the "personal" and the "political". But how can a whole group of women meet for only two days and relate their experiences to each other's for the first time?'[99]

These organisational issues became even more pressing when activ-ists began to think about recruitment. Anxiety about the failure to attract new women to the movement emerged in discussions in the mid- to late 1970s. Yet the anti-structural attitude of the WLM, at times, prevented new women from engaging with feminist activities and debates. Fiona Forsyth expressed this concern most eloquently in her review of the 1978

Scottish WLM conference in St Andrews. She argued that the weakness of the movement lay in its 'spasmodic pattern' where women would meet once or twice a year at conferences and 'in between times we carry on as individuals or in small groups, oblivious of what others are doing or have done in the past'. She worried that this led to cliques in the movement as those attending conferences tended to stay with women they were familiar with. Fiona Forsyth asked, 'but what about the lone woman who may have come from Glenrothes or Falkirk or Inverness?' and the movement appeared to have no answer to this question.[100]

Challenging southern domination

Another area of discussion for feminists based in Scotland, which led to a growing disillusionment with British conferences in particular, was the domination of the movement by groups operating in southern England. A major concern for feminists active in Scotland was the fact that most British women's liberation conferences were held in cities in England which were miles away from their homes. Paula Jennings and Frankie Raffles appeared to speak for the entire movement in Scotland when they published an article in *WIRES*, which argued that 'Scottish women are being put down and dominated. We are being isolated from the Movement, London holds power in the Women's Liberation and Scotland is suffering.'[101] Elspeth McLean recalled the long journeys to British women's liberation conferences and that women in Scotland never felt fully included in the wider WLM in Britain. She described travelling to a conference in England:

> we went down in a minibus overnight. So, we – were absolutely exhausted when we got there. And we were really grumpy all the time we were there. And they must have dreaded the Scottish women coming because we were so grumpy. But one of the things we were grumpy about was that everything was very London-centred. And I remember Frankie had drawn a map with a sort of women's liberation London view of where Scotland was and like it was kind of nowhere. And we were saying wanted to have the next one in St Andrews or Dundee. And I remember thinking, Frankie please don't say that, how are we going to organise a conference?! And there she was up at the front of hundreds and hundreds of women saying we're going to have it [in St Andrews or Dundee] … there was a vote about where the next conference was going to be, – [and] it didn't come to Scotland. I'm glad because there was only about four or five – women in our group and not that many in St Andrews. Well we would have been able to do it because people do.[102]

There is evidence to suggest there was widespread discontent about this issue which was focused not just on conferences but on how the British WLM was organised. For example, Aspen, an activist in St Andrews also wrote to *WIRES* to ask, 'could feminists please try and stop referring to thi [*sic*] whole of thi [*sic*] British Isles as "England"? ta.'[103]

This resentment was also expressed during interviews conducted for this research. Sandie Wyles of Aberdeen women's liberation group said the WLM was:

> so London-centric. It was incredible. They had no idea about life beyond the Watford Gap. And we found that when we went to London. They didn't know that there was a women's movement in Scotland and that there had been a history of suffrage.[104]

Sandie admitted that this made women in Scotland feel angry.[105] The women's group in Aberdeen also held regular film nights which showed films from Sweden and Norway, such as *Take It Like a Man*. The group rented these films from a distributing company in London which would send both the film and the equipment required to show it. Sandie remembered:

> there was a film that we had ordered and it hadn't appeared. So I had to phone – Cinema of Women in London. And she couldn't make out a word I was saying, of course with my Scottish accent. And she says 'oh, don't worry about it, she says it's just, we've just put it on the train now'. 'The train now', I said, 'the film's being shown in two hours' time!' She said, 'oh it'll get there, don't worry, it'll get there.'[106]

This illustrated to women in Aberdeen the extent of the 'London-centric' mentality of some activists in the WLM in Britain. This was a constant complaint made by activists in Aberdeen, who felt the movement was dominated by those in the South of England. The anger about this domination seemed to increase the further away a woman was located from London. Chris Aldred felt that if she wanted to network with feminists beyond Aberdeen then she would have to travel as very few national women's liberation events were held in towns and cities near to Aberdeen.[107] Irrespective of whether women had been born in England, many Scottish-based feminists expressed outrage at the London/Southern domination of the movement.

From the late 1970s onwards a small number of Scottish women also began to express fears about English women dominating local workshop discussions. A member of Aberdeen women's liberation group published an article in *The Scottish Women's Liberation Journal* in 1978 titled 'A Scottish Movement?' She argued that 'the WLM in Scotland is not Scottish', as it was dominated by middle-class English women. She supported the creation of a workshop on 'Scottish culture and feminism' held at the Scottish women's liberation conference in 1978.[108] She reported this was a well-attended workshop and that women admitted they 'often found it a habit to keep quiet and be led, allowing the more articulate and confident English women to set the pace'.[109] In order to overcome this timidity she suggested that they should establish separate CR sessions for Scottish women only. She urged the WLM:

> At this time we should take our heads out of the sand – the wheels are grinding slowly towards devolution and thereafter (I myself believe) to an independent Scotland. How we can say that party politics are of no use to us. We live here, are subject to the whims of our politicians and although independence will not be a golden age, there is such a tremendous opportunity for government not only to reflect the needs of the people more closely, but those of women as well.[110]

Although this appeared to be a minority view within the WLM in Scotland, this activist was not alone in her protests. Elspeth King, a member of Glasgow women's liberation workshop, declared after one Scottish women's liberation conference that the Trade Descriptions Act should be enforced, given that it was billed as a Scottish women's liberation conference and yet Scottish women were in the minority and 'their voices drowned by the predominant South of England accents'.[111]

These discussions were underpinned by a growing feeling of difference for feminists active in Scotland as they often felt that Scottish culture seemed particularly backward and hostile to women's demands. Indeed, feminists in Scotland felt, unlike many feminists in England, that the Westminster Parliament was actually offering them a degree of protection. Women involved in the WLM in Scotland felt 'male domination [was] more institutionalised in Scotland' and there was a definite fear that if more power was granted to Scottish politicians it would lead to a backlash against the WLM.[112] Additionally, male domination and oppression of women were viewed as being rooted in the peculiar nature of Scottish society. Breitenbach argued that 'the wrath of the righteous fell heavily on the Scottish people, but it fell most heavily on the female sex'.[113] Indeed the patriarchal nature of Scottish society has been noted by a wide range of commentators.[114]

A symbol used by the WLM north of the border to illustrate the patriarchal tendencies of Scottish society was the character Ma Broon. *The Broons*, a popular cartoon series published by D.C. Thomson in Dundee, told the story of a supposedly 'quintessential' Scottish family in which the mother, Ma Broon, is portrayed as looking after the family, especially her husband Pa Broon, and viewed by some feminists in Scotland as the typical downtrodden housewife. The WLM parodied this cartoon by drawing its own version. As Figure 5.1 shows, its storyline differed significantly from the D.C. Thomson original. In the WLM version there was a new character Granny McGreer, based on Germaine Greer, and Ma Broon finally awakens to feminism, declaring to her family, 'I'll not be call Maw anymore – a woman should na be defined by her child-bearing role'.[115]

Ma Broon featured in discussions about the women's movement in Scotland once more during the 1970s. In *The Scotsman* journalist Julie Davidson's article 'Time of Political Reckoning for the Modern Ma Broon' she wondered why women, especially those associated with the WLM, had remained silent over the question of devolution.[116] Introducing her article Davidson argued that the character Ma Broon and what she represented continued to haunt

> the sculleries and parlours of Scotland's social history like an irreversible curse. She patrols our psyche like a bossy traffic warden, comic incarnation of the authoritarian drudge … Despite her apparent power, despite her control of the domestic fiefdom, Ma Broon probably asks Pa Broon how she should vote; if she votes at all. Her power is private, internal, compressed and dictated by pragmatism. The dutiful daughters of Scotland hold the head of the country's impoverished manhood at the cost of holding their own outside the home.[117]

Using Ma Broon as her example, Davidson questioned the prevailing myths about Scotland. She also questioned why feminists had failed to engage with the debates about devolved power in Scotland in the late 1970s and argued that women's voices 'could have been powerful' in these discussions. She challenged the belief of many women's liberation activists north of the border that more political power for Scotland would have

> been a triumph for the McNasties; for the kind of meanness and mediocrity which has characterised some areas of Scottish public life; for the flexing of machismo muscles in an amphitheatre of reaction and repression. With no nice times for women.[118]

A vote was held in 1979 to determine whether the people of Scotland wanted to see more power devolved away from the Westminster parliament to a Scottish Assembly based in Edinburgh, conducted against a political backdrop which had witnessed a resurgent Scottish National Party (SNP). The 1970s was a decade in which people north of the border were assessing the implications of more political power and considering what it was to be Scottish.[119] Yet, Breitenbach has stressed that 'there is little evidence of active engagement of feminists in the debate on devolution

Figure 5.1 Women's liberation parody of D.C. Thomson's *The Broons*

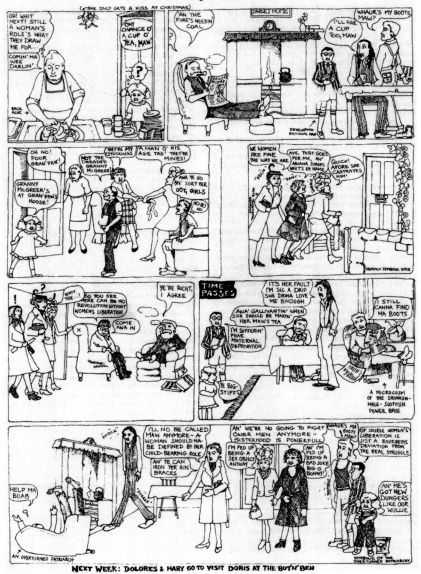

Source: *Scottish Women's Liberation Journal*, no. 4, 1978, p. 16.

in 1979'.[120] The silence about devolution in the WLM is not surprising considering that many active feminists were not party political and had more in common with those groups which operated in a political culture where politics was conducted on the streets rather than in parliaments. The parliamentary nature of the devolution campaign, therefore, would not have interested many active feminists, although smaller women's liberation groups, like the Campaign for Legal and Financial Independence, did discuss it.

However, the two issues should not be confused. Women's liberation activists in Scotland could feel that the British movement was dominated by those in the South of England and that they had different issues to face and campaign on, while still displaying ambivalence about the devolution issue. Most activists viewed the WLM as an international movement but one which should be more representative and should acknowledge the different issues women faced in different parts of the world while also recognising the similarities between women's experiences. Indeed, active feminists in Scotland were not alone on this issue. An Irish woman described her feelings when she moved to England to work for *Spare Rib*. She described how she thought

> the British women's movement ... would be different, that it would be another home, and I would be welcomed. I was wrong. Slowly it sank in. I was supposed to adapt and become part of *their* movement, culture, politics. I was never asked about what was happening in Ireland, whether things were different or the same. It didn't matter.[121]

A feeling of being overlooked contributed to a growing disillusionment with British women's liberation conferences and encouraged women in Scotland to consider their own particular experiences, leading to the creation of literature, newsletters and conferences focused more specifically on the Scottish context.

Conclusion

As elsewhere in the USA and Western Europe, there were a number of intense discussions in the WLM in Scotland which altered the ways in which women thought about and interacted with the movement over time. Reflecting concerns amongst the wider movement in Britain, women debated sexualities and feminist ideologies. Scottish-based feminists were also concerned with the organisation of the movement and its impact on recruitment, and the additional problem of the domination of the British movement by groups in London and the South of England. While the debates outlined in this chapter often negatively affected the experiences of some feminist activists, it is clear that women reacted to these issues in different ways and the impact of these debates was less clear cut than has often been described.

Furthermore, while it is evident that in Scotland women were changing their approach to women's liberation, and large conferences and meetings were becoming an increasingly frustrating experience because they could not meet the needs of every woman, this did not mean that women's liberation activists gave up discussing and organising around feminist themes. Instead they began to experiment with the organisation of conferences in an attempt to re-energise the movement. Furthermore, many activists began to focus on issues which mattered to them most. Women were experiencing intense personal change both because of changes within their own lives and also because of their involvement in the WLM. As they changed they often looked to other like-minded women to support them, moving into groups which were smaller and often focused on a single issue.

Notes

1 *The Student*, 27 April 1972, p. 1.
2 E. Breitenbach, "'Sisters are doing it for themselves": The Women's Movement in Scotland' in A. Brown and R. Parry (eds), *Scottish Government Yearbook 1990* (Edinburgh, 1990), p. 211.
3 Transcript of interview with Chris Aldred (CA), 30 August 2007, p. 21.
4 *Edinburgh Women's Liberation Newsletter*, August 1976, p. 5.
5 Transcript of interview with Ellen Galford (EG), 2 April 2007, p. 29.
6 *WIRES*, no. 9, February 1976, p. 1.
7 *MsPrint*, no. 1, August 1978, p. 19.
8 Transcript EG, p. 11.
9 Transcript CA, pp. 21–2.
10 E. Setch, 'The Women's Liberation Movement in Britain, 1969–79: Organisation, Creativity and Debate' (unpublished PhD Thesis, University of London, 2000), p. 13.
11 *Scottish Women's Liberation Journal*, issue 3, November 1977, p. 16.
12 *MsPrint*, no. 1, August 1978, p. 19.
13 Ellen Galford in E. Galford and K. Wilson, *Rainbow City: Stories from Lesbian, Gay, Bisexual and Transgender Edinburgh* (Edinburgh, 2006), p. 102.
14 Transcript of interview with Ruth Miller (RM*), 27 April 2007, pp. 10–11.
15 E. Breitenbach, 'Scottish Feminism in Print', *Cencrastis*, no. 21 (Summer 1985), p. 45.
16 A. Coote and B. Campbell, *Sweet Freedom: The Struggle for Women's Liberation* (London, 1982), p. 45; 'The Women's Issue', *The Observer Review*, 7 December 2008, p. 3.
17 D. Bouchier, *The Feminist Challenge: The Movement for Women's Liberation in Britain and the United States* (London, 1983), p. 101.
18 Coote and Campbell, *Sweet Freedom*, p. 45; *WIRES*, no. 76, August 1979, p. 1.
19 *Catcall*, issue 1, 1976, p. 1.

20 Breitenbach, "'Scottish Feminism'", p. 45.
21 Bouchier, *The Feminist Challenge*, p. 103.
22 Breitenbach, "'Scottish Feminism'", p. 45.
23 Breitenbach, "'Scottish Feminism'", p. 45; Bouchier, *The Feminist Challenge*, p. 98.
24 *Scottish Women's Liberation Journal*, issue 4, Spring 1978, p. 3.
25 *Nessie*, issue 1, May 1979, front cover.
26 *Scottish Women's Liberation Journal*, vol. 1, issue. 1, Spring 1977, p. 1.
27 Ibid., p. 3.
28 Breitenbach, "'Sisters are doing it for themselves'", p. 214.
29 Transcript of interview with Esther Breitenbach (EB), 24 May 2007, p. 22.
30 *Scottish Women's Liberation Journal*, vol. 1, issue 1, Spring 1977, p. 1.
31 *Scottish Women's Liberation Journal*, issue 3, November 1977, p. 1.
32 Ibid., issue 4, Spring 1978, p. 25.
33 Ibid., issue 2, Summer 1977, p. 1.
34 Bouchier, *The Feminist Challenge*, p. 1, p. 122 and pp. 129–36; Whelehan states that the radical/socialist tension led in Britain to a destructive split: I. Whelehan, *Modern Feminist Thought: From the Second Wave to 'Post-Feminism'* (Edinburgh, 1995), p. 61.
35 Coote and Campbell, *Sweet Freedom*, p. 27.
36 J. Lovenduski and V. Randall, *Contemporary Feminist Politics: Women and Power in Britain* (Oxford, 1993), p. 96.
37 *Scottish Women's Liberation Journal*, vol. 1, issue 1, Spring 1977, p. 18.
38 *Scottish Women's Liberation Journal*, issue 2, Summer 1977, p. 22.
39 *Scottish Women's Liberation Journal*, no. 3, November 1977, p. 27.
40 Transcript AJ and PJ, p. 35.
41 *WIRES*, March 1978, no. 47.
42 *Nessie*, issue 1, May 1979, p. 8.
43 *Nessie*, issue 1, May 1979, p. 2.
44 *Scarlet Women*, March 1978, no. 47, p. 3.
45 *Edinburgh Women's Liberation Newsletter*, May 1978, p. 2.
46 Ibid., p. 9.
47 Ibid., p. 10.
48 *Whatever Happened to the Scottish Women's Liberation Journal?*, 1978, p. 2.
49 Ibid., p. 3.
50 Breitenbach, "'Sisters are doing it for themselves'", p. 214.
51 Transcript EB, p. 21.
52 *Scottish Women's Liberation Journal*, issue 2, Summer 1977, p. 26.
53 *Tayside Women's Liberation Newsletter*, 1978, p. 20.
54 S. Rowbotham,, *Women in Movement: Feminism and Social Action* (London, 1992), p. 313.
55 Transcript RM*, p.12.
56 L. Segal, *Is the Future Female?: Troubled Thoughts on Contemporary Feminism* (London, 1987), p. 65.
57 Whelehan, *Modern Feminist Thought*, p. 19.
58 It must be pointed out that Bouchier admitted that this distinction was over-simplistic before then analysing the movement in terms of this division, arguing that the strategies of socialist feminism were reformist campaigns and radical feminism was CR and communes: *The Feminist Challenge*, pp. 130 and pp. 83–8.

59 *Edinburgh Women's Liberation Newsletter*, July 1978, p. 15.

60 Coote and Campbell, *Sweet Freedom*, p. 29, and M. Pugh, *Women and the Women's Movement in Britain 1914–1999* (Basingstoke, 2000), p. 332.

61 Breitenbach, "'Sisters are doing it for themselves'", p. 215.

62 Transcript EG, p. 21–2.

63 Transcript of interview with Pauline Robinson* (PR*), 6 December 2006, p. 24; E. Hamer, *Britannia's Glory: A History of Twentieth-Century Lesbians* (London, 1996), p. 194.

64 Transcript PR*, p. 24.

65 Transcript of interview with Paula Jennings (PJ), 15 October 2007, pp. 20–1.

66 Transcript PR*, p. 28.

67 *Scottish Women's Liberation Journal*, no. 4, Spring 1978, p. 26.

68 Transcript EB, p. 24.

69 *Scottish Women's Liberation Journal*, issue 2, Summer 1977, p. 23.

70 Transcript EG, pp. 23–4.

71 *Scottish Women's Liberation Journal*, issue 4, Spring 1978, p. 26.

72 *Nessie*, issue 1, 1979, p. 17.

73 *MsPrint*, no. 2, 1978, p. 22.

74 *MsPrint*, no. 3, 1979, p. 24.

75 Ibid., p. 26.

76 Ibid.

77 *Tayside Women's Liberation Newsletter*, vol. 1, no. 4, October 1977, p. 7.

78 Transcript SW and AMcG, p. 31.

79 There are numerous examples in the literature. While Gelb acknowledges that structureless groups presented problems, she states that it was the divisions between radical and socialist feminists which 'have prevented national conferences from meeting since 1978': J. Gelb 'Feminism in Britain: Politics without Power' in D. Dahlerup (ed.), *The New Women's Movement: Feminism and Political Power in Europe and the USA* (London, 1986), pp. 108–9. While Martin Pugh acknowledges the importance of the wider economic and political context in the movement's development, he discusses both radical and socialist feminists and the splits over sexualities as being prime reasons for the movement ceasing to function as a national co-ordinating presence: *Women and the Women's Movement*, p. 332. Lynne Segal has also cited the debates between feminists at the 1978 conference for ending this particular mode of organisation: *Is the Future Female?*, p. 56.

80 *Edinburgh Women's Liberation Newsletter*, October 1976, p. 9.

81 *Women's Report*, vol. 2, issue 5, July–August 1974, p. 19.

82 Breitenbach, "'Sisters are doing it for themselves'", p. 221.

83 Transcript EB, p. 20.

84 *Scottish Women's Liberation Journal*, issue 4, Spring 1978, p. 25.

85 Setch, 'The Women's Liberation Movement in Britain', p. 83.

86 *Women's Report*, vol. 2, issue 5, July–August 1974, p. 19.

87 *Women's Report*, vol. 2, issue 6, September–October 1974, p. 18.

88 *MsPrint*, no. 2, 1978, p. 13.

89 Problems with conference organisation have also been explored by J. Rees, 'A Look Back at Anger: The Women's Liberation Movement in 1978', *Women's History Review*, 19:3 (2010), p. 350.

90 J. Freeman, *The Tyranny of Structurelessness* (New York, 1970), p. 3.

91 Setch, 'The Women's Liberation Movement in Britain', p. 30 and p. 91.

92 Z. Fairbairns, 'Saying What We Want: Women's Liberation and the Seven Demands' in Z. Fairbairns, H. Graham, A. Neilson, E. Robertson and A. Kaloski (eds), *Saying What We Want: Women's Demands in the Feminist 1970s and Now* (York, 2002), p. 20.

93 *Edinburgh Women's Liberation Newsletter*, June 1975, p. 4.

94 Ibid., p. 2.

95 Transcript of interview with Zoe Fairbairns (ZF), 5 June 2007, pp. 15–16.

96 Freeman, *The Tyranny*, p. 5.

97 Transcript of interview with Anne Jackson (AJ) and Paula Jennings (PJ), 27 August 2007, p. 36.

98 Transcript RM*, p. 16.

99 *Scottish Women's Liberation Journal*, issue 4, Spring 1978, p. 25.

100 *Scottish Women's Liberation Journal*, issue 4, Spring 1978, pp. 25–6.

101 *WIRES*, no. 32, 1977, 18–19.

102 Transcript of interview with Elspeth McLean (EMcL), 9 August 2007, p. 12.

103 *WIRES*, 71, June 1978, p. 20. The spelling in this extract reflects the efforts of some radical feminists to challenge the gendered nature of the English language – any word which included, for example, 'he' or 'his' would be replaced with another word. The word 'the' would, therefore, become 'thi'.

104 Transcript of interview with Sandie Wyles (SW) and Anne-Marie McGeoch (AMcG), 18 September 2007, p. 39.

105 Transcript SW and AMcG, p. 40.

106 Transcript SW and AMcG, p. 39.

107 Transcript CA, p. 19.

108 *Scottish Women's Liberation Journal*, no. 4, Spring 1978, p. 3.

109 Ibid.

110 Ibid.

111 LSE (MCINTOSH 1/15), *A Record of the Scottish Women's Liberation Conference, Glasgow, October, 1976*, p. 36.

112 Ibid., p. 4.

113 Ibid., p. 24.

114 Bouchier, *The Feminist Challenge*, p. 178; J. Macleod, P. Bell and J. Forman 'Bridging the Gap: Feminist Development Work in Glasgow' in E. Breitenbach and F. Mackay (eds), *Women and Contemporary Scottish Politics: An Anthology* (Edinburgh, 2001), p. 35.

115 *Scottish Women's Liberation Journal*, no. 1, Spring 1977, p. 1.

116 With thanks to the Trustees of the National Library of Scotland for granting permission to use this material. National Library of Scotland (hereafter NLS), Acc 9395, Box 6/5, *The Scotsman*, 19 February 1979, as found in Scottish Convention of Women Archive.

117 Ibid.

118 Ibid.

119 N. McGarvey and P. Cairney, *Scottish Politics: An Introduction* (Basingstoke, 2008), pp. 29–30. G. Brown, 'Introduction: The Socialist Challenge' in G. Brown (ed.), *The Red Paper on Scotland* (Edinburgh, 1975), p. 7; D. Gow 'Devolution and Democracy' in Brown, *The Red Paper*, p. 58–9.

120 E. Breitenbach, 'Feminist Politics and Devolution in Scotland' (unpublished paper, Colloque Franco-Britannique, Lyon, March 2007), p. 3.

121 As quoted in H. Kanter, S. Lefanu, S. Shah and C. Spedding (eds), *Sweeping Statements: Writings from the Women's Liberation Movement 1981–1983* (London, 1984), p. 282.

6

Abortion: a woman's right to choose

ccounts of the WLM in Britain have often argued that the
debates discussed in Chapter 5, especially those between radical
and socialist feminists and over sexualities, led to the fragmentation of the movement, which then resulted in a 'dramatic decline' of
the WLM at the end of the 1970s.[1] Fragmentation is often portrayed as
undermining the unity and strength of women's liberation politics. For
example, Bouchier argued that 'the limited appeal and fragmentation
of the British movement are indisputably signs of weakness' and Weir
and Wilson posited that the focus on separate identities and single-issue
campaigns led to the movement's 'political muscle' being 'weakened by its
non-existence as a *national* movement'.[2] These debates it would seem had
such a negative impact that they led to the dissolution of the movement
with no further British women's liberation conferences being held after
1978. Bouchier concluded that the movement 'fell into the doldrums
by 1978' owing to the 'conflicts of the first decade' and Lynne Segal
also concluded that the 'second wave of feminism … grew rapidly as a
mass social movement, peaking in the mid-1970s before dissolving as a
coherent organization by the end of that decade'.[3] This book seeks to revise
these arguments by illustrating that far from fragmentation automatically
signalling the decline of the movement, it often opened up fruitful areas
of feminist activism in the 1970s and consequently widened the appeal of
women's liberation ideas. Debates and disagreements were, therefore, not
as detrimental as some accounts have contended. Far from being in the
doldrums, as Bouchier suggested, or 'peaking in the mid-1970s' as Segal
as described, activists within the WLM in Britain, at least north of the
border, were finding ways to revitalise the movement from the mid-1970s
onwards and the debates outlined in the previous chapter were part of
this process. Setch identified that the movement in London was 'very far
from defunct by the end of the 1970s, for the changes and challenges it

went through were part of its development, not its demise' and the same can be said of the WLM in Scotland.[4]

A good illustration of the development of the movement in Scotland during the 1970s is that while British conferences ceased there were actually two further women's liberation conferences held in Glasgow and Edinburgh in 1987 and 1989. Organised by women working within the field of violence against women, these conferences could be seen as a negative development as discussions were focused on a single issue. However, over 260 women attended 1987's event indicating continued enthusiasm for women's liberation ideas. Those who attended represented 'a cross-section of the Women's Liberation Movement in Scotland' with many women who had been active in the groups in the 1970s participating. The second conference in Edinburgh attracted two hundred women, and Breitenbach has argued that 'it indicated a resurgence of interest in feminist ideas in Scotland'.[5] Indeed in some respects Scotland may have differed from other areas of Britain. This will not be known until more research is conducted into women's liberation in other parts of the British Isles but it would seem that, as Lovenduski and Randall highlighted, Scotland still witnessed a growth in women's liberation activism at the end of the 1970s.[6] Why does the evidence from Scotland appear to contradict those accounts of the British movement which argue that women's liberation politics were in decline during the late 1970s? The final two chapters explore this question. It will be argued that, far from the movement declining, it actually fragmented into a number of different campaigns, which in many ways was a positive development as it widened the appeal of women's liberation ideas and made them more relevant to women beyond the activist core. The account presented here supports the recent findings of Dean, who questioned 'melancholic narratives' which portrayed the movement as going into decline in the late 1970s owing to a loss of 'vitality and energy' and instead offers a more optimistic account of the development of women's liberation politics at the end of the 1970s.[7] Instead it will be shown that, far from abandoning the ideas of women's liberation, most women sought smaller and more intimate gatherings which were focused on a narrower theme or were organised in their own towns and cities. Far from being an entirely negative development, therefore, fragmentation can be seen in some ways as constructive, ensuring the influence of women's liberation ideas beyond the activist core and beyond the confines of the movement's newsletters, and continuing after the last British conference in 1978.

In seeking a reappraisal of the fragmentation of the movement, the final two chapters will explore the abortion and violence against women campaigns in order to show how feminist activism developed in the late 1970s. Of course there were many other important areas which feminists continued to campaign on, including, for example, the women who gathered at Greenham Common to protest against nuclear weapons.[8] Moreover women were involved in a number of single-issue campaigns simultaneously. But it is argued here that abortion and violence against women were of central importance to the development of feminism and women's liberation in Scotland during the late-1970s and beyond. Vast numbers of active feminists became involved in these campaigns. Of the twenty-nine women interviewed for this research, all but two were involved in the groups and protests focused on violence against women and abortion rights. Moreover these campaigns accentuated the feelings of difference which feminists in Scotland felt within the context of the British WLM, encouraging them to consider women's liberation from the perspective of women in Scotland and in doing so illustrating that women north of the border often had different issues to face.

Abortion in Scotland before 1967

As Drude Dahlerup has contended, 'the issue of abortion was to the new women's movement of the 1970s what the suffrage issue had been to the feminist movement around the turn of the century'.[9] This was particularly true in Scotland, where abortion rights were defended in the attempts by a small number of politicians and anti-abortion groups to tighten up the 1967 Abortion Act. Observing these developments, Neil Williamson commented that abortion was becoming 'a major issue in political life in Scotland' in the late 1970s.[10] Abortion was not only a priority for women's groups but was also ranked as an important campaign by trade unions, the Labour Party and other groups and movements on the left of the political spectrum. This was an important development for the WLM. While some commentators portray fragmentation of the movement as a weakness, it will be shown that in terms of the Scottish movement it enabled the WLM to make or to strengthen alliances with other sympathetic political groups and introduced the ideas of women's liberation to new women and to men, ensuring their continued influence.

The influence of women's liberation ideas can be seen in debates focused on abortion during the 1970s. Before the arrival of the WLM in the late 1960s, abortion had been liberalised through the 1967 Act. This Act has been characterised as one part of a broader liberal consensus permeating British politics in the 1960s and 1970s.[11] But far from being an entirely liberalising law, rooted in the 'permissive' 1960s and aimed at extending rights for women, the 1967 legislation was a result of a long campaign for legal abortion dating back to at least the 1930s.[12] Early campaigns had focused on eradicating the unsupervised practice of backstreet abortions. Forming an almost 'secret' female culture, women had often ended pregnancy themselves. Furthermore, abortion was viewed as one part of women's wider contraceptive routine. Advice was passed from mother to daughter, as women learned that to aid a miscarriage it was helpful to take caraway seeds, nutmeg or gin. Some even used knitting needles to abort a foetus, with many left haemorrhaging and permanently damaged.[13]

Clearly the methods used by many women to end pregnancy before 1967 were unsupervised, extremely primitive and unhygienic. Attempting to gain control, legislators introduced a variety of legislation aimed at combating the number of deaths caused by botched backstreet abortions. In 1939 an abortion was performed on a fourteen-year-old girl who had become pregnant as a result of rape. In what became known as the Bourne decision it was ruled that abortion, before the twenty-eighth week, might be legal if a doctor decided that either the mother's physical or mental health was at risk. Setting an important legal precedent, this decision allowed for mental health justifications to be used in decisions over abortion.[14] In Scotland the situation was further complicated by the practice of common law. For example, the Lord Advocate would order to have a case investigated by the Procurator Fiscal. This meant that even before 1967 a doctor who carried out an abortion would not be charged with a crime unless a definite complaint was made. This anomaly in common law meant that many obstetricians in Scotland were performing abortions before 1967 without any real fear of prosecution. The Bourne decision, therefore, had less impact in Scotland where common law already afforded doctors more freedom. But it was an important decision as it set a precedent and helped to encourage the British government to extend the law in the form of the Abortion Act of 1967.[15]

A desire to see the state intervene in this matter became more pressing as information about backstreet abortions became known. For example, it was estimated that in 1960 alone there had been sixty-two deaths caused by women having backstreet abortions in Britain.[16] Despite the risks associated with this procedure, some women would still go to any lengths to end pregnancy. This was partly because of the social stigma attached to children born out of 'wedlock'.[17] It is estimated that around a hundred thousand illegal abortions were performed annually in Britain before 1967.[18] Collections of papers emanating from the WLM recorded some of these experiences, with, for example, one woman describing how when she was twenty years old she discovered she was pregnant. She felt trapped and unprepared and decided not to continue her pregnancy. She described how she and her boyfriend

> made contact with someone who could help. I never knew the name of the woman who did it – with a syringe and carbolic soap in the middle of a bright October afternoon. That part wasn't horribly painful, only very uncomfortable and with one sharp pain. Within a couple of hours I had started losing a small amount of blood and by late evening the loss was well-established.[19]

After several hours of pain a doctor was called and she was eventually admitted to hospital where it was discovered that the placenta had to be removed. After the procedure she was chastised by the doctor. She described being left 'in no doubt about his view of my "immoral" behaviour'.[20]

Not every woman had to place her life in the hands of a backstreet abortionist. The procedure was also offered at private clinics, most notably on Harley Street in London. Costing around £3000, it was incredibly expensive but it did ensure that the procedure was done properly. Private clinics offered abortions on a highly secretive basis and it was, therefore, very difficult for a woman to be able to make the necessary arrangements. Pauline Robinson, who would become an activist for the Dundee branch of the National Abortion Campaign (NAC), remembered having to go to a clinic in London when abortion was still illegal. She recounted her experience with the psychiatrist:

> [He] really got to the heart of it. I would injure myself rather than go home with this and I already knew my friend ... had aborted herself, using quinine, of a four month foetus in her college room. One, two, three of my friends had had backstreet abortions. They wouldn't tell me, nobody would give me the information. But I would have found it if I hadn't had this abortion. So eventually the abortionist agreed to abort me ... but I had to get my consent form signed ... But I couldn't go to my mum or dad, those days you had to get a signature until you were twenty-one ... And I can remember signing my own form, thinking what will they do if they get checked over? Who will get arrested? But by then – if he was going to give me an abortion that was all right by me. I mean I'd have – done anything. I so badly didn't want to be pregnant.[21]

Pauline's relief at obtaining an abortion was evident throughout her transcript where she described how she 'had got rid of this burden, absolute burden. And never thought of it as a baby. Never. Never. Never for one minute ... I had got rid of this burden. I was no longer a shame and a disgrace in the eyes of my dad'.[22] It was becoming evident that there was always going to be a demand for access to abortion facilities, either on

Harley Street or in the backstreet. And it was this realisation that encouraged the government to liberalise the abortion law in order to control and supervise the situation and avert the unnecessary deaths of countless women.

Debating abortion

The Act of 1967 established a twenty-eight-week upper time limit in which an abortion could be carried out. It also legislated that 'a person shall not be guilty of an offence under the law relating to abortion when a pregnancy is terminated by a registered medical practitioner'.[23] The legislation also ruled that abortion was permissible if continuing the pregnancy would involve risk to the 'physical or mental health' of the woman or if there was a risk the child would be born with physical or mental abnormalities. Moreover, the second clause stated that 'account may be taken of the pregnant woman's actual or reasonably foreseeable environment'.[24] This made it possible for medical practitioners to judge cases of abortion on medical and social grounds and meant that the 1967 Act was 'an enormous improvement on what had gone before'.[25]

The Bill's proposer, David Steel, the son of a Church of Scotland minister, argued during the Bill's third reading that 'anyone advancing the Bill has in no way been advocating abortion ... The main case for the Bill and for clarifying the law rests on the grounds that we are hopeful that the scourge of criminal abortion will be substantially removed from our land'.[26] The Act, therefore, did not recognise a woman's right over her own body but rather introduced legislation in order to combat the 'scourge' of the backstreet abortionist.[27] This is an important distinction. Placed in a wider context it is evident that the British approach was more conservative than, for example, that in the USA where laws pertaining to abortion had at least recognised a woman's right to privacy.[28] Indeed, Lovenduski and Randall have illustrated that the Bill's sponsors had to drop an additional clause which would have allowed doctors the right to perform abortions on women who were judged to be under excessive strain.[29] Nonetheless the Act appeared to be quite successful as by 1970 the number of deaths caused by botched backstreet abortions had been reduced to thirty-two.[30]

Before 1967 the main abortion campaign group was the Abortion Law Reform Association (ALRA). Formed in 1936 by seven women, including prominent feminist campaigners Dora Russell and Stella Browne, it was successful in creating a broad-based campaign.[31] In the 1960s twenty-five national groups supported ALRA's work including many supposedly 'traditional' women's groups.[32] The National Union of Townswomen's Guilds (TGs) supported a degree of abortion law reform in 1965, aligning themselves with ALRA's work. This decision 'caused quite a stir in the press, whose stereotyped image of the TG members were clearly upset'.[33] Local branches began to distribute ALRA leaflets and lobby local politicians.[34] Courting groups like the TGs, who were viewed as 'traditional', ALRA was able to present itself as a credible representative of a wide range of opinion.[35] With the emergence of the NAC, however, ALRA was to become much more radical.

Discussions about abortion, therefore, did not begin with the arrival of the WLM. Yet the WLM was extremely important in shifting the terms of the debate and in radicalising the campaign, mainly by demanding a woman's right to self-determination. It was also active in the late 1970s in defending the 1967 law against the attempts of James White, William Benyon and John Corrie, who introduced parliamentary Bills to reduce the upper time limit in which a woman could legally obtain an abortion. Abortion was an early campaigning priority for the WLM in Britain. Its importance was signified by the adoption of the fourth demand at the first national women's liberation conference in 1970, arguing for the procedure on demand.[36] The issue was partly understood in the wider context of patriarchy where, it was argued, like rape and domestic violence, the failure to recognise abortion on demand was an illustration of the effect of men's domination of women.[37] Anne-Marie McGeoch, an activist of the Aberdeen women's liberation group, argued that abortion 'was really the main flashpoint ... defending women's right to have an abortion was something that was kind of fundamental ... it was a focus for everything that was wrong really. You know here were men making laws about women.'[38] Conceptualised in terms of the body politic, one activist argued that 'the state has no right in a woman's body'.[39]

Yet as Rowbotham argued, 'there is not a universally accepted feminist case for abortion'.[40] Some Scottish-based women's liberation activists exhibited a deep disquiet about the issue. Susie Innes of St Andrews women's liberation workshop said in 1972 she was 'happy to use any name – baby, embryo, foetus ... this is unimportant. The question is that of when is an embryo/baby held to be a human being, with whatever rights are accorded to humans, particularly the right to life.'[41] This diversity of opinion in the WLM over the issue is not always represented in the literature on the topic. Two active members of the WLM in Scotland reviewed the NAC conference in Sheffield in 1978 and described how some participants were uneasy about abortions being offered up until full term. They reported that:

some sisters in the group felt anxiety about conference discussion and decisions on the question of positive legislation. In particular we were disappointed at the vote that NAC should not at the time support the Abortion Law Reform Association's effort to get their model bill through Parliament but should draft its own bill specifying no time limit on abortion on demand ... Some were uncertain whether terminating a viable foetus late in pregnancy could even be properly termed an abortion ... [There are those who] incant the right to choose principle as if that were the start and finish of the argument.[42]

Nonetheless most discussions by Scottish-based feminists were consistent with those elsewhere in Britain: abortion was seen as being inextricably linked to women's rights. Indeed during the 1970s the WLM's litmus test to ascertain the extent to which a particular society was 'feminist' was whether or not it had legalised abortion.

Opposition to a woman's right to choose

The main opposition to the WLM's campaign for abortion on demand came in the form of a number of pro-life groups. These included LIFE and the Society for the Protection of Unborn Children (SPUC). Democratically but hierarchically structured, there were 250 local branches of SPUC in Britain in the 1970s. It also had a central council and executive and a membership of 26,000 people by 1980. LIFE was organised along similar lines but proved slightly less popular, with a membership of 20,000.[43] Branches of SPUC and LIFE could be found throughout Britain. SPUC witnessed an increase of 14 to 33 branches in 1976 alone.[44] Its political strength was drawn from the Catholic Church. The other major advantage for groups like SPUC was that they were able to secure strong financial backing, raising at least £250,000 per year.[45] They spent this money on publicity, including numerous poster campaigns and distributing leaflets. It was also used to mobilise support during general elections. Eveline Hunter, a Scottish-based feminist, argued that 'in recent by-elections the Society for the Protection of Unborn Children (SPUC) has used its hysterical propaganda to make candidates waver on their support for legal abortions. They know that an anti-abortion stance is an easy way of winning the Catholic vote.'[46] The groups secured support in two ways. First, they encouraged priests, from the pulpit, to persuade their congregations to write to MPs in order to secure their support for opposing abortions.[47] Second, they drafted letters and got them signed by representatives of, for example, the Salvation Army and Scottish Lay postolate. Led by high-profile Dumbarton lawyer George Crozier, these letters were then sent to hundreds of MPs.[48]

The Catholic Church became a particular focus for frustration for the WLM in Scotland. This is not surprising given its vocal and fervent opposition to abortion. In contrast the Church of Scotland provided a far more equivocal response to the issue, neither supporting nor condemning it.[49] However, no one was left in any doubt about the Catholic Church's stance on the matter. The pages of *The Scottish Catholic Observer* were packed with articles updating its readership on the issue. Even innocent school competitions emphasised their opposition. In 1979 the newspaper ran an essay competition for schools on the theme of 'Why Not Abortion?' The winning entry was by a student from St Saviour's High School in Dundee who had argued that 'abortion is wrong. It is violent and primitive. It is "birth prevention" not "birth control". It is murder.'[50] It was reported that anti-abortion groups frequently went 'into schools with lurid pictures and films of abortions.'[51] In Ireland too, where Catholicism was an even stronger force, SPUC transported pictures and models of embryos around schools.[52] Anti-abortionists used emotive language, frequently linking abortion with murder. For example, one priest in Dundee described how the thought of 'foetuses being consigned to the dustbin frankly turns my stomach and I can clearly understand why many people describe abortion as murder.'[53]

Esther Breitenbach, writing in the *Scottish Women's Liberation Journal* in 1978, summed up the WLM's response. She described how the Pope had opposed abortion, even if continuing the pregnancy put a woman's life in danger. Breitenbach argued that concealed behind the Pope's pronouncement was 'support for the right to oppress women by ensuring that they remain domestic slaves and reproductive machines.'[54] A woman's right to choose was, therefore, opposed by the pro-life lobby which argued that the child's right to life was more important than a woman's control over her own body. These two contrasting positions would find little to compromise on.

Defending not demanding: establishing the NAC

Although the WLM was important in establishing the links between abortion and broader feminist theories, it quickly realised 'that none of the existing organisations ... had the forces to initiate mass action' on the issue. Consequently some feminists from the WLM became active in the NAC.[55] Forming one part of the international movement for abortion rights, NAC was formed in 1975 and aimed to 'build a mass national campaign on the basis of a woman's right to choose.'[56] The NAC built a broad-based campaign and was mixed-sex. Nevertheless, there was substantial crossover in terms of membership of the NAC and the WLM in Scotland. Many women recalled that they were introduced to the activities of the NAC through women's liberation politics. Furthermore, in the late 1970s the abortion campaign was an effective recruiter of women into broader women's liberation politics.[57] Sandie Wyles and Anne-Marie McGeoch remembered being introduced to broader feminist campaigns in this way.[58] The two groups also tended to share meeting places, with the Glasgow branch of the abortion campaign convening in the women's centre on Miller Street.[59]

The NAC had a clearer structure than the WLM. It was co-ordinated by a steering-committee but allowed local groups a large degree of autonomy.[60] Branches were formed throughout Scotland; by the late 1970s there were groups in Aberdeen, Dundee, Glasgow, Stirling and Edinburgh and many more women were receiving its literature in places such as Shetland. Glasgow was the first branch to be formed in Scotland, established in 1975, followed by Edinburgh. By the end of the period women living in towns such as Paisley had also expressed an interest in establishing a group.[61] In the latter half of the period a distinct Scottish Abortion Campaign (SAC) was formed, although it was still broadly aligned to the wider British organisation. This aimed to 'deal with special problems in abortion facilities in Scotland'.[62] Prevented from applying for charitable status, the abortion campaign, unlike SPUC and LIFE, always struggled to survive financially. To overcome this problem, members were encouraged to take out standing orders and they also undertook a range of fund-raising initiatives, including asking the general public for donations.[63] Despite its precarious financial situation the NAC was effective in building alliances with influential individuals and groups.

An important group in this regard was Doctors for a Woman's Choice on Abortion (DWCA). A UK body, originating in Edinburgh, it was set up and run by Judy Bury and Nadine Harrison, both of whom were doctors and, in Nadine's case, also an active member of a local women's liberation group. Established in 1976, this group aimed to highlight that 'a large number of doctors would favour a change in the law to give women the right to make the abortion decision' and 'to answer at a medical level the arguments of anti-abortionists'.[64] Forty people attended the group's first planning meeting in 1977 and by the late 1970s it boasted a membership of six hundred. Any qualified doctor, sympathetic to the campaign's aims, was invited to join and associate membership was also open to medical students. Leading figures in this campaign were Wendy Savage and Peter Huntingford, Professor of Obstetrics and Gynaecology at London Hospital. His and other doctors' support afforded the abortion campaign a new legitimacy. Members campaigned to change the law in order to reflect the demand of a woman's right to choose. They wrote to MPs and attended parliamentary sessions on abortion.[65]

The second major group which the abortion campaign was effective in building alliances with was the labour movement. Historically women had been poorly represented in the Labour Party, the Scottish Trades Union Congress (STUC) and trades councils. The links between the WLM and labour movement are complex. Although there was some crossover with women active in both the WLM and trades unions, their work tended to be separate and distinct with little interaction between the two groups. A major reason for this was that, as Chapter 2 outlined, some women felt their issues and concerns were trivialised by the labour movement. For example, Isabelle Kerr, who was active in feminist politics in Glasgow, recalled that:

> it was quite difficult, I think there was still – that – kind of round the table in the smoky rooms. – There's Margaret at the end of the table and she'll do the women's issues and make the tea, Margaret while you're there ... Lots of posturing and you know, I'm certainly not afraid to say it, a lot of posturing, and oh yes, 'these women are oor brothers' ... but heaven help these women if they ever really did want to be their brothers.[66]

However during the late 1970s a number of feminists became active once again in the labour movement, probably owing to the increasingly hostile political and economic climate which the WLM was operating in. As one activist described, for some feminist activists, 'it meant back to the organisations we had left some years before'.[67] It was clear to many feminist activists that the only way to defend women's reproductive rights was to ally with those fighting for working-class issues. Abortion could be clearly defined as a working-class issue. Women who had enough money to pay for abortion had always been able to undergo the procedure in a private clinic, albeit on a highly secretive basis. But working-class women had little choice. For example, it was asked by one woman 'how many working-class women have a choice between the cash and the knitting needle.'[68] Linking this issue to class politics was important, and political engagement with left-wing activists, therefore, became a key strategy in turning the abortion campaign into a mass movement.[69]

Coote and Campbell have argued that 'the relationship between the NAC, the unions and the women's movement as a whole was not entirely comfortable'.[70] Suspicion about the motivations of left-wing men led to some feminists asking whether the NAC was a feminist campaign. This distrust led to the Edinburgh branch of the NAC splitting over the issue in 1976. The members of this local group decided to distance themselves from left-wing groups and align their work more directly with the WLM as there were only six members who regularly attended meetings and they were all women. They concluded that 'many of us feel we should have organised the campaign differently from the beginning'.[71] Furthermore, those aligned with radical feminism resented links with the labour movement, frequently accusing those women involved in building such an alliance of 'selling out'.[72] Distrust was not one-sided. Some activists in the labour movement also kept a distance from the WLM, believing it to be middle-class, bourgeois and individualistic.[73]

Yet some women's liberation activists were actively engaged with both the labour movement and left-wing groups, and were directly responsible for influencing their agendas. In this regard they appeared quite successful. As early as 1970 the Communist Party (CP) in Scotland declared that one of the three campaign priorities for that year would be abortion and contraception.[74] Rafeek has described how there was growing support for the NAC amongst women in the CP in Scotland. However, it is evident that men were a little more reticent and 'this often reflected the influences of religious backgrounds and a social conservatism'. Despite this the CP became an important contributor to the work of the abortion campaign.[75]

While it has been recognised that the International Socialist (IS) group was important in the development of women's liberation politics in Britain it can be seen that the International Marxist Group (IMG) also lent support. Whilst only having around eighty members in Scotland in the late 1970s, the IMG was among the first to take an active interest in the WLM.[76] This was true for other social movements too. As Robinson recognised, 'of all the groups IMG was the most prepared to direct its energies into picking up activists engaged in the peace movement, feminism and other sorts of single issue politics'.[77] Pamphlets and internal discussion papers in the IMG's archives reveal that it believed itself to be the antidote to the organised labour movement, which it felt was sidestepping the abortion issue. In 1973 it argued that it was important for the IMG to 'show more support' than its counterparts in the trades unions and Labour Party.[78] There is a sense that during the 1970s, left-wing groups were courting the WLM in order to attract more women to their particular causes and to boost their own membership.[79] Whatever its motivations were for supporting abortion, the IMG was an important part of the wider coalition campaigning for women's rights. Indeed, as early as 1971 it listed abortion, alongside Iberia and unemployment, as their campaign priorities for the year. It viewed the NAC as an effective way to campaign on 'the class struggle' more generally, and courted the women of the WLM, viewing them as 'the organised expression of the radicalisation of women'.[80] The IMG's support was significant for one further reason: it openly defended 'a woman's right to choose'. For them abortion was not merely a way to eradicate the scourge of backstreet abortions but was an important aspect in the wider liberation of women.[81]

Unlike the IMG, the Scottish Labour Party, far from backing a woman's right to choose, adopted a more pragmatic approach. In contrast, the Party in the UK overwhelmingly passed a resolution in favour of defending the 1967 Act with a majority of 4,666,000 to 73,000 in 1978. The Catholic Church in Scotland reacted angrily to this decision, declaring that it was considering an extensive campaign in Labour constituencies to urge MPs to speak out against the Party's abortion policy. In the Garscadden by-election of 1978 this strategy can be clearly seen. Despite his party's support for the 1967 Abortion Act, it was reported in the *Scottish Women's Liberation Journal* that the Labour candidate and future First Minister of Scotland, Donald Dewar, opposed abortion law reform as, according to women's liberation campaigners, he believed it would alienate Catholic voters in his constituency.[82] Furthermore, the records of the Scottish Council of the Labour Party reveal that a subcommittee on abortion recommended:

(i)   That at some point the Party's position would have to be made explicit;
(ii) That the best course in the short term was to adopt 'a low profile';
(iii) That in light of (ii) the request for a spokesman from the BBC to be turned down and the BBC be informed that 'the matter was still under consideration'.[83]

Women's liberation activists saw this reaction as selling out, accusing the Labour Party of being blackmailed by the Catholic Church.[84] Abortion put tremendous pressure on the Labour Party as, every time there was a vote in the Houses of Parliament over the issue, the *Scottish Catholic Observer* would list the names of those MPs who had voted against its agenda.[85] Furthermore, influential churchmen like Cardinal Gray of Edinburgh urged members of the STUC and Labour Party to vote in line with the interests of the Catholic Church.[86] Despite the pragmatic response, abortion was still crucial in bringing feminist activists closer to the Labour Party, indicating that individual members must have been more supportive of abortion rights than the minutes of subcommittee meetings reveal.[87]

The Catholic Church also actively courted the trades unions in Scotland. Press releases issued by the Scottish Catholic Press Office frequently argued that the Labour Party and trades union movement were running contrary to both the UN declaration on the Rights of the Child and the Law of God.[88] Although many trades unionists appeared immune to such statements, they did have an effect. For example it was claimed at the STUC annual conference in 1980 that people were resigning 'from the Movement on conscience if the issue of abortion is adopted.'[89] Furthermore some feminists believed that, although the trades union movement passed resolutions which mandated members to support the abortion campaign, it did very little to actually promote these demands.[90]

Yet, despite some individual dissent, the STUC was an important voice in the NAC. By aligning itself with the campaign it legitimised it. Elspeth McLean, a member of the Educational Institute of Scotland (EIS) and active feminist in Dundee, believed 'trade union support for the NAC campaign was really important because normally – people weren't interested – And just thought we were – a bit mad and very scruffy and hippy type people.'[91] Chris Aldred, who was a women's liberation activist and had actively tried to involve trades unions in the struggle for greater abortion rights, argued in an article in the *Scottish Women's Liberation Journal* that by including members of the trades unions 'we can expand our own vision of women's struggle' and encourage them to 'take up feminist ideas'. She further added that by securing their backing they could expand their own support base to include ten million more people.[92] Women's liberation activists were not alone in recognising the importance of enlisting trades union support. The IMG also argued that parliamentary tactics would not be enough to secure a victory for abortion on demand but that the campaign 'also need[ed] the mobilisation of the TU movement in extra parliamentary action'.[93]

Support by the unions was visible at protests and demonstrations. They also provided financial backing, paying transport costs for people to travel to various demonstrations. They wrote letters to newspapers and expressed concern about SPUC's tactics. One such instance resulted in the Chairman of Aberdeen SPUC asking for an apology from an EIS representative of Aberdeen Trades Council who had reportedly argued that pro-life groups wanted to use 'working class girls … as breeding cattle for couples who cannot have their own children'.[94] The trades councils were especially supportive of a woman's right to choose. Glasgow and Dundee Trades Councils both backed a motion giving 'women the right to choose' at the STUC Women's Conference in 1979.[95] Arguments for self-determination in matters of abortion were not as widely supported amongst the STUC's general membership. Instead of arguing for women's right to control their own bodies, the STUC opposed changes to the Abortion Act of 1967 on the basis that they would disadvantage working-class women the most. Yet, whether or not they subscribed to women's right to choose, they were an important support for the broader campaign. Elspeth McLean felt the WLM and the trades unions were particularly united in Scotland. Once she had moved to Cambridge and Liverpool she realised that neither place had 'that kind of real solidarity' evident north of the border.[96] The feminist perspective had a clear impact on the workings of the trades unions, with Beale arguing that 'many issues first debated within women's groups have expanded the agenda of union thought and action'.[97] This point was illustrated in the newspaper *Dundee Standard*, which stated in 1979 that support for abortion within the trades unions prior to the 1970s would have been 'met with looks of astonishment, possibly followed by howls of derision' indicating how far the trades union movement had come on the issue.[98]

Defending the accessibility of abortion facilities, therefore, high-lighted the mutual interests of feminists and left-wing activists. No other issue in the 1970s united groups of women and left-wing campaigners quite so effectively. These alliances legitimised feminist campaigns and enabled them to carve out space politically. Furthermore, by working with groups like trades unions and the Labour Party they were often able to influence their mode and operation.

The NAC in action

Throughout the 1970s there were a number of challenges made to the Abortion Act of 1967. Some politicians attempted to pass legislation which would cut the time limit in which women were lawfully allowed to have an abortion. This was because the 1967 legislation had proved to be extremely controversial, leading to debates over the decline of the family and the emergence of a 'permissive society'. The first challenge to abortion rights came in 1974 in the form of a Parliamentary Bill intro-duced by James White, Labour MP for Glasgow Pollok. White argued that no abortion should be permitted after twenty-four weeks. The bill was unsuccessful but the challenge was perceived to be so serious that the NAC was actually established in response to White.[99] However, more serious challenges were to emerge. The first was William Benyon's Bill in 1977. The Conservative MP for Buckingham wished to cut the upper time limit to twenty weeks. The WLM in Scotland argued this would:

mean suffering and misery for thousands of women for whom it will become more difficult to obtain safe, legal abortions ... They will be forced to continue with an unwanted pregnancy, or to suffer at the hands of the dangerous, illegal, back-street abortionists.[100]

The bill also aimed to force women to notify their GPs if they were planning to have an abortion, and the giving of any advice to women under sixteen would have to be done in the presence of their parents. Benyon also wished to extend the conscience clause to allow doctors and nurses more grounds to refuse to perform an abortion.[101] The Scottish WLM's newsletters frequently updated their readership on the developments of this bill.

The most serious attack on abortion provision came in the form of the Corrie Bill, which was introduced in 1979.[102] John Corrie, Conservative MP for North Ayrshire, wanted to modify the 1967 Act in order to eliminate what he felt were abuses of the law. This included lowering the upper time limit, taking away the charitable status from organisations like the British Pregnancy Advisory Service and making the 'grounds for termination' more rigid.[103] Of all the attempts to reform abortion legislation in this period Corrie's bill came the closest to achieving success. This was because the Conservative government had a comfortable majority and the likelihood of the bill being passed was extremely high. A major reason why it did not succeed was a 'lack of parliamentary time'.[104]

The controversial nature of Corrie's bill led to a hardening of positions on both sides of the debate. *WIRES* reported that there had been two hundred pro-choice letters sent to Parliament in 1979 but this had been eclipsed by several thousand letters by pro-life campaigners. In this respect it would seem that 'the women's movement [had] a lot to learn from Catholic activism'.[105] The TUC and STUC were extremely important in galvanising support for the anti-Corrie campaign. They financially supported NAC's efforts and organised demonstrations and they also paid protestors' travel costs. The most significant protest was the TUC's Right to Choose demonstration against Corrie in London in October 1979 which included women's groups and NAC representatives. Described by Lovenduski as the 'NAC's most publicised success', it attracted around a hundred thousand protestors.[106] This march has been described at length in Coote and Campbell's book *Sweet Freedom*. When the TUC's General Secretary, Len Murray, decided he would lead the procession he was challenged by feminists. They were outraged by a 'woman's' issue being hijacked by men and voiced their complaints, much to Murray's anger.[107] The protest had been organised into columns. Leading the march were representatives from the TUC. They were followed by the NAC, Labour

Party members and all other demonstrators, including those from Lesbian Line. Spurred on by their anger at being put at the back of the march, a group of two hundred women edged to the front of the protest with a London WLM banner.[108] Accusations were exchanged: the TUC felt the WLM was taking over the struggle and feminists were angered at the TUC's blatant disregard for them. According to Coote and Campbell, 'for the women in the NAC who had worked so hard for this movement it was an excruciating ordeal to be caught between elements of mutual distrust and intolerance in the two movements they wanted to bring together.'[109] However, other feminists describe an altogether more positive experience of marching with trades unionists. Elspeth McLean remembered:

> going to a demo in London, which was sponsored, [by] the unions … The unions were behind it and sponsored a train, I think probably starting in Aberdeen all the way down to London. And I think the train was free. I think they paid for all these women … For us all to go all the way down to London and all the way back again. And I remember when we got back to Edinburgh, – we'd missed the last train or something had happened. So, they put on a special train, just for us. For about six of us, to get back to Dundee. And I had to get out at Cupar and the train stopped for me … and that was because it was a trade union sponsored thing. Even though it was a very contentious issue, really. And I remember at the time thinking this is real solidarity, you know?[110]

Setch has shown how this dispute led to some women leaving the NAC in London, citing the dominance of men from the labour movement as their major problem.[111] In Scotland this did not appear to cause as much outrage with women returning from large demonstrations in London struck by how much support they had received from trades unionists. This is a good example of how oral histories and case studies challenge or add to published narratives of the WLM in Britain.

Indeed, there were some important differences between the abortion campaign in Scotland and in the rest of Britain. Whilst the NAC was organised at a British level with the focus on Westminster, it was always a decentralised group. Campaigners in Scotland had always organised separate NAC conferences. However, from the mid-1970s onwards activists north of the border felt there was an urgent need for more action on a Scottish basis. The SAC was established to discuss and work on issues facing women in Scotland.[112] Differences in opinion within the broader NAC organisation emerged in the late 1970s. These focused on which campaign issues should be prioritised. The consensus in NAC was that they should widen the focus of their campaigns, to include reproductive and birth control issues.[113] The SAC disagreed with this decision, believing that the primary task of its campaign was to get the 1967 Act fully implemented. It argued that although abortion was readily available in London the same could not be said for certain areas in Scotland.[114] The NAC eventually split over this issue, with the Scottish organisation opting to remain within the original framework.[115] A splinter group emerged: the Women's Reproductive Rights Campaign, which also stressed issues like the limited availability of birth control.[116]

The reason why the SAC wanted the focus to remain on the 1967 Act was the patchy nature of NHS abortion facilities. This became a key campaigning issue for activists in the late 1970s. For example, it was argued in *WIRES* that 'until we have enough National Health Service facilities "the right to choose" means nothing'.[117] In 1977 abortion provision in Birmingham, England was thought to be so bad that the NAC organised a demonstration to highlight the issue.[118] Regional variations were also deeply felt in Scotland. It was reported by some feminist activists in the *Scottish Women's Liberation Journal* that the poor NHS facilities in certain areas of Scotland had forced nearly one thousand women every year to travel to England to obtain an abortion.[119] Clearly the availability of facilities varied throughout the United Kingdom with, for example, women travelling to England from Northern Ireland, where the 1967 Act did not apply and abortion was, therefore, still illegal. According to

Table 6.1 Legal abortions from NHS local authorities (1976 figures) (rates per thousand women aged between 15 and 44)

Region	Rates per thousand
Arygll and Clyde	3.6
Ayrshire and Arran	5.3
Dumfries and Galloway	5.7
Fife	7.2
Forth Valley	4.9
Greater Glasgow	6.6
Grampian	11.2
Highlands	10.5
Islands	1.6
Lanarkshire	2.7
Lothian	9.5
Tayside	10.7

Source: E. Hunter, *Scottish Woman's Place* (Edinburgh, 1978), pp. 124–5.

Hunter, a major issue in Scotland was that many local health boards were controlled by chief consultant gynaecologists who did not favour a liberal interpretation of abortion laws.[120] Within Scotland there was a clear East/West divide. As can be seen from Table 6.1 Grampian region witnessed the highest rates of abortion, whilst the Islands and Lanarkshire areas had the lowest with only 1.6 and 2.7 per 1000 live births respectively. It is not surprising the Islands had the lowest figure in Scotland given the conservative nature of society there. Moreover, as Chapter 4 showed,there was a lack of available funding for local services in this area, with women's groups campaigning for improved child-care facilities, amongst other issues. Margaret Elphinstone remembered that any woman who lived in the Shetland Islands who wished to terminate her pregnancy had to travel to Aberdeen. The women's liberation group in Shetland decided

> [to do] something about abortion. In Shetland [this] was a very problematic thing because girls had to go to Aberdeen on the plane to … the hospital in Aberdeen. – Which made it very public. Because, you know what Shetland's like. You know, people would spot, oh so and so's just gone … you know, this was not confidentiality and I can't remember quite how that went but that was another of the issues we addressed. And I think maybe that's when we lobbied the county council .[121]

In contrast to the situation in Shetland, Aberdeen had long been known as the 'abortion capital' of Scotland. The city had a family planning clinic as early as the 1920s. This came under local authority control in 1946 and became Scotland's first and Britain's second such facility.[122] Taking advantage of the freedom afforded doctors under common law, Dr Dugald Baird, Head of Obstetrics and Gynaecology in the 1930s, performed 233 abortions during his tenure. Baird had been a doctor in the Glasgow slums and believed that abortion was justifiable in certain circumstances. His approach to abortion was carried on by his successors and was evident in the 1970s, with Thompson arguing that 'Aberdeen appears to have retained its reputation of liberality in abortion.'[123] The availability of abortion provision in the local context was clearly shaped by individuals within the medical community. The disparity in abortion facilities throughout Scotland forced those in the WLM and trades unions to campaign on the issue. The STUC's Women's Advisory Committee in 1977 urged the 'General Council to seek improvement in NHS provision in Scotland to ensure proper implementation of the '67 Abortion Act'.[124] Similarly, the Women's Legal and Financial Independence Group, an offshoot of the WLM in Scotland, demanded in its Women's Charter in 1978 that 'each Area Health Board should be obliged to provide abortion facilities, in the form of NHS abortion clinics.'[125]

The SAC was also concerned with the tendency of politicians north of the border to vote comparatively conservatively on issues to do with reproduction. There was a commonly held belief that Scottish MPs, on the whole, were more reactionary and anti-feminist than their English and Welsh counterparts in terms of parliamentary voting records.[126] Voting records from the time appear to support this interpretation. Abortion campaigners were particularly effective in publishing booklets which listed how MPs voted on the issue, what their religious beliefs were thought to be and what action was needed in order to convince them to support NAC and ALRA's arguments. ALRA's publication *A Woman's Right to Choose: Action Guide* indicated that, from a sample of Scottish MPs at Westminster, thirty-seven were against abortion, sixteen supported it and the views of the remaining thirteen were 'unknown'. Beside each name comments like 'retreats behind the fence' and 'needs information and lots of letters' were included. They also assigned 'RC' beside the names of those MPs who were known to be Roman Catholic.[127] Another useful source of information was Chambers and Cossey's *How MPs Voted on Abortion*, which listed how politicians had voted on the Benyon Bill of 1977, which proposed to cut the upper time limit to twenty weeks. Of the Scottish MPs they included, sixteen had voted in favour of Benyon and only four against.[128] The *Scottish Catholic Observer* claimed the margin was even wider, reporting that Scottish representatives had voted thirty to five in favour of the bill.[129] These voting records fed into a perception amongst feminist campaigners in Scotland that women north of the border had greater obstacles to overcome than their English and Welsh counterparts as 'the wind blowing through much of Scottish culture [was] cold and hostile to women's lives and values'.[130]

This perception was especially strong amongst abortion campaigners. There was a keen sense of Scottish 'backwardness' in terms of issues to do with sex and reproduction. Callum Brown has argued that 'in Scotland ... there was still a sense of a puritan Christian culture until the late 1970s' and the abortion issue effectively illustrated this point.[131] The James White Bill, for example, had been supported by many Scottish MPs, including seven SNP representatives.[132] Furthermore, two of the three main challenges to abortion rights in the 1970s were led by politicians representing constituencies north of the border: James White and John Corrie. For women's liberation activists these two politicians became the perfect illustrations of Scottish social conservatism. The Corrie Bill was the most effective in galvanising support for the abortion campaign in Scotland because activists were particularly incensed by the fact that Corrie was a Scottish MP. In 1979 *MsPrint* noted that 'in Scotland, the NAC groups, which had been at a low ebb up until the Corrie Bill, are now flourishing, and the Scottish coordinating meetings have been revived'.[133] Pauline Robinson, who was active in Dundee NAC, cited Corrie's Bill as a crucial factor in her politicisation over the issue as it created a

> little group of about eleven or twelve and there's us four stuck together all the way through the anti-Corrie march ... that galvanised me about abortion. John Corrie was a Catholic Western Scottish MP, tried to reduce women's access to abortion. And that was my first ... understanding of how important abortion was.[134]

Abortion polarised Scottish society. Rallies organised by anti-abortionists and held in major Scottish cities were always countered by the protests of smaller groups of feminists, trades unionists and others who supported abortion rights. The largest rallies were always organised by pro-life campaigners and were held at the People's Palace on Glasgow Green. In 1975 five thousand pro-life supporters attended a rally with only a minority of pro-choice protestors present. Speakers at these rallies included politicians, churchmen and medics. For example at 1975's event a former doctor described those aligned with the WLM as being beneath animals. News reporters were also shown slides of aborted foetuses before the start of the event.[135] A silent march was also held and white wreaths were laid to symbolise the number of abortions conducted since the 1967 Act. It was reported that only two hundred people had turned up to oppose the rally but they had countered their small numbers with 'vociferous heckling'.[136]

The second major anti-abortion rally to be held in Scotland during the 1970s was in Dundee in 1979. Coinciding with the fierce debates raging over Corrie's Bill, this event attracted three thousand people. Speakers included Archbishop Thomas Winning of Glasgow and the Right Reverend Mario Conti, Bishop of Aberdeen. The day began with two thousand anti-abortion campaigners marching from Riverside to Caird Hall in the centre of Dundee.[137] Both sides of the abortion debate attempted to capitalise on this event. *Spare Rib* reported that one hundred supporters of abortion rights picketed the rally and handed out 3,500 leaflets in Dundee.[138] On the other hand the *Scottish Catholic Observer* portrayed their picket as 'a mere 100 or so pro-abortion demonstrators, mainly students who awaited their arrival outside the hall. On being refused admission they soon dispersed'.[139] A speaker at the event characterised supporters of abortion as 'elitist, racist and genocidal ... whose attitudes and opinions were very similar to those held in Hitler's Germany'.[140] Furthermore, Archbishop Thomas Winning wondered 'if there was a connection between the increased number of armed robberies, physical assaults and cowardly planting of bombs that killed and mutilated and this cheapening of human life by the public authorities.'[141]

Women in the WLM recalled the tactics used by groups like SPUC. Nadine Harrison, who was prominent in both NAC and DWCA, described how:

> the anti-abortion people [could] be really really nasty. – I mean I'm quite shocked at how horrible they can be. You know – they kind of think they've got the high moral standing, you know – we think more about foetuses than you do or something. And yet they will – heckle at meetings ... and send threatening letters and you know stuff like that. Nasty letters.[142]

At one NAC conference in Stirling in 1979, two SPUC members were found to be in the audience, secretly recording the discussions.[143] They would also attend open meetings of NAC in order to heckle and challenge the speakers. Pauline Robinson recalled one meeting:

> There was a whole line of SPUC supporters. We knew who they were. They'd file in late looking very righteous and at the end of my talk about my experiences, one woman stood up and said 'and when you look at your lovely little boy and your lovely little girl', so they'd done their homework and found out who I was. 'Do you never grieve for the child you killed all those years ago?' Their tactics were appalling.[144]

NAC supporters also attended SPUC meetings. Lorna Peters described her experience:

> it was really, really difficult to keep quiet. And – because we were two young women who weren't known, I think they were very curious about this. But I mean I just came out, I was almost physically sick.[145]

The two opposing camps kept a close eye on each other. In Aberdeen, for example, the local NAC branch and trades union members picketed the opening of an Innocents counselling centre, which, it was reported, was mostly staffed by SPUC representatives. They lobbied Grampian Health Board to close the centre but this request was refused on the grounds that the board had no jurisdiction to take such an action. Local pressure on this issue was maintained through the organisation of small marches. For example in 1980 Dundee NAC and representatives from the labour movement organised a protest from the Hilltown to the city centre.[146] The campaign for abortion rights borrowed the street theatre tactics of the WLM. Ellen Galford described the protest methods of the Glasgow branch of NAC:

I was part of the group who started doing some odd and inventive things like SPUC, which was the Society for the Protection of the Unborn Child, would have these huge rallies where they would often spill out of the churches, the buses would be waiting for the people left from the Sunday churches to take everybody to Glasgow Green for a big, you know, Save the Unborn Child thing. And there was one of these huge rallies happening, because there were at that stage, there were periodic waves of legislation struggling to get – any sorts of rights for legalised abortion. But – there were also, as things get liberal, you get some nasty politician who would you know arise, things would crystallise around, you know, this amendment or that amendment. So a bunch of us, I remember, decided to do a little agitprop street theatre. So somebody worked, it must have been in one of the hospitals and got a bunch of doctor's coats which we splashed with red paint to create blood-stains and then we went to the rally on Glasgow Green for SPUC, carrying big signs saying 'Backstreet Abortionists say thank you to SPUC'. As all these people as they got off their buses from their various religious services – thought at first we were all about oh poor foetuses … I mean nobody beat us up, nobody got the police … Things were still quite kind of douce.'[47]

This form of campaigning ensured that the abortion debate was kept in the public eye throughout the late 1970s and early 1980s. The role of the WLM was crucial in radicalising this debate through their campaign tactics, protest methods and their recognition of the importance of women's control over their own bodies.

Conclusion

'No return to the backstreets' was a major campaign slogan for the WLM in Scotland. This encapsulated the movement's shift from demanding to defending abortion rights and this shift must be understood in terms of the wider political context of the late 1970s, in which abortion rights were constantly under attack. In ensuring that some form of abortion provision continued to be available to women during the late twentieth century, pro-choice campaigners can be seen to have been crucial in influencing and shaping both public opinion and the political agenda. This is further illustrated by the fact that the abortion debate today includes some recognition of its links with women's rights. However, as with many other issues, there was a diversity of opinion in the WLM. Whilst the WLM has frequently been portrayed as a movement which called for abortion on demand, up until full term, in fact there was a wide variety of views. However, most, if not all, women in the movement agreed about the importance of recognising a woman's right to choose as being fundamental to any feminist agenda.

The NAC became an effective forum in bringing together all those feminists who wished to campaign on this issue. Effectively radicalising ALRA, this organisation also built important alliances with those on the left of the political spectrum and with the medical community, affording their campaigns a new legitimacy. The WLM formed a major part of this campaign. The WLM is often portrayed as being hostile towards the state and parliamentary process but some feminists frequently engaged in lobbying and by becoming NAC activists they formed close relationships with Labour MPs and trade union members. The NAC can, therefore, be seen as an effective opposition to the better-financed pro-life movement and in providing this opposition it helped to foster debate over the issue in Scotland.

Those feminists who became involved in the NAC campaigned on a specifically Scottish basis. The fact that opposition to the 1967 Abortion Act usually came in the form of a Scottish politician illustrated to many active women's liberation campaigners the conservative nature of Scottish society. This galvanised them as they believed that in some ways feminists in Scotland had more to fight for than their English sisters. By discovering a different set of priorities, feminists in Scotland were able to create campaigns on their own terms, leading to an intensification of activity in the later part of the period. The campaign for abortion rights is, therefore, a good example of the positive aspects of a fragmentation of women's liberation politics in the later 1970s.

Notes

1 E. Setch, 'The Face of Metropolitan Feminism: The London Women's Liberation Workshop, 1969–1979', *Twentieth Century British History*, 13:2 (2002), p. 171.

2 D. Bouchier, *The Feminist Challenge: The Movement for Women's Liberation in Britain and the United States* (London, 1983), p. 217, and A. Weir and E. Wilson, 'The British Women's Movement', *New Left Review*, 148 (November–December 1984), p. 78.

3 Bouchier, *The Feminist Challenge*, p. 147, and L. Segal, *Why Feminism? Gender, Psychology and Politics* (Cambridge, 1999), p. 9.

4 Setch, 'The Face of Metropolitan Feminism', p. 171.

5 E. Breitenbach, '"Sisters are doing it for themselves": The Women's Movement in Scotland' in A. Brown and R. Parry (eds), *Scottish Government Yearbook 1990* (Edinburgh, 1990), pp. 221–2, p. 215.

6 J. Lovenduski and V. Randall, *Contemporary Feminist Politics: Women and Power in Britain* (Oxford, 1993), p. 95.

7 J. Dean, *Rethinking Contemporary Feminist Politics* (Basingstoke, 2010), p. 2.

8 Women from Scotland were present at this protest and also raised funds for the women at the camp. Transcript of interview with Chris Aldred (CA), 30 August 2007, p. 32. For an overview of this campaign see S. Roseneil, *Common Women, Uncommon Practices: The Queer Feminisms of Greenham* (London, 2000).

9   D. Dahlerup, 'Introduction' in D. Dahlerup (ed.), *The New Women's Movement: Feminism and Political Power in Europe and the USA* (London, 1986), p. 10.

10 N. Williamson, 'Ten Years After – The Revolutionary Left in Scotland' in H.M. Drucker and N.L. Drucker (eds), *The Scottish Government Yearbook 1979* (Edinburgh, 1978), p. 76.

11 J. Lovenduski, 'Parliament, Pressure Groups, Networks and the Women's Movements: The Politics of Abortion Law Reform in Britain (1967–83)', in J. Lovenduski and J. Outshoorn (eds), *The New Politics of Abortion* (London, 1986), p. 51.

12 J. Issac, 'The Politics of Morality in the UK', *Parliamentary Affairs*, 47:2 (1994), p. 175.

13 A. Holdsworth, *Out of the Doll's House: The Story of Women in the Twentieth Century* (London, 1988), p. 98.

14 A. Cohan, 'Abortion as a Marginal Issue: The Use of Peripheral Mechanisms in Britain and the United States' in J. Lovenduski and J. Outshoorn (eds), *The New Politics of Abortion* (London, 1986), p. 37.

15 S. Millns and B. Thompson, 'Constructing British Abortion Law: The Role of the Legislature, Judiciary and European Institutions', *Parliamentary Affairs*, 47:2 (1994), p. 192.

16 *Scottish Women's Liberation Journal*, no. 1, Spring 1977, p. 21.

17 L. German, *Material Girls: Women, Men and Work* (London, 2007), p. 21.

18 M. Turner, *The Women's Century: A Celebration of Changing Roles* (Kew, 2003), p. 123.

19 M. Sjoo, 'Abortion Accounts' in S. Allen, L. Sanders and J Wallis (eds), *Conditions of Illusion: Papers from the Women's Movement* (Leeds, 1974), pp. 35–6.

20 Sjoo, 'Abortion', p. 36.

21 Transcript of interview with Pauline Robinson (PR*), 6 December 2006, pp. 7–8.

22 Ibid.

23 *MsPrint*, no. 2, 1978, p. 16.

24 Abortion Act 1967, www.opsi.gov.uk/acts/acts1967/pdf/ukpga_19670087_en.pdf, accessed December 2009, *MsPrint*, no. 2, 1978, p. 16.

25 Bouchier, *The Feminist Challenge*, p. 39.

26 As quoted in Cohan, 'Abortion as a Marginal Issue', p. 34.

27 Issac, 'The Politics of Morality', p. 176. M.D Read, 'The Pro-Life Movement', *Parliamentary Affairs*, 51:3 (1998), p. 446.

28 In America, abortion was formally recognised by the Roe *v.* Wade decision in 1973. The challenge to the Supreme Court was based on a women's right to privacy as written in the American constitution.

29 Lovenduski and Randall, *Contemporary Feminist Politics*, p. 222.

30 *Scottish Women's Liberation Journal*, no. 1, Spring 1977, p. 21.

31 J. Lewis, *Women in England 1870–1950: Sexual Divisions and Social Change* (Brighton, 1984), p. 33.

32 E. Meehan, 'British Feminism from the 1960s to the 1980s' in H.L. Smith (ed.), *British Feminism in the Twentieth Century* (Aldershot, 1990), p. 200.

33 C. Merz, *After the Vote: The Story of the National Union of Townswomen's Guilds in the year of Its Diamond Jubilee* (Norwich, 1988), p. 47.

34 S.F. Browne, '"Dreary Committee Work?": The Work of Established Women's Groups in the North East of Scotland c.1960–c.1970s' (unpublished MLitt dissertation, University of Dundee, 2006), p. 43.

35 Meehan, 'British Feminism', p. 200.

36 *NAC Newsletter*, March 1977, p. 1.

37 *Catcall* 9, March 1979, p. 5.
38 Transcript of interview with Sandie Wyles (SW) and Anne-Marie McGeoch (AMcG), 18 September 2007, p. 33.
39 *Dundee Standard*, 18 January 1980, p. 2.
40 S. Rowbotham, *The Past Is Before Us: Feminism in Social Action since the 1960s* (London, 1989), p. 86.
41 *AIEN*, 8 November 1972, p. 2 (Courtesy of the University of St Andrews Library, StALF1119.A2).
42 *MsPrint*, no. 1, August 1978, p. 19.
43 Lovenduski, 'Parliament, Pressure Groups', p. 222.
44 *Scottish Catholic Observer*, 7 January 1977, p. 5.
45 Lovenduski, 'Parliament, Pressure Groups', p. 58.
46 E. Hunter, *Scottish Woman's Place: A Practical Guide and Critical Comment on Women's Rights in Scotland* (Edinburgh, 1978), p. 5.
47 *Scottish Catholic Observer*, 18 February 1977, p. 1; *Spare Rib*, no. 35, May 1975, p. 19.
48 *The Scotsman*, 6 January 1979, p. 5.
49 J.L. Hogg, 'How Did the Church of Scotland React to the Change in Women's Rights in the 1950s and 1960s?' (unpublished MA dissertation, University of Dundee, 2009), p. 21. The same can be said of the Church of England: Read, 'The Pro-Life Movement', p. 450.
50 *Scottish Catholic Observer*, 23 February 1979, p. 9
51 Abortion Law Reform Association (ALRA), *A Woman's Right to Choose – Action Guide* (London, n.d.), p. 43.
52 E. Manon, 'Women's Rights and Catholicism in Ireland' in M. Threlfall (ed.), *Mapping the Women's Movement: Feminist Politics and Social Transformation in the North* (London, 1996), p. 196.
53 *Dundee Standard*, 1 February 1980, p. 6.
54 *Scottish Women's Liberation Journal*, no. 3, Nov. 1977, p. 3.
55 *NAC Newsletter*, March 1977, p. 1.
56 National Abortion Campaign: *Aims and Structures* (London, 1982), and A. Coote and B. Campbell, *Sweet Freedom: The Struggle for Women's Liberation* (London, 1982), p. 113.
57 Transcript of interview with Margaret Adams (MA*), 3 May 2007, p. 10.
58 Transcript SW and AMcG, p. 4.
59 *A Woman's Right to Choose*, Newssheet of the West of Scotland NAC, undated but probably c.1978, p. 2.
60 *NAC Newsletter*, March 1977, p. 2.
61 *Scottish Women's Liberation Journal*, no. 4, Spring 1978, p. 28.
62 *MsPrint*, issue 6, 1980, p. 16.
63 Transcript of interview with Pauline Robinson (PR*), 4 January 2007, pp. 3–4.
64 DWCA leaflet (undated), Private Collection: Nadine Harrison.
65 *The Student*, 22 February 1977, p. 6; DWCA leaflet (undated), Private Collection: Nadine Harrison; *The Student*, 3 February 1977, p. 9. Transcript of interview with Nadine Harrison (NH), 12 June 2007, p. 6; Letter from M. Rifkind to Nadine Harrison, 5 July 1979, Private Collection: Nadine Harrison.
66 Transcript of interview with Isabelle Kerr (IK), 21 August 2007, p. 17.
67 E. Breitenbach, ' "Sisters are doing it for themselves": The Women's Movement in Scotland' in A. Brown and R. Parry (eds), *Scottish Government Yearbook 1990* (Edinburgh, 1990), p. 218.

68 *Brig*, March 1975, p. 5.

69 M. Barrett, *Women's Oppression Today: The Marxist/Feminist Encounter* (London, 1998), p. 258; S. Rowbotham, *Women in Movement: Feminism and Social Action* (London, 1992), p. 275.

70 Coote and Campbell, *Sweet Freedom*, p. 114.

71 *Edinburgh Women's Liberation Newsletter*, November 1976, p. 15, p. 16.

72 Weir and Wilson, 'The British Women's Movement', p. 78.

73 S. Rowbotham, 'The Beginnings of Women's Liberation in Britain' in M. Wandor (ed.), *The Body Politic: Women's Liberation in Britain 1969–72* (London, 1972), p. 98.

74 N. Rafeek, *Communist Women in Scotland – Red Clydeside From the Russian Revolution to the End of the Soviet Union* (London, 2008), p. 183.

75 Rafeek, *Communist Women*, p. 185.

76 Williamson, 'Ten Years After', p. 61.

77 L. Robinson, *Gay Men and the Left in Postwar Britain: How the Personal Got Political* (Manchester, 2007).

78 Glasgow Caledonian University Archives (hereafter GCUA), IMG Scotland Post-Conference Aggregate May 17/18, document 7, p. 5, Tony Southall Collection, Box 1E, *Socialist Woman*, May–June 1973, p. 7.

79 *IMG: International Bulletin*, October 1979, p. 4.

80 GCUA, Tony Southall Collection, Box P10, IMG-Misc Women Focus Papers, c.1979, p. 3; Tony Southall Collection, Box 1E, IMG Scotland Post-Conference Aggregate, May 17/18, document 7, p. 1.

81 London School of Economics, International Marxist Group Archive 4/4 Various Pamphlets on Abortion Issue, Turn Words into Action Leaflet.

82 *Scottish Women's Liberation Journal*, no. 3, 1978, p. 3.

83 Mitchell Library (TD1384/1/12), Minutes of Meeting of Executive Committee of Scottish Council of Labour Party, 12 November 1977, p. 3.

84 *Scottish Women's Liberation Journal*, no. 3, November 1977, p. 3

85 For example, *Scottish Catholic Observer*, 14 March 1977, p. 13.

86 *Scottish Catholic Observer*, 26 October 1979, p. 1.

87 S. Rowbotham, *A Century of Women: The History of Women in Britain and the United States* (London, 1999), p. 245.

88 GCUA, GB1847 STUC, no. 553, Women's Advisory Committee Papers, 1976–80, Catholic Church in Scotland Press Release, Glasgow, c.1979.

89 GCUA, GB1847 STUC, STUC 83rd Annual Report, Perth 21–25 April 1980, p. 488.

90 NAC, *A Woman's Right to Choose – Newssheet of West of Scotland NAC*, p. 3.

91 Transcript of interview with Elspeth McLean (EMcL), 9 August 2007, p. 14.

92 *Scottish Women's Liberation Journal*, Spring 1978, no. 4, p. 15.

93 *IMG International Bulletin*, June 1979, p. 5.

94 *Evening Express*, 18 August 1975, p. 6, GCUA (IMG – Aberdeen Branch Archives: National Abortion Campaign).

95 GCUA, GB1847 STUC, no. 553, Women's Advisory Committee Papers, 1976–80, Women's Advisory Committee Agenda, 52nd Scottish TUC Women's Conference, Edinburgh, November 1979, p. 9.

96 Transcript EMcL, p. 15.

97 J. Beale, *Getting It Together: Women as Trade Unionists* (London, 1982), p. 11.

98 *Dundee Standard*, 23 November 1979, p. 2.

99   *Scottish Women's Liberation Journal*, no. 1, Spring 1977, p. 21, Rowbotham, *The Past Is Before Us*, p. 67.

100 *Scottish Women's Liberation Journal*, No. 1, Spring 1977, p. 21.

101 Ibid.

102 Lovenduski, 'Parliament, Pressure Groups', p. 55.

103 *MsPrint*, no. 4, 1979, p. 11.

104 Read, 'The Pro-Life Movement', p. 452.

105 *Spare Rib*, no. 35, May 1975.

106 Lovenduski, 'Parliament, Pressure Groups', p. 61.

107 Coote and Campbell, *Sweet Freedom*, p. 148.

108 A. Garthwaite and V. Sinclair, 'The TUC's Right to Choose' in Feminist Anthology Collective (eds), *No Turning Back: Writings from the Women's Liberation Movement 1975–1980* (London, 1981), p. 36.

109 Coote and Campbell, *Sweet Freedom*, p. 148.

110 Transcript EMcL, pp. 4–5.

111 E. Setch, 'The Women's Liberation Movement in Britain, 1969–1979: Organisation, Creativity, Debate' (unpublished PhD thesis, University of London, 2000), p. 277.

112 *MsPrint*, no. 6, 1980, p. 16.

113 Lovenduski and Randall, *Contemporary Feminist Politics*, p. 227

114 *MsPrint*, no. 6, 1980, p. 16.

115 NAC, 'NAC: The Case for Change: Two Views' in H. Kanter, S. Lefanu, S. Shah and C. Spedding (eds), *Sweeping Statements: Writings from the Women's Liberation Movement 1981–1983* (London, 1984), p. 236.

116 Setch, 'The Women's Liberation Movement in Britain', p. 277.

117 *WIRES*, no. 69, May 1979, p. 26.

118 *Scottish Women's Liberation Journal*, no. 3, November 1977, p. 5.

119 The total number of women travelling to England in 1976 was 925. *Scottish Women's Liberation Journal*, no. 1, Spring 1977, p. 22, *MsPrint*, no. 2 , 1978, p. 18.

120 Hunter, *Scottish Woman's Place*, pp. 124–5.

121 Transcript of interview with Margaret Elphinstone (ME), 21 November 2007, p. 15.

122 *Spare Rib*, June 1980, p. 24.

123 B. Thompson, 'Problems of Abortion in Britain – Aberdeen, a Case Study', *Population Studies*, 31:1 (March, 1977), p. 143 and p. 153.

124 GCUA (GB1847 STUC), STUC 81st Annual Report, Aberdeen 21 April 1978, WAC Falkirk, 16 November 1977, p. 33.

125 Edinburgh and Glasgow Women's Legal and Financial Independence Groups, *Scottish Women's Charter – Proposals Designed to Extend Women's Control over Their Lives* (Edinburgh, 1978), p. 5.

126 Breitenbach, "Sisters are doing it for themselves", p. 216.

127 ALRA, *A Woman's Right to Choose*, pp. 29–35.

128 J. Chambers and D. Cossey, *How MPs Voted on Abortion* (London, 1982), pp. 8–37.

129 *Scottish Catholic Observer*, 14 March 1977, p. 13.

130 C. Craig, *The Scots' Crisis of Confidence* (Glasgow, 2004), p. 158.

131 C.G. Brown, *Religion and Society in Twentieth-Century Britain* (Harlow, 2006), p. 283.

132 *Scottish Women's Liberation Journal*, no. 1, Spring 1977, p. 6.

133 *MsPrint*, no. 4, 1979, p. 11.

134 Transcript PR*, p. 17.

135 *The Scotsman*, 22 April 1975, p. 1.
136 Ibid., 22 September 1975, p. 1.
137 Ibid., 23 April 1979, p. 7.
138 *Spare Rib*, June 1979, p. 12.
139 *Scottish Catholic Observer*, 27 April 1979, p. 1.
140 *The Scotsman*, 23 April 1979, p. 7.
141 Ibid.
142 Transcript NH, p. 7.
143 *MsPrint*, no. 6, 1980, p. 17.
144 Transcript PR*, p. 22.
145 Transcript of interview with Lorna Peters (LP*), 4 September 2007, pp. 8–9.
146 *Dundee Standard*, 18 January 1980, p. 2; *The Evening Telegraph*, 12 January 1980.
147 Transcript of interview with Ellen Galford (EG), 2 April 2007, pp. 6–7.

7

Violence against women

The second major campaign area for women's liberation activists in Scotland from the mid-1970s onwards was violence against women. Like abortion politics, this was important in raising the Scottish movement's profile, highlighting some of the specific needs of women north of the border, and in creating alliances with other sympathetic groups. However, it was also successful in introducing the ideas of women's liberation to new women through organisations like Women's Aid (WA) and Rape Crisis Centres (RCCs). Furthermore, as was discussed in Chapter 6, the violence against women issue was important in providing a focus for two further women's liberation conferences in the 1980s in Scotland. In this way these campaigns illustrate that, whilst women's liberation groups no longer regularly met up at large British conferences from the late 1970s onwards, the ethos, philosophy and, to some extent, the organisational principles of the movement were carried on into the 1980s. In order to understand one of the ways in which the movement developed in the late 1970s this chapter will outline the theoretical and practical responses to the issue of violence against women.

Theoretical responses to violence against women

Internationally the WLM played a leading role in theorising the issue of violence against women.[1] Women in Scotland offered few theoretical innovations but are an interesting case study in demonstrating how feminist ideas were interpreted by individual women's liberation groups. Early discussions on this issue tended to focus on the impact of domestic violence or the problem of 'battered wives' as it was more commonly described in the 1970s. A central premise was that every woman, no matter what her sexuality, colour or class, was at risk of domestic violence; women had more to fear from the man they lived with than from the stranger on the street.[2] Social researchers at the University of Stirling Rebecca and Russell Dobash were extremely influential in exposing the prevalence of violence in the home. They succinctly argued, 'it is within marriage that a woman is most likely to be slapped and shoved about, severely assaulted, killed or raped'.[3]

The clearest theoretical position on this issue was provided by revolutionary feminists. This group of feminists has been accused of creating sharp divisions and destabilising the movement by playing a central role in some of the debates discussed in Chapter 5. However, in recent years their disruptive reputation has been challenged. Jeska Rees has illustrated that, particularly in the area of violence against women, this ideology offered a theoretical clarity which other feminisms failed to provide.[4] Lynne Segal has also argued that 'revolutionary feminism was the most influential beyond feminist circles in its analysis of rape and violence towards women'.[5] Revolutionary feminism viewed society through the prism of patriarchy and argued that the state was complicit in the maintenance of male power by failing to address the issue of violence against women – one of the key ways in which men cemented their power over women. An influential voice in the British context was Jalna Hanmer.[6]

In contrast, socialist feminists preferred to emphasise the destructive impact of capitalism. They contended that violence in society occurred as a result of people feeling exploited and disempowered. Furthermore, capitalism had turned sexual activity into a commodity to be bought and sold. Combining these two ideas, socialist feminists argued that, in raping women or abusing their wives, men were both indicating their frustration at a lack of control over their own lives, as well as demonstrating the belief that women were just another form of property.[7] When it came to the issue of violence against women this focus on the relations of production under a Marxist framework never resonated with women's liberation activists in quite the same way as the theories about patriarchy. For example, the Legal and Financial Independence groups in Edinburgh and Glasgow emphasised the importance of male power when they argued rape was

> not the result of overpowering sexual desire. It is instead the logical extension of the way men treat women in our society, a method by which men demonstrate their power over women and put into practice the ultimate fantasy of male expression and female submissiveness.[8]

They also argued in 1973 that rape would not stop until women had equality and were regarded as more than just mere 'sex objects, to be leered at, joked about and treated with contempt'.[9]

The feminist definition of rape was also expanded in the later 1970s to include, not only physical sexual assault but any acts of sexual degradation, including catcalling, pornography and the use of sexual imagery in advertising. As was argued by the London Rape Action Group in 1979, every man could use the weapon of rape:

> and men know it too. The man who utters obscenities at us in the street knows it, the local greengrocer who insists on calling us love (although we have objected) knows it, the wolf-whistling building workers know it, the man on the tube reading page three and grinning at us knows it.[10]

This broadening of the definition led Scottish-based feminists, as elsewhere in Western Europe and America, to the understanding that 'all men are potential rapists'.[11] This phrase became an effective précis of the revolutionary feminist theory. Aileen Christianson, a member of Edinburgh women's liberation workshop and Rape Crisis activist, recalled this idea being formative in her development:

> [I] felt that all men were potential rapists, not that I thought that they were going to rape but that every single man at some point benefits from a woman moderating her behaviour because of the fear of being sexually assaulted.[12]

Active feminists in Scotland were influenced by discussions and theoretical developments in England, France and the USA and contemporary news stories also proved to be highly influential. For example, the media coverage of the Yorkshire Ripper, Peter Sutcliffe who in the late 1970s murdered thirteen women, provided ammunition to feminist campaigns against violence against women. Sutcliffe's killings created a culture of fear in the local area with the police advising women to stay indoors and avoid walking alone at night. Feminists were angered by this advice believing it punished women by curtailing their freedom. Women's liberation activists in Scotland were dismayed by the press coverage of this news story as they felt a double standard existed in the print media – specifically the coverage of the largest-selling Scottish daily newspaper, Glasgow-based *The Daily Record*. It was pointed out in *MsPrint* that, whilst the newspaper had included a 'daily report' on the Ripper trial, it had also continued to publish pictures of topless women on page three. Active feminists argued that this coverage illustrated the inherent contradictions surrounding the issue of rape and how *The Daily Record* was only one small part of a wider problem in the media, which it was contended continued 'the scandal press's tradition of condemning the crime and creating the motive'.[13]

'Opening Doors': Women's Aid and the 'battered wife'

The movement in Scotland, as elsewhere in Britain, responded in two main ways to the issue of violence against women. The first was the establishment of a network of WA groups and refuges. Founders of local WA branches in Scotland were influenced by revolutionary feminist thinking. For example, one WA activist argued that 'we saw that "domestic violence" was the extreme extension of the submission forced on all women by men. For women to be liberated no woman could live in fear in her own home.'[14] WA sought to break this cycle of violence through the provision of refuges, educating the general public on the issue and taking discussions out of the 'shadowy, uninvestigated underworld of crime' and on to the front pages of newspapers and the agenda of government.[15]

There were a number of factors which encouraged women to provide practical responses to the domestic violence issue. First, women involved in the WLM found that participating in CR sessions led to a desire to find practical solutions. For example one WA activist in Edinburgh recalled that 'in 1972 the Edinburgh women's liberation workshop, which had a room down in Fountainbridge, was getting a bit dissatisfied by the way they seemed to be doing a lot of talking and no action.'[16] Similarly a member of WA's Central branch described how she 'was attracted to something practical' and this sentiment was echoed by a Glasgow WA activist who expressed the desire to move on from just sitting 'in talk-shops'.[17] Indeed, the first co-ordinator of Scottish WA and a founder member of the Edinburgh branch, Fran Wasoff, recalled:

> [it sprang from] a concern of wanting to – do something practical and it was obvious that there was a need for some practical emergency accommodation for women trying to escape violence. So it was (a) the wish to do something practical, (b) to engage more working-class women and more mothers and we – could see the opportunity was there. So I mean those were really my motivations.[18]

Second, there was a growing awareness of the high levels of violence that women in Scotland were experiencing on a daily basis. For instance, by 1978 the Legal and Financial Independence Groups in Scotland reported that domestic violence constituted 25 per cent of all reported violent crime and that 'its actual incidence is much higher since many cases go unreported'.[19] Feminists in Scotland began to link the high levels of domestic violence with what they felt were the peculiarities of Scottish culture, attempting to find explanations as to why this form of violence existed. As Hunter said:

Scotland likes to boast of her romantic reputation, a history of kilts and pipes, brave Highlanders and Red Clydesiders. The reality has been poverty and oppression, clan massacres, the eviction of the Highlanders by their clan chiefs for profit, religious bigotry, and an aggressive unromantic treatment of women.[20]

Historically, domestic violence had been an accepted part of Scottish culture. It was considered a private issue between husband and wife. Indeed, eighteenth-century Scottish law recognised a man's right to beat his wife, given that upon marriage she was viewed as an extension of her husband's property.[21] An added legal complication was the peculiarity in Scottish law of corroboration which required more evidence than one woman's word. The legal system's failure to punish such actions adequately continued into the contemporary period. As the Scottish Legal and Financial Independence Group recognised in 1978, 'at present the law affords little protection ... The police often refuse to interfere with what they regard as "private" domestic quarrels'.[22]

Although statistics were extremely powerful evidence in galvanising support for campaigns, some feminists also brought personal experiences of abuse to discussions. A combination of domestic violence statistics with these personal histories created potent reasons for campaigning on the issue. For example, Pauline Robinson, a member of Dundee Women's Liberation group and volunteer for Dundee WA, remembered

> going to early meetings of the Women's Aid group ... It was when I was admitting a woman to the refuge she said to me, has this ever happened to you? And I said no. And suddenly just got an image of myself being kicked around my flat by a boyfriend whom I'd finished with but had come round and I wouldn't have sex with him. And you know having him chasing me around the room and eventually getting me on the ground and I was fighting him off and he was kicking me. Being too bruised, too bruised to function really and then going out with him that night because we were going to the theatre with three friends of his. And not saying anything and the horror of that, – and realising that ... it's something that happens, it's something that's universal, even if it's the odd comment in the street from somebody who doesn't know you. You know we've all experienced it. Not that men haven't. It's just that women have.[23]

The final major motivating factor for feminists in Scotland to create campaigns against violence against women was the examples of women's groups elsewhere in Britain. In this regard feminists in Scotland drew on the inspiration of Erin Pizzey, who set up the first refuge in Britain in 1971. Pizzey's group in Chiswick began almost by accident, emerging out of the protests by a group of women against the rising prices of staple foods in their local area. From this campaign a group decided to start a community centre. It became apparent that some of the women who attended the centre were being abused by their husbands and Pizzey decided this was an issue that needed further exploration. She converted the community centre into Britain's first refuge. By 1973 thirty women were resident.[24] The media took a keen interest in this initiative and for the first time domestic violence was being openly discussed by the general public.[25]

Despite providing an inspiration for other groups, Pizzey became a controversial figure in the British WLM. Many activists believed that she 'was monopolizing the publicity, keeping too much of the money for her own refuge and wanting too much personal control'.[26] Pizzey was also branded by one feminist in England as a woman who had 'no scruples'.[27] Much of this criticism was based on the fact that her ideas about violence against women diverged from the analysis set out by the WLM. For example, she argued that some women had an addiction to violence as she had 'never met a woman who enjoyed the actual beating, but I have come across women who need to live on an "adrenaline high" who describe the moment before being hit in terms of a substitute for sexual climax'.[28] This contrasted with the WLM's arguments, which wanted to shift the blame from the behaviour of women to men. Pizzey's viewpoint, it was felt, reaffirmed the negative stereotype of a woman 'asking for it' and she admitted that it turned her 'into a figure of hate'.[29]

Pizzey's example was influential to the WLM, therefore, not for its theoretical underpinnings but for the practical example it set. This influence was evident when women from the Edinburgh women's liberation group travelled to Chiswick in 1972 to determine if the model could be replicated in their city. On their return they applied to Edinburgh City Council for a house to run as a centre for women and children. Their bid was successful and they were given a three-bedroom flat in a block of four but with the proviso that if they had been unable to fully establish their group within six months the centre would be closed. The imminent closure of the facility seemed inevitable when in the first two weeks of opening no one had contacted the refuge. One of the volunteers recalled, 'then one wonderful morning there came a bang on the door and there was a lassie who had travelled all the way down from Wick with her three children and we were in business. It was a terrific relief.'[30] A few weeks later the refuge had thirty-five residents.[31] Securing adequate accommodation for refuge space became critically important for groups throughout the 1970s. Fran Wasoff described the difficulties involved in trying to convince local authorities to support such initiatives:

we asked then for another house and [a local councillor] was really furious that we had overcrowded the place because he said we were violating the tenancy conditions and our feeling was too bad ... We said what tenancy agreement? We never signed anything and he realised that we were right, they'd forgot to get us to sign a tenancy agreement. So we were given another flat on the condition that we sign a tenancy agreement for both and agreed to observe [a] no overcrowding rule as well. We were more observant than in week one but we were never all that observant because – unless you allow the place to overcrowd you can't make the case the demand exceeds the supply. So it was a constant tension.[32]

The establishment of the first refuge in Scotland stirred a group of sixteen women in Glasgow to found one too. They created a campaign group in spring 1973. The refuge, named Interval House, opened its doors on 6 February 1974 in a five-bedroom flat with one kitchen and toilet area and 'almost from the day it was opened Interval House was overcrowded'.[33] In its first year this refuge had to turn away one hundred women and children, indicating the need for such a service.[34] The Glasgow and Edinburgh examples encouraged women in Dundee to take action when a group, associated with the local women's liberation workshop, formed a WA branch in 1974.[35] A refuge was set up in the same year called Rainbow House. The running of the Dundee facility differed significantly from other refuges throughout Scotland; it combined the work of both volunteers and three paid members of staff, funded by the Job Creation Scheme.[36] Dundee WA was in a constant battle with the local authorities over the provision of adequate refuge space. It moved into a new and bigger refuge in 1976 but only after a protracted two-year battle with the Dundee Corporation and Tayside Regional Council, who, according to women's liberation activists, both refused to take responsibility for the issue.[37] Despite this the Dundee group provided refuge space for 99 women and 227 children in the period March 1978 to April 1979 and, like the facilities in Glasgow and Edinburgh, had to turn away many more women for lack of space.[38]

A refuge was also established in Aberdeen some time around 1974. A small group of women lobbied the council in order to secure some accommodation. This was because, as elsewhere in Scotland, they faced fierce opposition to their proposals.[39] Women who lobbied on this issue in Aberdeen were directly linked with women's liberation activities but there were also women from outside the movement. For example Lorna Peters remembered:

one woman who was in her 60s or 70s. And she'd been battered for years. She was utterly fantastic. You know, she just was so strong, – had kind of come through it. She'd put up with it all that time. I think actually her husband had died or something ... So there were a few women that were coming in through, – that sort of route. And – that made me much more comfortable, because you felt it wasn't just students and it wasn't just kind of professional women who were involved.[40]

WA was, therefore, effective in expanding the reach of 1970s feminism. Groups were set up in smaller towns in Scotland to establish refuges. In Falkirk, for example, in June 1975 a public meeting was held in order to ascertain if there was an interest in establishing a WA group. Sixty people attended this meeting and in February 1976 a refuge was opened. During its first year the group admitted twenty-seven women to the refuge but crucially had to turn away thirty-two.[41] By 1977 there were fifteen refuges throughout Scotland in places such as Perth, Stirling, Clackmannan and Kirkcaldy.

There were concerns expressed at this early stage that WA was too urban and women in rural areas were being left alone to cope with domestic violence. This problem was noted by the first Scottish WA's co-ordinator.[42] WA branches in cities, therefore, tried to set up refuges in other locations. For example, Edinburgh WA tried to establish a refuge in the Lothians in 1976. Ruth Miller remembered that this proved quite difficult given the local council's opposition:

> we had to go and present ourselves to [the councillors] and – it was a council with ... pretty right-wing thinking, traditional male councillors mainly and we had to try and convince them that there was a reason for it ... I mean that was hard work, it took a year to set that up, we got an office fairly quickly in Dalkeith and we eventually got a refuge but it was such hard work, it was such a battle.[43]

As WA extended its reach in Scotland the calls for a central co-ordinating body became louder. This led to the establishment of Scottish Women's Aid in 1976. Women's Aid groups north of the border had always been loosely affiliated at a UK level with the National Women's Aid Federation, which had been formed in 1974, but as local groups were created in Scotland they saw the need for networking amongst themselves.[44] This initiative was partly funded by the Scottish Office. The idea of a central co-ordinating body diverged from the structure-less ethos of the WLM, which WA had grown out of, but women such as Fran Wasoff realised that if they formed into 'a Scottish Women's Aid organisation [then the government would] support you, we will fund you. We'll pay for a co-ordinator and a secretary, so we drew up a constitution and got an office.'[45] This national body attempted to nurture new groups throughout Scotland and also supported existing branches by providing help with funding applications and training.

Yet the expansion of the WA movement was somewhat problematic. Local branches had to continually negotiate funding with local authorities, usually on an annual basis, and therefore it was difficult to make long-term plans.[46] Furthermore, each branch had to prove to the local authorities that there was a need for a refuge but it was very difficult to prove the prevalence of domestic violence when it was usually conducted in the privacy of people's homes. Many women recalled facing opposition from local authorities. One Women's Aid activist described how she

> was in one of the first meetings in the City Chambers in Glasgow and I remember two Councillors met us. They took us very light-heartedly. We got sniggering comments [about battered women] such as 'they like it'. The Councillors also accused Women's Aid of breaking up families.[47]

Those local authorities that did provide support for refuges usually offered 'a dilapidated structure slated for demolition and located in an area distinguished by its lack of amenities'.[48] Despite these conditions many publications of the time recorded that women still found refuges a great source of support. For others, however, the overcrowded conditions would prove insurmountable and some women voluntarily left the refuge.[49] Unable to cope with the ever-increasing number of residents, a group of women from the refuge in Glasgow organised a squat. A combination of this strategy and the evidence of overcrowding in Interval House eventually encouraged the local Social Work and Housing Department to provide fifty houses for homeless women.[50] Indeed, Dobash and Dobash have noted that squatting was a tactic used by other local groups in their attempts to expand facilities in their area.[51]

WA groups frequently ran their services on a shoestring. Owing to the short-term and precarious nature of local authority funding, women in the refuge were asked to contribute any benefits they received. Rent for the council flat in Edinburgh was £11.50 a fortnight and in order to meet this cost WA divided the rent by the number of families in the house, encouraging each to pay their fair share in the running and upkeep of the refuge.[52] WA also ran along collectivist lines, indicating its theoretical link with the broader WLM. The organisation emphasised the democratising effect of the refuge, arguing that every woman should have an equal say in how it was run.[53] As the Dobashes convincingly argued, this emphasis on self-determination would 'allow a woman to regain her self-confidence and begin to manage her own life'.[54] In practice this meant that there had to be weekly house meetings, which included assigning each woman a share of the daily chores. Volunteers had a number of tasks to undertake. One of the most important jobs was staffing the phone line. Most WA branches had an open phone line which any woman who was suffering from domestic violence could ring. It was organised and run by volunteers who prior to receiving calls were educated on the seriousness of the task. Pauline Robinson described the point at which she realised the importance of this job:

> [I was told that] women should really take it seriously when they're on call, when you chat to your friends there might be a woman trying to get through to you and for her it is a matter of life and death. Talk about a knife to the heart. For any time that you'd answered the phone and it wasn't and you'd let your pal chat for a bit because you know if you're on call you dreaded every call. Awful. Just dreaded every call. I remember a woman ringing from Blairgowrie and asking, just asking for help, he was coming home soon and hearing him crash through the door and having her put the phone down. And you didn't know where she was. You didn't know what she was going through. She could be dead.[55]

In the early days of WA there was limited support for volunteers. Those working on the phone lines worked very long hours and were confronted with horrendous stories of domestic violence. Volunteering for WA was a serious undertaking in which volunteers admitted that they were often not very good to themselves:

> we – used to have an on-call system where everyone had to be on call overnight and over weekends and we had no – kind of sense of proper working conditions ... And you were at the end of the telephone and there'd be two of you usually, one person to be at the end of the phone and another person with a car if they had to go and get someone. 'Cause often we did have to go out and get people. And of course the statutory services assumed that we had proper shifts and would phone us at three in the morning or whatever but we were just working like that.[56]

Some groups also offered mediation between couples, although this practice was eventually abandoned in the 1980s as Women's Aid became a woman-focused organisation. This decision was also taken out of a fear for personal safety as it could involve great risk for volunteers. Training and support was limited during WA's early days and volunteers were, therefore, left to take action on a very ad hoc basis. As Ruth Miller of Edinburgh branch recalled:

> I went with my colleague out to – East Lothian at the time and we went to the woman's house and she said he's not back from – the pub yet and

we said oh that's fine we'll go and get him. And I just think I wouldn't do that but we did, we went down to the local pub, where's so and so? Oh there he is in the corner, we've come to see you, you know, like the heavies? And it was just ridiculous ... and he came – with us and I think he was so taken aback ... And there were other things that we did, I can remember, you know going several times to women's houses to help them get away-and one woman came to us and said I really want to go back, I need to go back and get a few things, I just want to do that and will you come with me? And it was me and one other person said okay we'll go with you but we'll call the police to come and – accompany us, we don't want to just go on our own. And they did, they came with us but we got to the house and she went to unlock the door and there was a chain on in the inside so we couldn't get in, even though she had the key and the police were ready just to turn around ... I took a pair of nail scissors out of my bag and opened the lock just quickly like that and we were in and they, the police were just sort of standing there, and I thought oh I guess I probably shouldn't have done that but we were in and they just kind of ignored us. And we started filling black bags as quickly as we could and suddenly the guy came back and he was really drunk and he was very violent and he was just going for this woman and we had to get out of there really quickly. And the police were not of any help, they sort of ran into their cars. So, we ran and with our bags into our car and sped into town, this was on one of the outskirts, sped into town where our office was and sort of ran in to the office. And the guy tried to follow us and he didn't quite make it but I mean it was pretty crazy. So we used to do that because we were just quite young and foolish and – so passionate about what we were doing and we took big risks.[57]

Despite volunteers giving up a lot of time and often putting themselves at great risk, WA still attracted some unwelcome publicity. The overcrowded conditions of refuges led to complaints from neighbours who reportedly rang WA volunteers to complain and some even contacted the newspapers to publicise their grievances.[58] In Dundee, the group admitted that they received 'some complaints from neighbours but it [was] understandable as there can be as many as twenty kids charging around out there'.[59] Some people also believed that WA workers were interfering in private matters between husband and wife and that they were troublemakers, leading to more serious accusations of being marriage-breakers. WA volunteers had to counter an increasing moral panic about the escalating levels of divorce and marital breakdown. A vocal opponent of WA was Evelyn Scott-Wallace, a Scottish Conservative local councillor, who in 1975 in an article in *The Guardian*, argued:

[WA was] just a group of amateur do-gooders without any professionally qualified help. And I think they are playing with fire if they attempt to interfere between a husband and a wife in this way ... Anyway some of these women might well deserve the batterings they get from their husbands.[60]

She was supported by Nicholas Fairbairn, Scottish Conservative MP for Kinross and Western Perthshire who, in the same year in the *Glasgow Herald*, stated that:

I know there are battered wives in Britain, but why should the Government get involved in a family squabble as the Courts are quite capable of dealing with violent husbands? Surely they could go to a neighbour or a relative for some time and think things over rather than run to the State to look after them.[61]

The media also seemed to have a particular inability to understand the severity of the issue. Given the novelty of the WA movement, newspapers were incredibly curious about refuges and frequently profiled them. This interest could at times infringe on the security of both the women living in the refuges and the volunteers helping to run them. In July 1978 Glasgow WA allowed a journalist from *The Evening Times* to visit the refuge in order to raise awareness about their work. It asked that, in return for its allowing access to the refuge, the journalist would not publish any identifiable details about the location of the refuge. Unfortunately *The Evening Times* did not adhere to this request.[62] Fran Wasoff, who was co-ordinator of Scottish WA at the time, recalled this episode, describing how the *Daily Record* had picked up the story and

published on the front page a photograph of the refuge in Glasgow and I thought this was absolutely outrageous. Anyway, later that day, some loony husband – I mean anyone who knew Glasgow knew exactly where this house was – a loony husband arrived with a gun and was shooting through the door and you know it was a complete coincidence that there was no child passing through getting killed. Anyway I complained to the Press Council, which had no teeth and still has no teeth, and I said this is an outrageous and life-threatening act and what are you going to do about it? And they said oh well we'll tell them it's not a good idea and I said well that's not very impressive, what else are you going to do about it? And they said well we could try to get a voluntary agreement that they won't publish identifiable details about refuges and – that was the best we could achieve.[63]

WA volunteers, therefore, faced an uphill struggle to convince the wider public of the merits of their campaign. In addition to setting up and running refuges, therefore, they also undertook important educational work. They believed that changing perceptions and informing people about domestic violence were the only way long-lasting change would be achieved. As is clear from the episode at the Glasgow refuge in 1978, Scottish WA had to balance the desire to attract publicity with trying to control what journalists wrote. On many occasions they opened up the refuge for journalists but in the end were left disappointed by the reporting of the events. A Dundee WA volunteer described how the group

> had a whole spate of press reports ... culminated in the autumn with a *News of the World* reporter coming round to the refuge. Our first instinct was to send the guy away but we thought if we did that he'll just speak to the neighbours and ... so we spoke to him ... that Sunday what should appear in the *News of the World* but a photograph of me that I didn't know they had taken under the banner headline which read – 'Saucy frolics rumpus at battered wives hostel!'[64]

As Dobash and Dobash pointed out, however, 'efforts to raise public awareness about the very existence of this abuse and its extent and severity required active involvement with the media and the public'.[65] Fran Wasoff described:

> people didn't believe how dangerous domestic violence was. I mean they just did not understand. I mean you are living in a completely different time. I mean domestic violence was seen as a private matter ... I mean the fact that, you know, women are at far greater risk of being murdered by their intimate partner than by anyone else was, although it was known by criminologists, it wasn't somehow put – together in the links to sexual violence ... I mean, you know, there was a real education job ... I just remember we did non-stop, got really tired of it. I mean you just after a while of making the same arguments and you get really bored with them.[66]

In order to raise awareness about domestic violence in Scotland, WA produced numerous pamphlets. *Battered Women in Scotland – Your Rights and Where to Turn for Help* was published in 1977 to 'provide information on the nature of Scottish law in this area, for doctors, social workers, police and others to whom battered women and other women in distress turn to for help'. It included sections on how the legal system operated, what money and benefits were available, the location of refuges and what would happen to women's homes after they left. Local groups also produced newsletters, of which Edinburgh WA's *Broken Rib* was notable. Research was also undertaken by Dundee WA, which analysed a sample of women in the refuge to find out why men battered women.[67] All of this led to a body of literature which challenged many of the basic assumptions underpinning the domestic violence issue. It helped, for example, to undermine the idea that violence and abuse occurred only amongst the working class. This was a persistent view and one which WA activists sought to challenge. Anne Wallace, Chairperson of Falkirk and Grangemouth branch, wrote that 'there exists a popular misconception that wife battering occurs only in socio-economic groups 4 or 5 … Among the women who have sought the help of Women's Aid in Scotland are the wives of the following; an MP, a University Professor, a research scientist, and an ex-priest.'[68]

WA believed the most important group to educate on the issue were those who enforced the law. They felt that the police were reluctant to get involved in domestic violence cases because they viewed it as merely a 'domestic'.[69] As Dobash and Dobash commented at the time, the 'police are actually more likely to arrest individuals involved in non-violent acts outside the home than they are to arrest husbands for violent offences committed within the home'.[70] These perceptions were backed up by statistics: in Glasgow in 1974 only 12 per cent of men arrested for domestic violence were imprisoned for assaulting their wives with 58 per cent being forced to pay a small fine or 24.6 per cent being admonished.[71] Indeed, it was observed by a volunteer at Glasgow WA that

> the police were extremely unsympathetic. The attitude was very much that [wife-abuse] was just domestic disputes … the police felt there was 'no point' in doing anything about reportings of domestic violence, because they held the mistaken and erroneous view that, in nearly all cases, the woman dropped her charges, Later, the group learned to counter this argument, backed with facts from research and information about 'correct' police procedure. But it took time to learn to react effectively.[72]

Marion Blythman, a Scottish WA spokeswoman, expressed her anger publicly, offering strong criticism of police procedures to a Parliamentary Committee, which had been set up in 1975 to investigate the issue of spousal abuse.[73] Many WA activists spoke to police groups to educate them on the theory behind the domestic violence issue. They hoped to achieve effective policing of the issue.

Despite the lack of police recognition WA had more success in terms of legislative reform. During the 1970s there were three major pieces of legislation passed by the British government in relation to domestic violence. First, divorce law reform made ending a marriage far simpler. At the beginning of the twentieth century divorce was both extremely difficult and expensive to obtain. From 1946 onwards, however, legal aid became more widely available and then in 1969 the Divorce Reform Act was passed for England and Wales, establishing the principle of irretrievable breakdown. Prior to 1969 in order to end a marriage there had to be an 'innocent party', who then sued for divorce. With the passing of this legislation there was no need for blame and the ending of divorce was, therefore, simplified.[74] Yet, as with so many legal reforms, Scotland would be slow to catch up. Divorce reform was not introduced north of the border until 1976 under the Divorce (Scotland) Act. Similarly, legislation of this kind was not passed in Northern Ireland until 1978, with Hill observing that this was because any reform was opposed by Free Presbyterians and the Catholic Church.[75] In Scotland there was also fierce opposition to these legal proposals, with the *Scottish Catholic Observer* believing it would open 'the floodgates' to marital breakdown.[76] According to women's liberation activists, the delay in the passing of reform in Scotland was further evidence of 'Scottish backwardness'.[77] The link between divorce reform and the problem of domestic violence was made by a Parliamentary Select Committee, which had been set up in 1975 to look at the introduction of such reform in Scotland. As one member commented, 'both in the criminal law and in the matrimonial law, the odds are stacked against the battered wife' and it was evident that better legislation would have to be introduced north of the border in order to protect women from the risk of domestic violence.[78]

Second, the Domestic Violence and Matrimonial Proceedings Act was passed in 1976. This gave police greater powers of arrest in the form of injunctions. Once again this act applied only to England and Wales.[79] This led to many in the women's movement declaring that 'Scots law is even more ineffective than English law' and that 'battered women in Scotland are still a breed apart, with little protective legislation on their side'.[80] The clear disparities in legal protection available to women in different parts of Britain compelled active feminists in Scotland to consider how well they were represented both by their local politicians and by the broader WLM in Britain. Under Scottish law, and the peculiarities of corroboration, in order for a domestic violence case to be taken to court, there had to be two witnesses to the event or proof of injuries. Quite clearly in many instances the gathering of evidence proved very difficult. There were two further civil remedies open to women north of the border. The first of these was the interdict, whereby the court could order a husband to refrain from threatening his wife but this entailed a lengthy legal process. The second remedy was 'lawburrows' where a man would lodge a sum of money as security for good behaviour. These procedures, however, came nowhere near to the effectiveness of the injunction backed up by the powers of arrest, which the Domestic Violence and Matrimonial Proceedings Act offered.[81]

Scottish WA campaigned on getting similar legislation passed north of the border. This was supported by SNP politician George Reid, who led a particularly relentless campaign to have effective legislation enforced in Scotland. Reid was forced to spend a night on the floor of the Public Bill Office in Parliament in 1979 to ensure he was first in line for a limited number of ten minute-rule bills. These were handed out to politicians to enable them to have a particular issue raised in Parliament. He introduced the Matrimonial Violence (Scotland) Bill which would have given power to the courts to exclude a man from his home if he was found to have abused his wife. Reid was an important voice in the debate, recognising the severity of the issue. Nevertheless the differences between England and Scotland in this regard also proved particularly effective in highlighting his wider political agenda of the benefits of greater political powers for Scotland.[82] He argued that devolved power for Scotland would, at the very least, lead to people having a greater say in political decisions which affected Scotland and they would not have to wait until politicians at Westminster found time to discuss 'Scottish' issues. This, it was argued, would lead to better protection for women and ultimately contribute to a greater recognition of women's rights more generally. Unfortunately this bill failed owing to a lack of parliamentary time.[83] Pressure on this issue was maintained, culminating in the passing of the Matrimonial Homes (Family Protection) (Scotland) Act in 1981. This included interdict backed up by the powers of arrest. Without the pressure from groups such as Scottish WA the British government would have been unlikely to ask the Scottish Law Commission to review the situation leading to the passing of this act.[84]

The final major piece of legislation introduced during the 1970s which applied to Scotland was the Housing (Homeless Persons) Act. This forced local authorities to house women who were made homeless through battering. According to women's liberation activists, this represented 'an important step forward' and paved a way to ease the congested conditions in many refuges. However both the police and housing authorities frequently failed to comply with these laws.[85]

It is interesting to consider how far WA influenced government policy. Coote and Campbell have argued that for politicians 'wife battering was different. Perhaps it pricked their consciences, or perhaps it genuinely shocked them.'[86] Fran Wasoff has also argued:

> who could be in favour of domestic violence really, you know? ...
> Abortion – is a controversial issue, rape even is a controversial issue,

> the rape crisis group had less success in getting support than domestic violence. I think partly because domestic violence involves children, and the state has a responsibility towards children. Whereas a lot of the other issues that we dealt with didn't ... involve children directly.[87]

WA was a highly effective organisation in attracting both the attention of the media and the public. It started the conversation about the impact of domestic violence on women, the family and the community. Key to WA's beginnings was the WLM, which through CR sessions explored the concept of patriarchy and male oppression and how this led to aggression against women. Margaret Adams of Dundee Women's Liberation workshop argued: 'I mean there wouldn't be Women's Aid if it wasn't for the women's liberation group – so it's definitely made an impact'.[88] It was particularly effective in challenging the concepts of dominance and power. Jennifer Kerr of St Andrews Women's Liberation group and Dundee WA described how some of the issues they talked about have now gained recognition:

> there are individuals and patterns used by individuals to abuse, that men abuse the power that they have over women. That men abuse the power that they have over children – and that this is wrong and that it is right to get out of those situations. That's a huge, huge change.[89]

The WLM's ability, through the organisation of WA, to create a body of literature about domestic violence clearly influenced the way the wider public viewed this issue and arguably represents one of the movement's greatest successes.

Setting up a Rape Crisis network in Scotland

In campaigning on the issue of violence against women, active feminists also undertook a second practical initiative. Inspired by the work of Women's Aid supporters, feminists established a Rape Crisis Centre (RCC) network in Scotland. In comparison to domestic violence, rape was a late addition to the WLM's agenda. As one woman, active in the movement in Britain, outlined in an article in the left-wing journal *The Leveller* in 1979, 'a sense of guilt creeps upon me that it is only recently that rape has ranked as an issue of crucial importance'.[90] Arguably, one reason for the earlier emphasis on domestic violence was that rape, as a crime, was viewed as somewhat more ambiguous, with questions asked by some people about the issue of consent.

A lack of clarity over rape was prevalent not only amongst the general public but also in the WLM. In the early 1970s, the movement did not develop a clear analysis of the issue. Many feminists openly admitted their disgust when they discovered that they had also blindly accepted social attitudes about rape. Zoe Fairbairns described how one St Andrews women's liberation session on rape had been

> a total eye-opener to me, because I'd never heard of it in that context. I'd never heard the idea, I mean, this was how dim and sheltered I was. I had never heard of the idea that a woman who was raped might have the fact of her chastity, or lack of chastity, used as evidence on trial. And that somehow, if she'd had consenting sex with another man, that might be taken as evidence that she consented this time.[91]

As was discussed earlier in this chapter, by the late 1970s, the revolutionary feminist theory of violence against women was gaining ground within the movement. Anti-rape activists echoed these arguments, contending that rape should be viewed as the ultimate expression of patriarchal relations. The London Rape Action Group argued that 'the threat of rape is a weapon which men use to perpetuate their dominance of women'.[92] Drawing on many of the theoretical developments in the wider WLM in Britain, the issue of sexual violence began to explode on to the pages of women's liberation newsletters in Scotland from the mid-1970s onwards. Of course, there had been some discussion of the issue before the late 1970s, but these tended to amount to a few fleeting references and were often shaped by local priorities. For example, the group at St Andrews began to discuss the issue after two students were sexually assaulted whilst attending St Andrews University in 1973. The arguments formulated against rape were forceful and angry. As Susie Innes wrote in 1973, links could be made between the cultural objectification of women and the act of rape, with every man complicit in this state of affairs, including

> the friendly guy who 'appreciates' your legs, to the professor who keeps looking at your breasts, to the dirty joker who talks of women as convenient receptacles for sperm, to the building workers shouting you'd be good in bed, to hubby forcing sex on his wife, to uncle feeling up his niece, to the rapist on the front page of the *Citizen*.[93]

Through women's liberation workshop discussions and CR groups feminists began to make links between the way society was constructed with the way men behaved towards women. Lovenduski and Randall summed up this process, describing that 'part of the source of women's anger was surprise. There is a huge and contradictory mythology that surrounds rape, and women born before 1970 were brought up in thrall to that contradictory mythology'.[94]

The central book in these discussions was Susan Brownmiller's *Against Our Will*, published in America in 1971. The British edition was released six years later. This was hugely influential, demonstrating how rape had been used throughout history as a weapon against women. Brownmiller effectively crystallised the arguments against rape by arguing that it was a method used by all men to ensure women remained in a perpetual state of fear. Moreover, this was a key text in demonstrating to feminists that, far from rape consisting of an attack by a sexually depraved stranger, as it was commonly understood, it was in fact the extreme expression of patriarchal values. Echoing the surprise of many feminist activists who were unearthing new theories about rape, Brownmiller wrote how she, at one time, had been completely ignorant of the issue. She described how her generation had been brought up to believe that 'rape is something awful that happens to females, it is the dark at the top of the stairs, that indefinable abyss that is just around the corner, and unless we watch our step it might be our destiny'.[95]

Brownmiller's book was widely read by feminists active in Scotland. Aileen Christianson, an influential member of Edinburgh RCC during the 1970s and 1980s, was overwhelmed by the clarity of the arguments contained in this book.[96] Women active in feminist politics in Scotland followed the developing discussions on rape, reading, amongst other material, works by revolutionary feminists in France. This group argued that women wanted 'to live without protection, bodyguards, fathers, brothers, husbands, policemen, managers and bosses',[97] again, evoking the notion that the fear of rape curbed the independence of women. Revolutionary feminists wished to see the focus of the debate shifted away from an emphasis on women's behaviour to that of the rapist.

In order to challenge the myths and double standards surrounding rape, the WLM in Scotland responded with three practical solutions: support work and campaigning; attempts to reform the law; and publicity. As with domestic violence, a key motivator in setting up centres in which women could seek advice was a growing awareness of the incidence of rape in Scotland. In 1972 twenty-nine people were proceeded against for rape, but by 1976 this had almost doubled to fifty-two. Furthermore, although there had been fifty-two prosecutions during 1976, there had actually been 184 instances of rape reported to the police, leading to a 28.3 per cent prosecution rate.[98] These statistics fired the fierce debates and discussions ongoing in the WLM in Scotland and encouraged women to take action. This took the form of creating and establishing RCCs. Inspiration came initially from America, where Rape Relief Centres had started during the early 1970s. Unlike WA, in Britain RCCs were generally a local phenomenon, with no central network. The first centre in Britain was established in North London in 1976. Five years later there was a total of sixteen such groups in Britain.[99] RCCs aimed to provide support and advice and they also provided support to women when complaining to the police or attending court.[100]

The first RCC in Scotland opened in Glasgow in 1976.[101] Located in the offices of the Scottish Council for Civil Liberties in Holland Street, this centre was set up to provide telephone support to those who had been raped. The office consisted of one room in which all the rape crisis work in Glasgow was conducted. It was not uncommon during collective meetings, therefore, for proceedings to be halted whilst a call was taken from a member of the public.[102] Two years later, a RCC was established in Edinburgh. The centre emerged from a three-phase preparatory process. First, a group of fifteen women met as part of a CR group to challenge their own and society's perceptions of rape.[103] During the second phase they invited speakers to talk to the group about rape and they also organised a training weekend conducted by representatives from London RCC. The final phase focused on setting up and establishing a centre.[104] The Edinburgh RCC opened on 1 July 1978 with a vigil on Princes Street to publicise the new telephone line. The initial collective was made up of several incomers to Edinburgh, mainly English and American women, but there was a smattering of Scottish women too.[105]

Women from the Glasgow and Edinburgh centres always 'went to great lengths to support women at considerable distances from their urban bases'. In the early 1980s, the rape crisis network expanded with groups established in Dundee and Aberdeen, both growing out of the campaigns against domestic violence and for abortion rights. Moreover a central Scottish RCC and a Highland group were set up in 1982, followed by a Kilmarnock branch in 1987. The roots of these individual groups were all 'clearly, unequivocally feminist', with links to the broader WLM.[106]

The women who joined a Rape Crisis group were generally rooted in the wider WLM. They were on the whole white, young, middle-class and with links to a university.[107] However, the diversification of the WLM in the later 1970s into single-issue campaigns encouraged new women to become active on issues linked with women's liberation. For example Isabelle Kerr recalled that joining the RCC had been

> a total accident. – I'd come from a very, very traditional working-class background, where – women look after the weans [children] and have a husband and that's all they do. And then they get a wee part-time job, – cleaning the shop down the road or something like that. Very, very traditional background. Brought up very much in that way ... There

was no question about it ... I mean any kind of – politics. Any kind of involvement in that, any kind of feeling that you were able to get involved in any kind of discussion that was in any way political did not belong to the kind of world that I grew up in. That was ... the domain of people who- stayed on at school. You know, they had qualifications and they knew what they were talking about and people like us didnae ... I got married when I was seventeen years old. And by the time I was twenty I had two children. But, – it was a pal of mine who said that she wanted to ... be a volunteer with Rape Crisis. And she said will you come with me, because I don't want to go myself? And, of course, I had sort of said well okay. Isn't it terrible? God love them all these poor lassies. Isn't it terrible? And I was like genuinely sympathetic ... And it was very much like I'll come along as well because I could always make the tea. That kind of approach. – and when it came down to it this woman never went along and I did! And that, that was the start of it ... Was totally sucked in to the issue, the politics ... I got much more interested in – quite a lot of issues. I really – got interested obviously in women's issues ... And it just – completely snowballed from that ... and I've never stopped since.[108]

The influx of working-class women challenged other feminists who had been active in the wider WLM for many years. Occasionally issues of class became a point of conflict. Isabelle Kerr described attending a Rape Crisis meeting with her two children in tow, who were

sitting in the corner of the, the room. At that time my husband worked shifts. – and they were drawing while the meeting was going on. So we were talking about the work we were going to do. And I said I really need to go. – can I phone a taxi? ... And – the women who had worked for the university said if you go into the next room, – there's – an office and you can just use the phone from there. So that's what I did ... And I came back and said I can't, I can't use the phone there's a wee padlock on it. – and one woman who was -, unbelievably posh, – said to me ... 'you're from Glasgow, you should be able to pick that lock no problem!' And I was so angry. – that, even though I felt really embarrassed, as you can imagine, I felt really embarrassed and, – upset about it. I was so angry.[109]

Despite this tension there was an early enthusiasm for the establishment of centres. Volunteers worked tirelessly to establish a network in Scotland although insufficient funds meant that collectives could not afford to spend excessively on the upkeep of centres. This was especially true in Edinburgh with Aileen Christianson recalling that the RCC

was in a basement room in Union Street off of Leith Walk, and the loo was across the area outside ... underneath the pavement. It was freezing, so we would come and we would sit ... absolutely freezing.[110]

Naomi Wolf detailed her experiences in a RCC. Her recollections were apparently based on her time spent volunteering in Edinburgh.[111] She described how she found the conditions to be especially challenging, as the

> concrete steps [were] sticky with rubbish. Once inside, you were met by the sight of sofas with their stuffing spilling out, rickety folding chairs flung on their sides and bare light bulbs, that made skin look dead white or liverish grey-brown.[112]

Wolf argued these conditions helped to underline a culture of misery in which the squalid conditions inculcated a feeling of piety amongst the volunteers, who gave up their time to work with women despite the appalling state of the centre.[113] During the late 1970s, however, a lack of adequate and sustained funding was always an issue for RCCs. Lack of financial security was, therefore, a more likely explanation for the conditions of the Edinburgh centre. In the period June 1978 to June 1980, for example, after paying their expenses, the workers were left with only £338.54. This had to cover volunteers' expenses, the running of the centre, the cost of the phone line and publicity material. They also had no guaranteed funding, as the donations they received were always so sporadic.[114]

The centrepiece of the work of the RCCs in Scotland was the phone line. Problems with funding also affected this service. Jan Macleod of the Glasgow group recalled that:

> if you got somebody on the phone that maybe had never really spoken to anybody or was quite distressed or had a lot of questions or whatever, you could easily be on the phone for an hour. And so that means that other people, you know maybe trying two, three nights. If they're unlucky, they think well that phone is always engaged, you get discouraged.[115]

When calls began to flood in, many of the volunteers were surprised to discover that they were speaking to women who were reporting that they had been raped many years before. The expectation had been that the phone line would be used by women who had just recently been raped.[116] An insight into the type of woman who called the centre in Edinburgh in its early days is revealed by research conducted by volunteers in 1981. It can be seen from Figures 7.1 and 7.2 that callers were mainly twenty-one to thirty-five years old and were likely to have known the man who raped them.[117]

Like WA activists, RCC volunteers also found they were not as busy as they had initially expected. Nadine Harrison recalled a lot of the time was 'just sort of sit[ting] there for hours on end and nobody phoned at

Figure 7.1 Age at time of attack of those women who rang the Edinburgh RCC phone line, 1981 (sample of 50 consecutive phone calls)

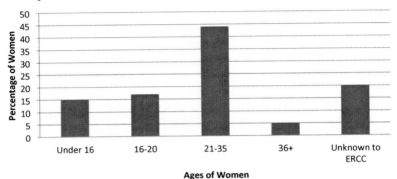

Source: Edinburgh Rape Crisis Centre, *First Report*, January 1981, Edinburgh, p. 9.

all'.[118] Nevertheless, contact rates did increase; in 1978 the annual number of calls made to Edinburgh RCC was ten and by 1979 this had increased to thirty-four.[119] No formal training was given to those on the phone lines. Support was provided by attendance at the weekly collective business meetings. Once a month Glasgow and Edinburgh RCCs also held open meetings which potential volunteers could attend to find out about their work.[120] Unlike WA, there was no central rape crisis organisation in Scotland. Instead centres preferred autonomy, indicating their theoretical links with the broader WLM. Glasgow and Edinburgh RCCs did meet infrequently to discuss issues that were consistent with the workings of both centres and to compare cases.[121]

Networking on the issue of rape was done, on the whole, through British groups such as Feminists Against Sexual Terrorism (FAST) which produced a monthly newsletter.[122] This group had been established at a British feminist conference on rape held in Bristol in 1978 and the newsletter was created to co-ordinate activities and to develop discussions amongst feminists who were working in the area of violence against women. Scottish women frequently contributed to the newsletter and also took an active part in the network.[123]

As the centres developed, so too did the theoretical understanding of the issue. It was decided to drop the word 'victim' in preference for 'survivor'. This was justified because 'after a woman has been raped, to call her a victim is to trap her into a passive stereotype'.[124] Similarly, volunteers were actively encouraged not to counsel or guide the female caller but to offer support and allow her to dictate what course of action she wanted

Figure 7.2 The relationship of the rapist to the woman

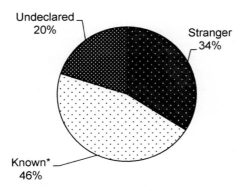

NB. * The rapist was known to the woman as, for example, a friend or lover.
Source: Edinburgh Rape Crisis Centre, *First Report*, January 1981, Edinburgh, p. 9.

Table 7.1 Percentages of all reported crimes and their prosecution rates
in Scotland, 1977–78

Crime	% of all reported offences where someone was apprehended, warned or traced		% of all reported offences when the case came to court	
	1977	*1978*	*1977*	*1978*
Rape	70.2	71.1	33.7	31.3
Assault with intent to ravish	48.7	57.3	23.0	28.0
Indecent assault	41.7	39.3	12.6	13.0
Murder	89.6	91.7	94.0[1]	106.0[1]
Attempted murder	91.9	91.4	100.0[1]	27.0[3]
Culpable homicide[2]	100.0	100.0	100.0	100.0
Assaults	52.5	59.2	32.0	43.4
Robbery	18.7	19.6	14.0	14.6
Theft	31.6	32.5	17.0	18.9

Notes: 1 Some cases left over from previous year
2 This crime is normally charged after someone is apprehended. It is rarely
reported as culpable homicide.
3 This low figure for 1978 is unusual.
Source: Edinburgh Rape Crisis Centre, *First Report*, January 1981, Edinburgh, p. 12.

to follow. Once a woman had phoned the centre there were a number of options open to her. She could decide to remain anonymous and continue contact with the centre by ringing the phone line. During the 1970s, however, volunteers from RCCs also met women to offer support work and accompany them to the police or VD clinic.[125]

The second main area that anti-rape campaigners concentrated on in the 1970s was to lobby government to reform the law. The London RCC group identified this as a key area, as in order to challenge 'ignorance about rape' there was a need 'for reliable and serious research pertaining to the British Isles'.[126] Activists played a crucial role in gathering research and statistics, which informed debates about the issue. As Table 7.1 shows, although a high number of rapes were reported to the police, many of these cases did not gain a full hearing in court. Moreover, in comparison with other serious crimes, such as murder, rape had a 'remarkably low conviction rate'.[127]

Armed with these statistics, feminists in Scotland engaged with the police and legal representatives to ensure that women got a fairer hearing in court. The first attempt to reform the law coincided with the devolution debates that were occurring in Scotland from 1978 onwards. Like WA volunteers, many anti-rape campaigners were frustrated by legal advice emanating from women's liberation groups in London and the South of England which was not applicable to the separate legal system in Scotland. Furthermore, there was a frustration that changes to Scottish rape law were interminably slow owing to the lack of parliamentary time afforded Scottish issues at Westminster.[128] For instance, the Sexual Offences (Amendment) Act of 1976 applied only in England and Wales. This defined rape, established a woman's anonymity and argued that the victim's past sexual experience should be admissible only at the discretion of the judge.[129] Calls for similar legislation to be passed in Scotland were led by Rape Crisis activists, the Edinburgh and Glasgow Legal and Financial Independence groups and the Campaign for Scottish Devolution.[130] Discontent about the tendency of some feminists in England to assume that legislation at Westminster applied to all parts of the United Kingdom began to emerge. In *Spare Rib* in 1974, for example, it was pointed out by one woman that a lot of the legal advice on rape published in the journal was not applicable to Scotland.[131] Aileen Christianson described how in order to overcome this RCCs north of the border would have joint meetings with groups in England but would 'not bother overmuch with "National" (i.e. English) campaigns'.[132]

The Scottish legal position differed in significant ways. Rape was a common law crime and, in order to have a hearing, a woman had to convince not only the police but also the procurator fiscal to take up her case. Furthermore, evidence in court had to be corroborated either by the unlikely event of another person being present or by medical evidence. There was also no legal obligation for newspapers to avoid printing the names of rape victims, although they did, on the whole, adhere to this practice on a voluntary basis.[133]

One of the main issues the women's movement campaigned on was to make it illegal for a man to rape his wife. In Scottish and English law a man could not be convicted of raping his wife as it was defined as a private matter. The women's movement interpreted this issue as being about ownership; under the laws of the land, it would seem that once a woman agreed to marry she gave up the right to say no.[134] The women's movement raised awareness of this issue through articles in women's liberation journals and writing to politicians. With legislation passed in Scotland in 1989, the campaign to outlaw rape within marriage was finally won. This was a full two years before similar legislation in England and Wales and was a rare occasion when the Scottish legal system led the rest of the UK.

The main issue that Rape Crisis campaigners concentrated on during the 1970s was the police's treatment of rape victims. Like Women's Aid activists, Rape Crisis volunteers found that the police could be aggressive and unhelpful. Rape Crisis argued that because women, who had been raped were regarded as the main witness to the crime, the police were allowed to put them under intense questioning. Dominant myths about sexual assault amongst wider society were also apparent amongst the police, such as women 'asking for it' or that many allegations turn out to be false.[135] RCC campaigners also found the police hostile to their work and spoke at the police training college in Tulliallan.[136] At these training sessions, the Rape Crisis activists recalled being met with widespread scepticism. During one session conducted by Glasgow RCC, the police asked questions ranging from 'can a husband rape his wife?' to 'do RCC give any thoughts to the men since nine tenths of rape allegations are withdrawn as false?'[137]

The third main area of RCC's work was publicity. Early reactions to the RCCs had generally been supportive. They publicised the opening of centres in student newspapers, including in *The Student* in 1976, where they argued that 'rape is fodder for the daily cartoon strip and joke page. It is romanticised and exploited at every level of film; literature; entertainment and issued as a successful selling point in advertising.'[138] RCC campaigners also tried to combat myths about rape. In a briefing document prepared by the Edinburgh group they listed a number of arguments that volunteers could use to counter these myths. Included in this list was that 'wearing a short skirt, going out alone at night or going hitchhiking are not invitations to sex'.[139] In these ways the feminist critique of violence in the 1970s provided 'a revolution' in the ways in which the general public thought about and understood the issue of rape.[140]

Reclaim the Night

For those women's liberation activists who did not campaign on the issue of violence against women through WA and RCCs, opportunities to become actively involved in the broader issue still existed, chiefly by attending Reclaim the Night (RTN) marches. These marches were an effective way of gaining publicity for both the violence against women issue and the wider WLM.[141] RTN was a direct challenge to the commonly held argument that to avoid sexual assault women should remain indoors and avoid walking alone at night. Using the example of the curfew placed on women in Yorkshire during the Ripper murders, the WLM in Scotland called on women to claim their independence and walk the streets at night. Women's liberation groups began to organise marches through city centres. The preferred chant on these marches was, 'however we dress, and wherever we go, yes means yes and no means no'.[142]

A precursor to the marches in Scotland had occurred in 1976 at an event called Witching the Meadows, held on Halloween. A group of women gathered on the Meadows in Edinburgh, dressed like witches and hexed a section of the park known to be particularly dangerous. They also hung an effigy of a rapist from a tree with a sign around its neck, which read 'an end to rape'.[143] A year later at a Radical Feminist Conference in Edinburgh some participants decided to spill out on to the streets and 'take back the night', protesting against the fear women felt when walking the streets alone. In doing so they inaugurated the first RTN march in Britain.[144] RTN marches were organised in locations throughout Scotland, including Aberdeen, Dundee, St Andrews, Glasgow and Edinburgh.

The year 1979 was a high point for RTN marches in Scotland. This indicates that feminism and feminist activism was flourishing despite the fact that no British conferences were being held after 1978. On 24 February 1979 around two hundred women gathered in Aberdeen. Anne Marie McGeoch, an active member of Aberdeen women's liberation group, described the RTN march route:

> [from] Old Aberdeen, which was where the old part of the university was. – girls had to walk through the park to get to the halls of residence and there – was a lot of attacks there. So the march was through, you

know started at Hillhead, came through the park, kind of along King Street and up round … they finished up in the centre of Aberdeen. But it was to draw attention to the fact that it, it was quite dangerous for girls to walk through, to get home at night. How were they going to get home? There was no buses. So you know it was all that, you know very basic things that you want to go out for the night. How are you going to get home if you're on your own or even two of you walking through – a park that was largely unlit?[145]

During the same month, a march was held in Dundee in conjunction with the NUS Women's Week. One hundred women assembled for this event. The women's group in Dundee had a particularly strained relationship with the police, who tried to prevent the women from gathering in the city centre. The women's group felt this prevented its message being promoted to the widest possible audience.[146] As was common on marches, large flaming torches were carried by the participants alongside banners and posters. As Elspeth McLean of Dundee women's liberation group described

big sticks, – great big thick sticks. And getting old sheets and wax, and making a big pan of wax, melting it. And, dipping the sheets in it and then winding the sheets round the stick. So we had this real flaming torch. And the first one we lit … and it of course lit and immediately we thought, oh my god, [we thought we were going to] set the whole building on fire! We had to stick it down the loo to make it go out. Anyway, we arrived at the march, wherever this was going to be. Lots of big, flaming torches and there were, I think the police appeared … of course, and I can see with hindsight, they were probably right, said – don't even think about lighting these torches.[147]

The police and the women's group in Dundee also failed to agree a route for the march. Many of the protestors refused to disperse and broke ranks, running around City Square continuing to protest.[148]

In Glasgow the route for the RTN march started from the West End and continued via Blythswood Square to George Square. After marching, there was usually an event to attend at a nearby venue. The women in Edinburgh in 1977 attended a women's disco at St Anne's Centre in the Cowgate.[149] Similarly a film was shown for women in Dundee in the Students' Union. Even at this event, however, the women challenged sexism. Fired up from the night's march, Pauline Robinson remembered challenging the male members of the Students' Union:

I can remember really well the leering men turning round to see this galaxy of women coming in … [and shouting] 'Gosh, she's nice', 'Look at them, wouldn't mind a bit of that', 'Like to wrap my arms around that'

... but [then we] started, 'Cor, look at him, isn't he lovely, I bet he's got a big one. I wonder if he'd take it out for us, go on get them off' ... Well they were just totally thrown off by this. It was – wonderful.[150]

RTN was also an effective method in mobilising women in other towns outside of the main urban centres of women's liberation politics. During August 1979, for example, women from around Scotland attended a march in Cumbernauld. They walked through many of the local housing estates and painted their faces in order to prevent being identified by the police. When evaluating this event doubts began to emerge about the effectiveness of RTN. Feminists from groups in Edinburgh began to question the effectiveness of RTN given that the police were spending their time overseeing the march when they could have been putting their energies into catching rapists.[151]

Reactions to campaigns against violence against women

Although violence against women activists had been influenced by revolutionary feminist thinking, most of their actions were more directly aligned to a reformist agenda. Had they adopted the revolutionary feminist approach in its entirety then they would have entered into direct conflict with the police, law courts and government. Instead they lobbied local government and, in the case of WA, adopted constitutions and created committees in order to secure funding to create refuges. Although direct action, like RTN marches, was an effective way to attract attention and generate publicity, it was by working within the system that feminists of the WLM were able to build alliances with representatives of the labour movement, MPs and other autonomous women's groups.

The issues they discussed and publicised transformed public understanding of women's rights. To raise awareness, RCC representatives gave talks to a variety of different groups including Business and Professional Women, Balerno Young Wives and the Communist Party Women's Group.[152] They also sent literature to the Scottish Trades Union Congress to distribute at its women's conference.[153] Scottish Women's Aid also established the Domestic Violence Action Group in March 1978 to bring together all voluntary groups which had an interest in campaigning for reforms in this area.[154] In this way they widened the coalition of groups working against violence against women. By conceptualising the issues of violence against women, women's liberation activists, through organisations like WA and Rape Crisis, were extremely influential in convincing others of the validity of their arguments. Women's groups that were deemed to be too traditional by some within the WLM, representing older women and therefore not relevant to the campaigns of women's liberation, were also influenced by these developing discussions. For example, groups such as the National Federation of Business and Professional Women urged the British government to 'encourage local authorities in co-operation with voluntary housing associations to provide sanctuary for battered wives and their children'. In Scotland WCAs, formed in the aftermath of the campaign for suffrage in the 1920s, took an interest in the opening of local WA refuges. Moreover, Dundee WCA introduced a resolution at the 1976 half-yearly meeting of the Scottish Council of WCAs to end the need for corroborative evidence in domestic violence cases.[155] Groups such as the WCAs and Business and Professional Women were typecast by some feminists of the WLM as committee women who had nothing relevant to add to debates about the role of women.[156] But on the contrary, the discussions of groups like the WCAs were important in creating a broad coalition and applying pressure on politicians.

Moreover not every feminist active in the broader WLM refused to work with established women's groups. The Scottish Convention of Women (SCOW) was set up after IWY in 1975, as a forum to which all women's groups and individuals could align themselves. It hoped to 'help women realise their own potential' as well as ensuring that 'the informed opinion of women in Scotland is given its due weight'.[157] A few women from the WLM worked with them, most notably Kath Davies of the liberation group Edinburgh Women in Media but also activists like Jill Rakusen, Aileen Christianson and Sheila Gilmore.[158] Alongside women's liberation activists were representatives from the Church of Scotland's Woman's Guilds, the Soroptimists, the WCAs and WA. SCOW was an important organisation in gaining publicity for the domestic violence debate. It was an integral part of the WA-created Domestic Violence Action Group and its also formed its own working group on the issue.[159] It scrutinised any developments in Parliament with regard to domestic violence and published accounts from Hansard in its newsletter, *Convention Notes*.[160]

Some left-wing organisations also lent support. As was made clear in Chapter 6 the IMG was particularly supportive of the campaigns of feminists in Scotland in the 1970s. Its archive reveals a continuing interest in the women's movement and particularly the issue of violence against women. In 1979 it made clear that 'building a woman's movement is not a tactic. It is a strategic goal and informs all our work'.[161] Its understanding of the violence against women issue diverged, unlike abortion, from the mainstream feminist analysis. In particular it argued against punishing individual men, clearly reflecting broader socialist theories. Nevertheless it did campaign for RCCs to be state-funded, self-defence classes to be offered in school and rape within marriage to be criminalised.[162]

Important voices in the debate about rape included the STUC's WAC which frequently raised the issue at its annual conference. In 1977, for example, a resolution was introduced by Falkirk's WAC which made clear that it viewed 'with alarm the increasing incidence of rape in this country'. This organisation was also effective in highlighting the plight of battered wives, introducing, at the same conference, a resolution which demanded that 'Government introduces as a matter of urgency legislation making it mandatory on local authorities to provide adequate accommodation for battered wives'.[163] The Scottish Labour Party was also vocal on both issues, calling in 1978 for changes to the law on rape and in 1975 urging local authorities to provide more assistance for domestic violence victims.[164] It is interesting to consider how much the WLM influenced these discussions as opposed to being a product of the same debates and discussions affecting politics more widely. Rafeek has argued that feminism changed the perspective of women in the Communist Party in Scotland, persuading them to view violence as a product not just of capitalism but of also of patriarchy.[165] The evidence presented here would back up Rafeek's interpretation. It is clear that the feminist ideas created and promoted by the WLM were an important influence on the way women (and men), not only on the left of Scottish politics but throughout Scottish society more widely, viewed the issue of violence against women.

Conclusion

There has been little consideration of the areas of convergence and collaboration between the WLM and autonomous women's groups and organisations on the left. This is an important area of research. From the mid- to late-1970s the WLM was reaching out, eager to share its findings on the high levels of violence against women in order to influence the agendas of other political groups and organisations. In this way it shaped public understanding of women and violence, leading to governmental support of initiatives like refuges and RCCs and greater protection under improved legislation.

It was an important issue for three further reasons. First, it helped to introduce women, who had not been involved in the WLM, to feminist theories and organisations. The diffusion of women's liberation thought and practice into wider society, through the violence against women issue, can be viewed as one of its major successes.[166] Second, violence against women was vital in providing a focus for the movement in the 1980s and beyond. Lovenduski and Randall described how they felt that the women's movement in Scotland in these decades was still 'lively, confident and inventive'.[167] As was shown in Chapter 6 one major reason for this perception was that two further conferences were held on violence against women in the 1980s. As Aileen Christianson, one of the three hundred women who attended, recalled, it did not feel 'as though the Women's Movement had broken up. It felt very powerful that after ten years of work we had survived and accomplished many changes'.[168] This perspective questions the notion that the fragmentation of the wider WLM was an entirely negative development and led to the end of the movement. Fragmentation actually meant the diffusion of feminist ideas, goals and to some extent practice throughout areas of government and society generally.[169] Finally, violence against women was important in raising the consciousness of feminist activists in Scotland. The slow progress made to pass legislation in Scotland tended to galvanise feminists north of the border and encouraged them to create their own campaigns. How far this slow progress was because of the broader WLM in Britain, dominated by groups in London, failing to consider the different situation of women in Scotland or due to a lack of appetite for the equalities agenda by Scottish politicians remains unclear. Whatever the reason, however, active feminists in Scotland slowly came to believe that whilst 'in England the struggle to end the oppression of women [was] going to be long and hard; in Scotland the challenge [was] even greater'.[170] In arriving at this conclusion, women's liberation activists contributed to the flourishing of feminist campaigning in Scotland in the later part of the 1970s and beyond.

Notes

1   J. Pilcher, *Women in Contemporary Britain – An Introduction* (London, 1999), p. 142.

2   For example, Ann Oakley argued that 'it is ironically true that they have more to fear from the men they "love" than from the strangers in dark alleys': *Subject Women: A Powerful Analysis of Women's Experience in Society Today* (London, 1981), p. 257.

3   R. Emerson Dobash and R. Dobash, *Violence Against Wives – A Case Against Patriarchy* (New York, 1979), p. 75.

4   J. Rees, 'A Look Back at Anger: The Women's Liberation Movement in 1978', *Women's History Review*, 19:3 (2010), p. 342.

5   L. Segal, *Is the Future Female?: Troubled Thoughts on Contemporary Feminism* (London, 1987), p. 102.

6   *Catcall*, March 1979, p. 23.

7   J. Lovenduski and V. Randall, *Contemporary Feminist Politics: Women and Power in Britain* (Oxford, 1993), p. 320.

8   Edinburgh and Glasgow Legal and Financial Independence Groups, *Scottish Women's*

Charter – Proposals to Extend Women's Control over Their Lives (Edinburgh, 1978), p. 8.

9 Edinburgh and Glasgow Legal and Financial Independence Groups, *Scottish Women's Charter*, p. 8.

10 *Feminists Against Sexual Terrorism (F.A.S.T.)*, no. 1, February 1979, p. 13; *The Revolutionary/Radical Feminist Newsletter*, no. 2, March 1979, p. 21.

11 *F.A.S.T.*, no. 1, February 1979, p. 15.

12 Transcript of interview with Aileen Christianson (AC), 26 April 2007, p. 11.

13 *MsPrint*, no. 7, 1980, p. 10.

14 K. Arnot, 'Leaving the Pain Behind – Women's Aid in Scotland' in S. Henderson and A. Mackay (eds), *Grit and Diamonds: Women in Scottish History 1980–1990* (Edinburgh, 1990), p. 78.

15 Oakley, *Subject Woman*, p. 257.

16 Scottish Women's Aid, *The Herstory of Women's Aid-Scotland* (Edinburgh, 1984), p. 2.

17 Ibid., p. 5, p. 7.

18 Transcript of interview with Fran Wasoff (FW), 20 February 2007, p. 11.

19 Edinburgh and Glasgow Legal and Financial Independence Campaign, *Scottish Women's Charter*, p. 6. Furthermore, the Scottish Home and Health Department sponsored research in this area and its conclusions highlighted that a quarter of all reported offences of violence in Glasgow and Edinburgh in 1976 were 'wife assaults', as quoted in E. Hunter, *Scottish Women's Place: A Practical Guide and Critical Comment on Women's Rights in Scotland* (Edinburgh, 1978), p. 103.

20 Hunter, *Scottish Woman's Place*, p. 11.

21 E. Gordon, 'The Family' in L. Abrams, E. Gordon, D. Simonton and E.J. Yeo (eds), *Gender in Scottish History* (Edinburgh, 2006), p. 255; Pilcher, *Women in Contemporary Britain*, p. 142.

22 Edinburgh and Glasgow Legal and Financial Independence Campaign, *Scottish Women's Charter*, p. 6.

23 Transcript of interview with Pauline Robinson (PR*), 4 January 2007, pp. 14–15.

24 E. Pizzey, *Scream Quietly or the Neighbours Will Hear* (Harmondsworth, 1974), p. 9 and p. 19.

25 M. Turner, *The Women's Century: A Celebration of Changing Roles* (Kew, 2003), p. 146.

26 A. Coote and B. Campbell, *Sweet Freedom: The Struggle for Women's Liberation* (London, 1982), p. 41.

27 *Spare Rib*, no. 127, February 1983, p. 5.

28 Pizzey, *Scream Quietly*, p. 148.

29 E. Pizzey, *This Way to the Revolution: A Memoir* (London, 2011), p. 83. See also pp. 94–5 in which Pizzey defends her analysis and discusses how it diverged from the women's liberation analysis of domestic violence.

30 Scottish Women's Aid, *The Herstory*, p. 3.

31 Dobash and Dobash, *Women, Violence and Social Change*, p. 64.

32 Transcript FW, p. 12.

33 Dobash and Dobash, *Women, Violence and Social Change*, p. 65 and Scottish Women's Aid, *The Herstory*, p. 8.

34 *Spare Rib*, November 1974, no. 29, p. 24.

35 *Dundee Courier and Advertiser*, 8 May 1975.

36 Scottish Women's Aid, *The Herstory*, p. 7.

37 *Spare Rib*, August 1976, p. 28; *The Scotsman*, 10 September 1975, p. 11.

38 *Dundee Standard*, 30 November 1979, p. 9.

39 Transcript of interview with Chris Aldred (CA), 30 August 2007, p. 8; Transcript of interview with Lorna Peters (LP*), 4 September 2007, pp. 3–4.

40 Transcript LP*, p. 4.

41 Scottish Women's Aid, *The Herstory*, p. 5.

42 *Scottish Women's Liberation Journal*, no. 2, Summer 1977, p. 17.

43 Transcript of interview with Ruth Miller (RM*), 27 April 2007, pp. 7–8.

44 Dobash and Dobash, *Women, Violence and Social Change*, p. 65.

45 Transcript FW, p. 21.

46 J. Cuthbert and L. Irving, 'Women's Aid in Scotland: Purity versus Pragmatism?' in E. Breitenbach and F. Mackay (eds), *Women and Contemporary Scottish Politics: An Anthology* (Edinburgh, 2001), p. 55.

47 Scottish Women's Aid, *The Herstory*, p. 7.

48 Dobash and Dobash, *Violence Against Wives*, p. 228.

49 Scottish Women's Aid, *The Herstory*, p. 8.

50 Glasgow Women's Legal and Financial Independence Group, *Women and Housing* (Aberdeen, n.d.), p. 20.

51 Dobash and Dobash, *Violence Against Wives*, p. 228.

52 Scottish Women's Aid, *The Herstory*, p. 3.

53 Arnot, 'Leaving the Pain Behind', p. 78.

54 Dobash and Dobash, *Violence Against Wives*, p. 225.

55 Transcript PR*, p. 15–16.

56 Transcript RM*, p. 10.

57 Transcript RM*, pp. 8–9.

58 Scottish Women's Aid, *The Herstory*, p. 7, p. 8.

59 *Dundee Standard*, 30 November 1979, p. 9. Transcript of interview with Mary Henderson (MH), 14 June 2007, p. 4.

60 *The Guardian*, 7 August 1975.

61 'MP Attacks Aid for Battered Wives', *The Glasgow Herald*, 22 September 1975, as quoted in Dobash and Dobash, *Violence Against Wives*, p. 227.

62 *Scottish Women's Liberation Journal*, no. 3, November 1977, p. 16.

63 Transcript FW, p. 15.

64 Scottish Women's Aid, *The Herstory*, p. 7.

65 R. Emerson Dobash and R. P. Dobash, 'The Response to the British and American Women's Movements to Violence Against Women' in J. Hanmer and M. Maynard (eds), *Women, Violence and Social Control* (London, 1982), p. 171.

66 Transcript FW, p. 16.

67 Scottish Women's Aid, *Battered women*, p. 7; Dobash and Dobash, *Violence Against Wives*, p. 230; *MsPrint*, no. 2, 1978, p. 9.

68 *The Scotsman*, 15 January 1979, p. 6.

69 Edinburgh and Glasgow Women's Legal and Financial Independence Campaign, *Scottish Women's Charter*, p. 6.

70 Dobash and Dobash, *Violence Against Wives*, p. 208.

71 Dobash and Dobash, *Violence Against Wives*, p. 220.

72 Scottish Women's Aid, *The Herstory*, p. 7.

73 *The Scotsman*, 8 May 1975, p. 11.

74 J. Lewis, 'Marriage' in I. Zweiniger-Bargielowska (ed.), *Women in Twentieth Century Britain* (Harlow, 2001), p. 72.

75 M. Hill, 'Lessons and Legacies: Feminist Activism in the North c.1970–2000', *Women's Studies Review*, 9 (2004), [Myrtle Hill's own copy], p. 3.

76 *Scottish Catholic Observer*, 7 January 1977, p. 1.

77 *Scottish Women's Liberation Journal*, vol. 1, no. 1, Spring 1977, p. 6.

78 *The Scotsman*, 19 September 1975, p. 11.

79 *Scottish Women's Liberation Journal*, vol. 1, no 1, spring 1977, p. 17.

80 *MsPrint*, no. 1, 1978, p. 5; *Spare Rib*, June 1980, p. 25.

81 *MsPrint*, no. 1, 1978, p. 5.

82 *The Scotsman*, 8 February 1979, p. 6.

83 *Spare Rib*, June 1980, p. 26.

84 Scottish Women's Aid, *A Guide to the Matrimonial Homes (Family Protection) (Scotland) Act 1981* (Edinburgh, 1981), p. 1.

85 For discussion of this development see: Arnot, 'Leaving the Pain Behind', p. 78, *MsPrint*, no. 1, 1978, p. 4, and Dobash and Dobash, 'The Response', p. 176.

86 Coote and Campbell, *Sweet Freedom*, p. 41.

87 Transcript FW, p. 22.

88 Transcript of interview with Margaret Adams (MA*), 3 May 2007, p. 17.

89 Transcript of interview with Jennifer Kerr (JK), 1 May 2007, p. 16.

90 *The Leveller*, no. 25, April 1979, p. 21.

91 Transcript of interview with Zoe Fairbairns (ZF), 5 June 2007, pp. 11–12.

92 *F.A.S.T.*, no. 1, February 1979, p. 14.

93 *AIEN*, 14 November 1973, p. 5 (Courtesy of the University of St Andrews Library, StALF1119.A2); 'the Citizen' refers to *The St Andrews Citizen*, which is the local newspaper in St Andrews.

94 Lovenduski and Randall, *Contemporary Feminist Politics*, p. 320.

95 S. Brownmiller, *Against Our Will – Men, Women and Rape* (Harmondsworth, 1977), p. 309.

96 A. Christianson, 'Making Choices – Scotland and the Women's Movement', in A. Sebestyen (ed.), *'68, '78, '88: From Liberation to Feminism* (New York, 1989), p. 208.

97 *Catcall*, issue 6, July 1977, p. 14.

98 *MsPrint*, vol. 1, 1978, p. 7. A briefing paper in 2003 showed that although the level of reporting for rape in Scotland had increased 300 per cent 1977–2001 there was only one more conviction in 2001 than in 1977 (www.rapecrisisscotland.org.uk/rcs.php?fileid=news_nov_2003.htm). The rape conviction rate still remains low in Scotland with the conviction rate in 2009 recorded as 3.7 per cent (www.rapecrisisscotland.org.uk/news.htm).

99 Lovenduski and Randall, *Contemporary Feminist Politics*, p. 322, Coote and Campbell, *Sweet Freedom*, p. 43, A. Christianson and L. Greenan, 'Rape Crisis Movement in Scotland 1977–2000' in E. Breitenbach and F. Mackay (eds), *Women and Contemporary Scottish Politics – An Anthology* (Edinburgh, 2001), p. 69.

100 Edinburgh Rape Crisis Centre, *Briefing Paper: Questions the Press May Ask*, undated but probably c. 1979, p. 1, Private Collection: Aileen Christianson

101 *WIRES*, no. 29, April 1977, p. 3.

102 Transcript of interview with Jan Macleod (JM), 10 July 2007, p. 2, pp. 7–8.

103 Edinburgh Rape Crisis Centre, *First Report* (Edinburgh, 1981), p. 1, Private Collection:

Nadine Harrison.

104 *F.A.S.T. – A Newsletter*, 1979, p. 25.

105 L. Greenan, L. Volpp and Aileen Christianson, 'Still a Long Fight Ahead – Edinburgh Rape Crisis Centre' in S. Henderson and A. Mackay (eds), *Grit and Diamonds: Women in Scottish History 1980–1990* (Edinburgh, 1990), p. 81.

106 E. Maitland (ed.), *Woman to Woman: An Oral History of Rape Crisis in Scotland 1976–1991* (Glasgow, 2009), p. 10, p. 35, pp. 51–63 and p. 99.

107 Transcript AC, p. 16.

108 Transcript of interview with Isabelle Kerr (IK), 21 August 2007, pp. 1–2.

109 Transcript IK, pp. 10–11.

110 Transcript AC, pp. 7–8.

111 Her experiences allegedly reflect time spent in Edinburgh RCC: Transcript AC, p. 6, and Maitland, *Woman to Woman*, pp. 178–9.

112 N. Wolf, *Fire with Fire: The New Female Power and How It Will Change the Twenty-First Century* (London, 1994), p. 164.

113 Wolf, *Fire with Fire*, p. 164.

114 Edinburgh Rape Crisis Centre, *First Report*, p. 10 and p. 11, Private Collection: Nadine Harrison.

115 Transcript JM, pp. 8–9.

116 Transcript of interview with Nadine Harrison (NH), 12 June 2007, p. 10. This led to women realising that there was a need for survivors' groups, focusing purely on those women who had been sexually abused as children. These groups began to be set up during the early 1980s.

117 With thanks to Aileen Christianson for granting permission to include these tables.

118 Transcript NH, p. 11. But, as she later pointed out, this radically changed later in the period.

119 Edinburgh Rape Crisis Centre, *Second Report*, July 1988, p. 5, Private Collection: Aileen Christianson.

120 Greenan, Volpp and Christianson, 'Still a Long Fight Ahead', p. 69.

121 Transcript AC, p. 23.

122 Lovenduski and Randall, *Contemporary Feminist Politics*, p. 324. F.A.S.T. was formed in 1979 and their newsletter was edited by a different geographical collective every month.

123 *F.A.S.T. Newsletter*, no. 1, February 1979, p. 1.

124 Edinburgh Rape Crisis Centre, *Second Report*, p. 1, Private Collection: Aileen Christianson.

125 Greenan, Volpp and Christianson, 'Still a Long Fight Ahead', p. 81

126 London Rape Crisis Centre, 'First Report' in Feminist Anthology Collective, *No Turning Back: Writings from the Women's Liberation Movement 1975–1980* (London, 1981), p. 210.

127 Edinburgh Rape Crisis Centre, *First Report*, p. 14, Private Collection: Nadine Harrison.

128 *Spare Rib*, December 1981, pp. 54–5.

129 Edinburgh Rape Crisis Centre, *Second Report*, p. 3, Private Collection: Nadine Harrison.

130 *Women's Devolution – What Women Can Achieve Through a Scottish Assembly* (Edinburgh, 1979), p. 4, Private Collection: Nadine Harrison; Edinburgh and Glasgow Women's Legal and Financial Independence Groups, *Scottish Women's Charter*, p. 8.

131 *Spare Rib*, February 1974, p. 30.
132 Christianson, 'Making Choices', p. 210.
133 Edinburgh Rape Crisis Centre, *First Report*, p. 17, Private Collection: Nadine Harrison.
134 Ibid.
135 *MsPrint*, no. 5, 1979, p. 4.
136 *MsPrint*, no. 5, 1979, p. 4; Transcript AC, p. 22, Maitland, *Woman to Woman*, p. 133.
137 *MsPrint*, no. 5, 1979, p. 4.
138 *The Student*, 14 October 1976, p. 2.
139 Edinburgh Rape Crisis Centre, *Briefing Document: A Rape Crisis Centre Is Opening*, undated but probably c. 1979, p. 1, Private Collection: Aileen Christianson.
140 Bourke, *Rape*, p. 140, p. 146.
141 E. Setch, 'The Women's Liberation Movement in Britain, 1969–79: Organisation, Creativity and Debate' (unpublished PhD thesis, University of London, Royal Holloway, 2000), p. 223.
142 Hunter, *Scottish Woman's Place*, p. 106; The Soho Sixteen Support Sisterhood, 'The Soho Sixteen and Reclaim the Night' in Feminist Anthology Collective (eds), *No Turning Back: Writings from the Women's Liberation Movement 1975–1980* (London, 1981), p. 223. A. Clark, *Women's Silence, Men's Violence: Sexual Assault in England 1770–1845* (London, 1987), p. 134.
143 *Spare Rib*, April 1980, p. 14; Lovenduski and Randall, *Contemporary Feminist Politics*, p. 318, Maitland, *Woman to Woman*, p. 148. Transcript of interview with Ellen Galford (EG), 2 April 2007, p. 15.
144 S. Rowbotham, *A Century of Women: The History of Women in Britain and the United States* (London, 1999), p. 407.
145 Transcript of interview with Sandie Wyles (SW) and Anne-Marie McGeoch (AMcG), 18 September 2007, p. 36. Also remembered by Chris Aldred, Transcript CA, p. 16.
146 *MsPrint*, no. 3, 1979, p. 11. Transcript MA*, p. 16. Transcript of interview with Pauline Robinson (PR*), 6 December 2006, p. 16.
147 Transcript of interview with Elspeth McLean (EMcL), 9 August 2007, pp. 5–6.
148 *MsPrint*, no. 3, 1979, p. 11; Transcript EMcL, p. 6.
149 *Scottish Women's Liberation Journal*, no. 3, November 1977, p. 35.
150 Transcript PR*, p. 16.
151 *F.A.S.T.*, no. 3, August/September 1979, p. 27.
152 Edinburgh Rape Crisis Centre, *First Report*, p. 7, Private Collection: Nadine Harrison.
153 GCUA, GB1847 STUC Women's Advisory Committee Annual Conferences 1976–1978, no. 003, Women's Advisory Committee Conference Literature, 1978.
154 *MsPrint*, no. 1, August 1978, p. 6.
155 S.F. Browne, '"Dreary Committee Work"?: The Work of Established Women's Groups in the North East of Scotland c.1960–c.1970' (unpublished MLitt dissertation,University of Dundee, 2006), pp. 38–9.
156 Nina Woodcock referred to such groups as 'middle aged, middle class ladies' who 'probably wouldn't have listened' to her anyway, *MsPrint*, no. 2, 1978, p. 26.
157 National Library of Scotland (hereafter NLS), Acc 9395, Box 6/5, Scottish Convention of Women, Special Paper Projects, SCOW Prospectus.
158 Various references in SCOW archive, NLS, Acc 9395.
159 NLS, Acc 9395, Box 3/8, SCOW 'Convention Notes', *Convention Notes (4)*, Spring 1979, p. 5.

160 For example, NLS Acc 9395, Box 3/8, SCOW 'Convention Notes', *Convention Notes* (2), 1977.

161 *Socialist Woman*, no. 1, 1972, p. 15.

162 GCUA, Tony Southall Collection, Box P10, IMG archive, Misc. Women Focus Papers, c. 1979, p. 11, Lovenduski and Randall, *Contemporary Feminist Politics*, pp. 303-4.

163 GCUA, GB1847 STUC, STUC, *81st Annual Report*, 17-21 April 1978, p. 33.

164 Mitchell Library (TD 1384/3/1/1), Scottish Labour Party Conference Reports and Resolutions, 1975, p. 19.

165 N. C. Rafeek, *Communist Women in Scotland - Red Clydeside from the Russian Revolution to the End of the Soviet Union* (London, 2008), p. 199.

166 The diffusion of feminism has been explored in other geographical contexts. For example, L.R. Wolfe and J. Tucker, 'Feminism Lives: Building a Multicultural Women's Movement in the United States' in A. Basu (ed.), *The Challenge of Local Feminisms: Women's Movements in Global Perspective* (Oxford, 1995).

167 Lovenduski and Randall, *Contemporary Feminist Politics*, p. 96.

168 Christianson, 'Making Choices', p. 210.

169 Lovenduski and Randall argue along similar lines. They said that 'there has been a diffusion of feminist values into public attitudes', *Contemporary Feminist Politics*, p. 365.

170 *Spare Rib*, April 1980, p. 15.

Conclusion

While there has been little written about the history of the WLM in Scotland, this book has shown that there was a lively cadre of feminists, who aligned themselves with the WLM, and who were engaged in a number of political campaigns focused on women's rights north of the border. Breitenbach and Mackay were clearly right to argue that when looking at women and Scottish politics, 'the lack of a record of feminist action must not be taken to demonstrate a lack of action in fact'.[1] Researching this activism is important as, while accounts of feminists active in large metropolitan centres such as London dominate narratives of the WLM, this book has shown that women's liberation had a much wider appeal, influencing women in many parts of Britain, not only those who lived in the 'big city'.

Much of what happened in the WLM in Scotland was not distinct. As a truly international phenomenon, the WLM campaigned on more or less the same issues and held similar discussions whichever country it took root in. This is also true of the movement in Scotland, where feminist activists adhered to the seven demands and many of the discussions and divisions apparent in places like London and Leeds also had an impact north of the border. Yet the WLM in Scotland also had distinctive features. Most important were the emerging discussions about the domination of the British WLM by groups in London and the South East of England. As early as 1972 women in Scotland were organising their own conferences and local newsletters and were, therefore, interested in exploring the different historical, cultural and political context north of the border. However, in the later 1970s there were also increasing concerns about the domination of the movement by groups in the South of England which led to women's liberation activists focusing much more on issues which affected women north of the border. These concerns emerged for two reasons. First, women were angered by a lack of recognition within the broader movement. This was especially the case when women had to travel long distances to conferences. In a movement which believed in equality, inclusivity and representation, it was felt that conferences should have been regularly rotated in order to include women from the far north of Scotland. Second, feminist activists in Scotland began to believe that in some respects they also had further to travel in terms of securing their demands. The conservative views of local politicians and the lack of parliamentary time afforded Scottish issues at Westminster combined, resulting in key pieces of legislation, such as those associated with sexual offences and divorce, not being passed until much later in Scotland. Furthermore, it was felt by some activists that the movement in Scotland was operating in a culture perceived to be more patriarchal and socially conservative, and, therefore, more hostile to feminist claims.[2] Case studies of the WLM, therefore, demonstrate that the movement in Britain was more complex and multifaceted than has hitherto been recognised.[3] It also points to the importance of the local context in shaping women's liberation demands and campaigns. While the movement had a national presence, primarily through conferences and newsletters, it was the local context which was arguably more important in shaping, limiting and challenging feminist demands. As this book has shown, local groups often emphasised different issues at different times and adjusted their approach to campaigning in order to fit the local context they were operating in.

Looking at the WLM in different parts of Britain also allows us to question the chronology of the WLM. As Chapters 2 and 3 demonstrated, far from emerging out of the 'short' historical context of the protest movements and youth culture of the 1960s, the WLM can also be positioned within the 'longer' historical context of the girlhood experiences of those women who became activists in the 1970s. Furthermore, many of the issues identified by the movement, as encapsulated in its seven demands, were not as radically new or innovative as may at first be thought. Continuing a social reform agenda, which had been intrinsic to many established women's groups of the 1950s and 1960s and to left-wing campaigns for equal rights and opportunities, the WLM can be viewed as a generational response to the general issue of women's rights. Themes of conflict and change were important in shaping a feminist consciousness. Approaching the roots of the WLM through the life stories of the women involved is important in ascertaining why certain campaign priorities emerged and were given precedence, and how change interacted with continuities. Indeed oral testimonies were important in understanding the development of a feminist consciousness. A sense of joy, wonder, excitement and discovery was evoked by many of the interviewees. The combination of interviews and documentary sources not only made 'research [a] lively and emotional experience' but it was also imperative in gaining a 'grass-roots' perspective of the movement's operation and campaigns.[4] While more work is now being done to collect women's liberation material, it is still the case that many stories still need to be recorded.[5]

The WLM, therefore, was not always important in inventing the issues. What was innovative was how it theorised and campaigned on them.

The WLM was incredibly important in providing a theoretical contribution, linking together issues in order to enhance understanding about women's oppression in society. Vital in this regard was CR as personal experiences became very potent reasons for campaigning. Explorations of childhood experiences led women to reflect upon how their own lives related to broader political theory. This made the movement more accessible and also provided it with an energy to move forward and campaign. Combining this personal aspect with the direct protest methods associated with the civil rights movement, the New Left and student groups, the women of the WLM successfully challenged gendered notions of public protest. This is probably what made them so newsworthy. The fact they were courted by the media, therefore, makes their relative invisibility in historical accounts even more puzzling.

Yet, despite the lack of in-depth historical research a basic narrative has been established mainly by sociologists and academics who were activists in the movement, and this narrative tends to focus on the intense debates of the mid- to late-1970s and how this led to the decline of the movement. By the late 1970s the concept of 'sisterhood', which had galvanised the movement in the early part of the period, began to come under pressure from groups which wished to emphasise other identities including sexualities, race and class. The identity of 'woman' was fractured, hoping to make the movement more representative of its membership. As Rowbotham has argued, this awareness of the differences amongst women 'pulled the rug from under feminism as politics' as it became increasingly difficult to unite under one banner.[6] Fragmentation is prominent in narratives of the British WLM in the 1970s.[7] Featured in these discussions are the impact of identities of class, race and sexualities. Although researchers such as Lovenduski and Randall, amongst many others, have drawn attention to the 'divisive' nature of race in which many black women felt that 'no account of their experience was taken by white feminists', this was not a theme to emerge from this research on Scotland.[8] The omission of ethnic minority voices in my oral history collection could confirm that the movement in Scotland was mainly white or that I interviewed networks which were not representative of the movement at large. Although oral history was an extremely effective way of understanding how women felt about the movement, concerns remain about which voices have been left out. Hopefully more interviewing of this kind will be undertaken by other researchers. Race certainly would appear to have become an issue for the women's movement in Scotland by the mid-1980s with, for example, the Black Women's Group formed in 1985. This would suggest that the impact of race as an issue was delayed north of the border.[9]

A focus on fragmentation in some narratives has tended to conflate the breaking up of the movement with weakness and decline. This book revises these arguments and has shown that 'fragmentation and diverse areas of activity are not in themselves a weakness'.[10] By the end of the 1970s national conferences, in both the Scottish and British contexts, were not being held with the same regularity or attended by large numbers of women and there was more focus on single-issue campaigns. The movement's development in this direction was not entirely negative. This argument is also emerging in research into WLMs in other countries. In the USA Wolfe and Tucker have shown that 'despite media assertions to the contrary, the women's movement in the United States was far from dead' and in fact it had become 'more diverse and diffuse'. Far from this diversity being a negative development it actually contributed to the 'movement's strength'.[11]

Not only does this book revise arguments about the movement's decline in Britain but it also asserts that the fragmentation of the movement cannot be entirely explained by the emergence of political divisions and seeks a reassessment of the reasons given for fragmentation. Disagreements over radical and socialist feminism and the role of sexualities in discussions have been cited as major reasons why the WLM declined in the later 1970s. While Chapter 5 showed that these discussions were influential in souring the experiences of some active feminists, we have seen that there were also other reasons why the movement fragmented in the later 1970s. British conferences became too large for a movement which emphasised the personal and individual. Going to events where three thousand women attended made it increasingly difficult for every woman to have a say in the development of the movement. This frustrated many feminists who had been introduced to the movement through the small group process and had been encouraged to believe that they had a stake in the WLM. Furthermore, many feminists wanted to socialise and campaign with women who understood their own political perspective. For example lesbian feminists wanted to socialise with other lesbians in order to find a supportive environment often during a period of intense personal turmoil. Chapter 6 also demonstrated that more generally many feminist activists wanted to move beyond theorising and towards practical action. CR had been highly effective in the movement's initial stages, helping women to relate their own lives to weighty political theories before then using these experiences to inform action. By the later part of the period, however, many activists wanted to put these theories into action and began to focus on areas such as violence against women and abortion. In this way, as Drude Dahlerup has argued of the Danish

WLM, 'division into many task-oriented groups was a way of getting things done'.[12]

While the reasons for and the impact of fragmentation need to be reassessed in narratives of the WLM in Britain, it is evident that it also needs to be placed in a wider historical perspective. Many studies of the movement view it from the perspective of internal movement politics and, while this is an important view, it is evident that strategies and approaches to women's liberation were also being shaped by wider economic, social and political developments. By the end of the 1970s feminist activists were operating in an entirely different political and economic climate from the one in which the movement emerged. The advent of the Thatcher Conservative government in 1979 challenged the WLM, as it did other political groups and social movements, forcing it into a defence rather than an articulation of women's rights, given deep and widespread public sector cuts.[13] Focusing on single-issue campaigns enabled it to defend gains made in the preceding period. This was similar for other women's movements throughout the world as feminists had to regroup and revise their campaign methods as from the late 1970s onwards in all countries they faced a state which had 'reshaped, relocated and rearticulated its formal powers and policy responsibilities'.[14]

While the reasons for fragmentation need to be reassessed, it is also evident that the impact of this fragmentation can be questioned. Had divisions been so debilitating to the movement at large then two further women's liberation conferences would not have been held in Scotland in the 1980s. Esther Breitenbach described how at the end of the 1970s the WLM in Scotland 'still felt like a growing, developing movement with enormous potential'.[15] Indeed Dahlerup would seem to be correct when she asserted in the late 1980s that 'the movement is still alive and active, but it certainly has changed since the first enthusiastic period of the late 1960s and early 1970s'.[16] Arguably, therefore, the appellation 'second wave' is a somewhat simplistic way to understand the complexities of women's liberation activism in the 1970s, failing to encompass the continuities between various women's groups and those on the left of politics, and in simplifying what happened at the end of the 1970s. An attempt to redefine the wave structure has been apparent in other research into the WLM. Donatella Della Porta has put forward the concept of a 'long wave' in which women's liberation campaigns were carried on into the 1980s and 1990s.[17] Yet, despite an increasing number of scholars questioning the first and second wave model, it continues to persist and more must be done to question these labels and how they relate to feminist political activism in order to allow a greater understanding of the continuities, as well as the changes, in the women's movement.[18] Questioning this model might also lead to a reassessment of supposed periods of abeyance, challenging media portrayals which tend to describe feminism as continually in need of rediscovery and reinvention.

By moving beyond the second wave label we can see that the chronology of the WLM is by no means a 'linear picture of rise and fall'.[19] In particular Chapter 4 argued that the movement was always in motion, with local groups throughout the 1970s experiencing peaks and troughs of activism and prioritising issues over others at different points in the 1970s. Chapter 5 outlined some of the major debates and discussions which the movement confronted in the 1970s. Far from being entirely negative, these divisions and debates helped to open up many new and fruitful areas for women's liberation campaigns. Important campaigns for the movement in Scotland were violence against women and abortion. They illustrated that in some legal and cultural respects feminists in the north felt they had further to go in terms of achieving success. By focusing on these campaigns, the movement in Scotland was able to attract new women to the idea of liberation. Women's groups throughout the history of twentieth-century women's movements have had a particular inability to attract younger women and new members to their cause. This is often because there is so much work to be done that there is little time left to dedicate to recruitment. Yet, with the creation of WA and Rape Crisis the diffusion of women's liberation ideas was effective in reaching other women who might not otherwise have been introduced to theories emerging from the movement. Indeed Rowbotham has noted that 'the ideas of women's liberation actually reached many more women in the 1980s than in the 1970s' and this would indeed seem the case.[20]

Abortion and violence against women were also important in building alliances with other sympathetic groups and movements. The WLM in Scotland was too small to operate on its own and this encouraged it to reach out to other organisations, as did the increasingly hostile political and economic climate it was operating in. In doing so it secured the support of a wide range of people, legitimising their campaigns and creating broad-based alliances to lobby government to acknowledge the validity of their arguments. It also ensured that their ideas influenced other women's groups and organisations on the left. In this way they transformed how women were discussed and understood in society, setting new standards for gender equality. What can be broadly concluded is that the way women's role in society was understood in the late 1960s differed substantially from how it was understood in the late 1970s. The WLM was important in challenging the dominant understanding of women's role.

While it did not achieve everything it wanted to, it was incredibly important in offering an alternative to women and in expanding the limited choices available to women before the 1970s.

Abortion and violence against women were also significant in shaping the Scottish WLM, leading to a flourishing of women's liberation research, activity and campaigning north of the border from the mid-1970s onwards. Although there had always been a focus on the distinct political and cultural issues facing the Scottish WLM, it is evident that from the mid-1970s onwards feminists north of the border were vigorously discussing and researching Scottish themes, and that there was a clearer 'focus on Scottish issues and Scottish experience by the women's movement in Scotland'.[21] The move towards single-issue campaigns was, therefore, not entirely negative. Certainly the euphoria of sisterhood prevalent in the early movement was over but the campaigns focused on a single issue were incredibly important in disseminating feminist ideas and in widening the coalition for women's liberation.

The influence of the WLM continued into the 1980s. Violence against women remained a central focus for feminist activists in Scotland. Important in this regard have been campaigns like Zero Tolerance. Frankie Raffles, an activist from St Andrews women's liberation workshop, pioneered work in this field. She developed a 'ground-breaking initiative' to challenge the attitudes to male violence against women and children and helped to found the Zero Tolerance Trust.[22] It was a highly effective campaign which, according to Fiona Mackay, generated 'high levels of public debate and pushed the issue of violence and sexual violence higher up the political agenda'.[23] Using photographs and posters, it challenged a number of dominant myths about domestic violence, including, for example, that it was a solely working-class phenomenon. Its ultimate success was that it led to the 'diffusion of feminist values which has changed the social and political context in which violence against women is discussed'.[24] It was formally launched by Edinburgh District Council in 1992. Indeed, local authority women's committees became important vehicles of change for the equalities agenda in Scotland in the 1980s. The first committee in Scotland was set up by Stirling District Council in 1984, and by 1995 there were eleven.[25] The abortion campaign also continued as a result of the introduction to Parliament in 1987 of David Alton's Bill, which aimed to bring down the upper time limit. Like the previous bills put forward by White, Benyon and Corrie, this was also defeated. Part of the wider British campaign was the Scottish Fight Alton's Bill group, which held protests, including a large one in Glasgow in January 1988. Indeed, the Scottish Abortion Campaign remained independent but with strong links to organisations south of the border.[26] Furthermore, in April 2009 there were attempts to re-establish the abortion campaign in Scotland, indicating its continuing importance to feminist politics.[27]

The WLM was, therefore, important in articulating arguments about women's role in Scottish society and in providing the energy with which to carry campaigns on. Many women's liberation activists worked in areas where feminism informed their work, further illustrating that, far from declining, the ideas of women's liberation have diffused. Narratives which focus on notions of post-feminism in the 1980s and beyond tend to overlook the important work which has continued since the 1970s. Women like Aileen Christianson, Fran Wasoff and Esther Breitenbach have followed academic careers, continuing to write and teach about women and gender in their respective fields. Jan Macleod and Isabelle Kerr still campaign against violence against women, working within organisations like Rape Crisis and the Women's Support Project. Others have followed a more creative path, including Zoe Fairbairns and Paula Jennings, who through their poetry and novels have explored women's role in society and the implications of identity politics. Far from fragmentation leading to a complete decline in the late 1970s, therefore, the ideas and theories raised by this movement have been carried on by the many women who were such enthusiastic early converts. As Della Porta has argued of the Italian example, the women involved in campaigns of the 1990s 'are mainly from the 1970s generation, their collective identity originates in the 1970s, and the origins of the movement are (proudly) set in the 1970s'.[28]

A major concern which emerged during interviews was the threat to the longer-term legacy of the WLM as 'older' feminists believed younger women now viewed feminism as unfashionable. Anne Jackson, for example, described how she believed young women viewed her generation of feminists: 'hairy old hippies with unshaved armpits and lesbians, ew!'[29] It would seem that many young women now take their opportunities for granted without realising the hard-fought campaigns which had to be created in order to secure those rights. Arguably this is because of the fact that very little history of women and political activism is taught in schools. Yet, in recent years, there has also been an emergence of a younger, more assertive generation of feminists who both reject the commercialisation of women's bodies and any notions of post-feminism, and in recent years have been actively engaged in campaigns against austerity and government cuts. In this regard the WLM has provided an important inspiration to a new group of women.[30] For example, we have witnessed the rise of SlutWalks, in which a new generation of feminist activists have reinterpreted the legacy of the WLM's RTN marches in order to fit the current political and cultural context.[31] Moreover, RTN marches have continued to be organised by feminist groups throughout Britain, indicating the continuing legacy and relevance of women's liberation. An understanding of past feminist activism is clearly important when analysing current developments.

This book has demonstrated that future research into the WLM must acknowledge the usefulness of looking at its impact in different areas of the United Kingdom as it has the potential to enrich our knowledge of feminist activism in the 1970s as well as questioning the ways in which women's liberation has been discussed and understood. In this case it has been shown that, at times, women in Scotland had different issues to face. These issues led them into alliances with groups in the labour movement and other women's groups in order to build a broad coalition. The WLM in Scotland, therefore, ensured that their political influence continued beyond the 1970s, transforming the way society both discussed and understood the role of women. Discussions which took place in the WLM diffused into wider society, helping to raise both women's aspirations and to expand their opportunities. For this reason alone, the WLM merits more detailed attention from historians.

Notes

1 E. Breitenbach and F. Mackay, 'Introduction' in E. Breitenbach and F. Mackay (eds), *Women and Contemporary Scottish Politics: An Anthology* (Edinburgh, 2001), p. 5.

2 This was also the case for other feminists operating outwith England. See, for example, D. Beddoe, *Out of the Shadows – A History of Women in Twentieth Century Wales* (Cardiff, 2000), pp. 179–80.

3 Fiona Mackay has also come to a similar conclusion in terms of what happened to women and Scottish politics in the 1980s and 1990s. F. Mackay, 'The State of Women's Movements in Britain: Ambiguity, Complexity and Challenges from the Periphery' in S. Grey and M. Sawer (eds), *Women's Movements: Flourishing or in Abeyance?* (London, 2008), p. 27.

4 J. Bornat, 'Oral History as a Social Movement: Reminiscence and Older People' in R. Perks and A. Thomson (eds), *The Oral History Reader* (London, 1998), p. 189.

5 See for example the Sisterhood and After website: www.bl.uk/learning/histcitizen/sisterhood/index.html.

6 S. Rowbotham, *Women in Movement: Feminism and Social Action* (London, 1992), p. 290.

7 See, for example, A. Lent, *British Social Movements since 1945: Sex, Colour, Peace and Power* (Basingstoke, 2001), p. 75.

8 J. Lovenduski and V. Randall, *Contemporary Feminist Politics: Women and Power in Britain* (Oxford, 1993), p. 79.

9 R. Arshad, 'The Scottish Black Women's Group' in S. Henderson and A. Mackay (eds),

Grit and Diamonds: Women in Scotland Making History 1980–1990 (Edinburgh, 1990), p. 118.

10 Rowbotham, *Women in Movement*, p. 283.

11 L.R. Wolfe and J. Tucker, 'Feminism Lives: Building a Multicultural Women's Movement in the United States' in A. Basu (ed.), *The Challenge of Local Feminisms: Women's Movements in Global Perspective* (Oxford 1995), p. 446 and p. 448.

12 D. Dahlerup, 'Is the New Women's Movement Dead? Decline or Change of the Danish Movement' in D. Dahlerup (ed.), *The New Women's Movement: Feminism and Political Power in Europe and the USA* (London, 1986), p. 230.

13 A. Dobrowsolsky, 'Shifting States: Women's Constitutional Organizing Across Time and Space' in L. A. Banaszak, K. Beckwith and D. Rucht (eds), *Women's Movements Facing the Reconfigured State* (Cambridge, 2003), p. 118, and D.S. Myer, 'Restating the Woman Question – Women's Movements and State Restructuring' in L. Banaszak, K. Beckwith and D. Rucht (eds), *Women's Movements Facing the Reconfigured State* (Cambridge, 2003), p. 283–4.

14 L. Banaszak, K. Beckwith and D. Rucht, 'When Power Relocates: Interactive Changes in Women's Movements and States' in L. Banaszak, K. Beckwith and D. Rucht (eds), *Women's Movements Facing the Reconfigured State* (Cambridge, 2003), p. 2. M. Sawer and S. Grey, 'Introduction' in S. Grey and M. Sawer (eds), *Women's Movements: Flourishing or in Abeyance?* (London, 2008), p. 8.

15 E. Breitenbach, '"Sisters are doing it for themselves": The Women's Movement in Scotland' in A. Brown and R. Parry (eds), *The Scottish Government Yearbook 1990* (Edinburgh, 1990), p. 215.

16 D. Dahlerup, 'Introduction' in D. Dahlerup (ed.), *The New Women's Movement: Feminism and Political Power in Europe and the USA* (London, 1986), p. 20.

17 D. Della Porta, 'The Women's Movement, the Left, and the State' in L. A. Banaszak, K. Beckwith and D. Rucht (eds), *Women's Movements and the Reconfigured State* (Cambridge, 2003), p. 49. Verta Taylor and Leila J. Rupp have also talked about looking at those periods outwith the 'waves' as being in abeyance: V. Taylor and L.J. Rupp, 'Preface' in S. Grey and M. Sawer (eds), *Women's Movements: Flourishing or in Abeyance?* (London, 2008), p. xiii. As this book was entering the production process Stephanie Gilmore published *Groundswell: Grassroots Feminist Activism in Postwar America* (New York, 2013) which by looking at local groups in the USA echoes the main arguments of this book: a grass roots and local perspective allows us to challenge the idea of the 'second wave'.

18 N.A. Hewitt, 'Introduction' in N.A. Hewit (ed.), *No Permanent Waves: Recasting Histories of U.S. Feminism* (New Brunswick, 2010), p. 7.

19 E. Setch, 'The Women's Liberation Movement in Britain, 1969–79: Organisation, Creativity and Debate' (unpublished PhD thesis, University of London, Royal Holloway, July 2000), p. 8.

20 Rowbotham, *Women in Movement*, p. 283.

21 Breitenbach, '"Sisters are doing it for themselves"', p. 217.

22 E. Ewan, S. Innes, S. Reynolds and R. Pipes (eds), *The Biographical Dictionary of Scottish Women* (Edinburgh, 2006), p. 296. See also F. Mackay, 'The Case of Zero Tolerance: Women's Politics in Action?' in E. Breitenbach and F. Mackay (eds), *Women and Contemporary Scottish Politics: An Anthology* (Edinburgh, 2001), p. 105.

23 Mackay, 'The Case', p. 105.

24 Ibid., p. 126.
25 Ibid., p. 113.
26 A. McChlery, 'Our Bodies, Our Lives, Our Right to Decide!' in A. Henderson and S. Mackay (eds), *Grit and Diamonds: Women in Scotland Making History 1980–1990* (Edinburgh, 1990), pp. 208–12.
27 A meeting was held in Edinburgh on 25 April 2009: www.abortionrights.org.uk, accessed 20 April 2009.
28 Della Porta, 'The Women's Movement', pp. 66–7.
29 Transcript of interview with Anne Jackson (AJ) and Paula Jennings (PJ), 27 August 2007, p. 39.
30 M. Turner, *The Women's Century: A Celebration of Changing Roles* (Kew, 2003), p. 153.
31 www.guardian.co.uk/society/2011/may/15/slutwalk-debate-sexual-discrimination, accessed 16 May 2011.

APPENDIX I

Short biographies of oral history interviewees

[* denotes the use of a pseudonym.]

Margaret Adams* was born in the 1950s and was an active member of the women's liberation group in Dundee in the 1970s.

Chris Aldred (b. 1950) was active in the Aberdeen women's liberation group. She was also active in a nursery campaign, the Women's Abortion and Contraception Campaign, the Scottish Abortion Campaign and the Workers Educational Association.

Esther Breitenbach (b. 1950) became involved in the WLM in Dundee in 1972. She was subsequently active in the groups in Glasgow and Edinburgh. She helped found the *Scottish Women's Liberation Journal* and was part of the *MsPrint* collective, and was active in the Legal and Financial Independence Campaign and Scottish Abortion Campaign.

Aileen Christianson (b. 1944) was a member of a CR group in Edinburgh 1976–78 and was also an active member of Edinburgh RCC in the late 1970s.

Kath Davies grew up in Wales. She was a member of Edinburgh Women in Media and was a branch equality officer with the National Union of Journalists. She is a board member of Engender.

Wendy Davies was born in 1949 in Wales. She was a member of Glasgow women's liberation workshop and became involved in the Legal and Financial Independence Campaign. She was also one of the first workers at Glasgow Women's Centre.

Judith Ekins (b. 1946) was active in the St Andrews women's liberation group.

Margaret Elphinstone (b. 1948) became a founder member of the Shetland Women's Group.

Zoe Fairbairns (b. 1948) was a founder member of the St Andrews women's liberation group in 1970. She worked at the Women's Research and Resource Centre (the Feminist Library) and at *Spare Rib*.

Caroline Florence (b. 1917) was a committed member of Arbroath WCA. She was President of this group in the late 1960s and 1970s.

Fiona Forsyth (b. 1952) was involved in the Aberdeen women's liberation group and the production of *The Scottish Women's Liberation Journal*, and also participated in the Women and Manual Trades group.

Ellen Galford (b. 1947) became involved in women's liberation politics in Glasgow in the mid-1970s. She campaigned for abortion rights and helped to establish a lesbian feminist group. She was also part of a women's writing collective.

Sheila Gilmore became involved in one of the first women's liberation groups in Edinburgh in 1970. She was also involved in the early stages of establishing a RCC in Edinburgh.

Nadine Harrison (b. 1950) was part of a CR group in Edinburgh and was also active in the National Abortion Campaign and Doctors for a Woman's Choice on Abortion.

Mary Henderson (b. 1934) was active in establishing a WA refuge in Dundee and was instrumental in the creation of a playgroup network in Tayside. She became the Chairperson of the Scottish Pre-school Playgroup Association and was also an active member of Engender.

Anne Jackson (b. 1953) was a member of St Andrews women's liberation group.

Paula Jennings (b. 1950) was a founder member of the women's liberation group in St Andrews and was an active radical feminist throughout the 1970s. She was a prolific writer, advancing many new ideas for the WLM, was an active campaigner against pornography and was involved in WA, amongst many other issues.

Isabelle Kerr (b. 1955) was active within Glasgow RCC and also helped to establish a centre with the trades unions and was a Welfare Rights Worker in the early 1980s.

Jennifer Kerr was active within St Andrews women's liberation group.

Jan Macleod (b. 1958) was a member of the Glasgow university women's group in the mid-1970s and it was through this involvement that she was introduced to the work of the RCC.

Anne-Marie McGeoch (b. 1957) started the women's action group at the University of Aberdeen in 1975.

Elspeth McLean (b. 1953) joined the local women's liberation group in Dundee. She was also a member of the EIS.

Ruth Miller* born 1946. She was a member of the Edinburgh Women's Liberation Group.

Lorna Peters* was born in the early 1950s and became an active member of the Aberdeen women's liberation group.

Pauline Robinson* was a member of the women's liberation group in Dundee. Through this she became an active member of the National Abortion Campaign and volunteered for WA.

Elizabeth Smith* was born in the mid-1950s in Scotland. She became an active member of the Labour Party in the 1970s.

Anne Ward* born in the early 1940s was an active member of the Glasgow Women's Liberation Group.

Fran Wasoff was a member of one of the earliest women's groups in Edinburgh and a member of the group of women who founded the first WA group in Scotland, helping to set up the first refuge.

Sandie Wyles (b. 1957) grew up in Stirling and was best friends with Anne-Marie McGeoch. She and Anne-Marie were important in jump-starting the women's group in Aberdeen in the mid-1970s.

APPENDIX II

The seven demands of the women's liberation movement in Britain

1. Equal pay
2. Equal education and opportunity
3. Twenty-four-hour nurseries
4. Free contraception and abortion on demand
5. Financial and legal independence[1]
6. An end to all discrimination against lesbians[2]
7. Freedom for all women from intimidation by the threat or use of male violence. An end to the laws, assumptions and institutions which perpetuate male dominance and men's aggression towards women[3]

Notes

1 Adopted at the National Women's Liberation Conference, Edinburgh, 1974.
2 Adopted at the National Women's Liberation Conference, Edinburgh, 1974.
3 Adopted at the National Women's Liberation Conference, Birmingham, 1978. The seven demands and their adoption dates can be found at www.feministarchivenorth. org.uk/chronology/appendixi.htm.

Bibliography

Oral history interviews

Adams, Margaret* interviewed in Dundee 3 May 2007
Aldred, Chris interviewed in Aberdeen 30 August 2007
Breitenbach, Esther interviewed in Edinburgh 24 May 2007
Christianson, Aileen interviewed in Edinburgh 26 April 2007
Davies, Kath interviewed in Edinburgh 12 December 2006
Davies, Wendy interviewed in Edinburgh 17 July 2007
Ekins, Judy interviewed in St Andrews 27 July 2007
Elphinstone, Margaret interviewed in Glasgow 21 November 2007
Fairbairns, Zoe interviewed in London 5 June 2007
Florence, Caroline interviewed in Arbroath 22 April 2006; 31 March 2007
Forsyth, Fiona interviewed in Glasgow 9 July 2008
Galford, Ellen interviewed in Edinburgh 2 April 2007
Gilmore, Sheila interviewed in Edinburgh 28 June 2007
Harrison, Nadine interviewed in Edinburgh 12 June 2007
Henderson, Mary interviewed in Dundee 14 June 2007
Jackson, Anne and Jennings, Paula interviewed in Fife 27 August 2007.
Jennings, Paula interviewed in Fife 15 October 2007
Kerr, Isabelle interviewed in Glasgow 21 August 2007
Kerr, Jennifer interviewed in Fife 1 May 2007
Macleod, Jan interviewed in Glasgow 10 July 2007
McLean, Elspeth interviewed in Edinburgh 9 August 2007
Miller, Ruth* interviewed in Edinburgh 27 April 2007
Peters, Lorna* interviewed in Aberdeen 4 September 2007
Robinson, Pauline* interviewed in Dundee 6 December 2006 and 4 January 2007
Smith, Elizabeth interviewed in Edinburgh 19 April 2007
Ward, Anne* interviewed in Edinburgh 28 August 2007
Wasoff, Fran interviewed in Edinburgh 20 February 2007
Wyles, Sandie and McGeoch, Anne-Marie interviewed in Edinburgh 18 September 2007

Unpublished primary sources

Glasgow Caledonian University Archives

International Marxist Group – Aberdeen Branch Archives: National Abortion Campaign (uncatalogued).
International Marxist Group – Misc Women Focus Papers, c.1979 (Tony Southall Collection, Box P10).
International Marxist Group Scotland Post-Conference Aggregate May 17/18 document 7 (Tony Southall Collection, Box 1E).

Scottish Trades Union Congress, Women's Advisory Committee records, Catholic Church in Scotland Press Release, Glasgow, c.1979 (GB1847 STUC, no. 553, Women's Advisory Committee Papers, 1976–80).

Scottish Trades Union Congress, Annual Reports, 1972–80 (GB1847 STUC).

Women's Advisory Committee Conference Literature, 1978 (GB1847 STUC Women's Advisory Committee Annual Conferences 1976–1978, no. 003).

London School of Economics

International Marxist Group Archive: Various Pamphlets on Abortion Issue: Turn Words into Action Leaflet (4/4).

Scottish Women's Liberation Conference 1976 – A Record of the Scottish Women's Liberation Conference, Glasgow, October 1976 (McINTOSH 1/15).

Mitchell Library, Glasgow

Minutes of Meeting of Executive Committee of Scottish Council of Labour Party (TD1384/1/12).

Scottish Labour Party Conference Reports and Resolutions, 1975 (TD 1384/3/1/1).

National Library of Scotland

Scottish Convention of Women, 'Convention Notes' (NLS Acc 9395, Box 3/8).

Scottish Convention of Women, Special Paper Projects, SCOW Prospectus (NLS Acc 9395, Box 6/5).

Private collections

Doctors for a Woman's Choice on Abortion minutes, reports and correspondence and misc items including leaflets like Women's Devolution – What Women Can Achieve Through A Scottish Assembly (Edinburgh, 1979) and Edinburgh Rape Crisis Centre, First Report (Edinburgh, 1981) (Nadine Harrison).

Various women's liberation newsletters and extensive archive of Rape Crisis briefing notes, newsletters and correspondence, including Edinburgh Rape Crisis Centre, Second Report (Edinburgh, 1988) (Aileen Christianson).

Various newsletters and women's liberation ephemeral including Edinburgh Women's Liberation Group, Nursery Report (Edinburgh, undated but probably c.1974) (Fiona Mackay).

Various newsletters including Tayside Women's Liberation Newsletters and other ephemeral material (Paula Jennings).

Published primary sources

Abortion Law Reform Association (ALRA), *A Woman's Right to Choose – Action Guide* (London, n.d.).

Beale, J., *Getting It Together: Women as Trade Unionists* (London, 1982).

Brown, G., 'Introduction: The Socialist Challenge' in G. Brown (ed.), *The Red Paper on Scotland* (Edinburgh, 1975).

Brownmiller, S., *Against Our Will – Men, Women and Rape* (Harmondsworth, 1977).

Bruley, S., 'Women Awake: The Experience of Consciousness-raising' in Feminist Anthology Collective (eds), *No Turning Back: Writings from the Women's Liberation Movement 1975–1980* (London, 1981).

Chambers, J. and Cossey, D., *How MPs Voted on Abortion* (London, 1982).

Dobash, R. Emerson and Dobash, R., 'The Response to the British and American Women's Movements to Violence Against Women' in J. Hanmer and M. Maynard (eds), *Women, Violence and Social Control* (London, 1982).

Dobash, R. Emerson and Dobash, R., *Violence Against Wives – A Case Against Patriarchy* (New York, 1979).

Edinburgh and Glasgow Women's Legal and Financial Independence Groups, *Scottish Women's Charter – Proposals Designed to Extend Women's Control over Their Lives* (Edinburgh, 1978).

Engels, F., *The Origins of the Family, Private Property and the State* (Moscow, 1968 edition).

Evans, S., *Personal Politics: The Roots of Women's Liberation in the Civil Rights Movement and the New Left* (New York, 1979 and 1989).

Firestone, S., *The Dialectic of Sex: The Case for Feminist Revolution* (Frogmore, 1973).

Freeman, J., *The Tyranny of Structurelessness* (New York, 1970).

Friday, N., *My Mother / My Self – The Daughter's Search for Identity* (Glasgow, 1977).

Garthwaite, A. and Sinclair, V., 'The TUC's Right to Choose' in Feminist Anthology Collective (eds), *No Turning Back: Writings from the Women's Liberation Movement 1975–1980* (London, 1981).

Glasgow Women's Legal and Financial Independence Group, *Women and Housing* (Aberdeen, n.d.).

Gow, D., 'Devolution and Democracy' in G. Brown (ed.), *The Red Paper on Scotland* (Edinburgh, 1975).

Hunter, E., *Scottish Woman's Place: A Practical Guide and Critical Comment on Women's Rights in Scotland* (Edinburgh, 1978).

Kanter, H., Lefanu, S., Shah, S. and Spedding, C. (eds), *Sweeping Statements: Writings from the Women's Liberation Movement 1981–1983* (London, 1984).

London Rape Crisis Centre, 'First Report' in Feminist Anthology Collective, *No Turning Back: Writings from the Women's Liberation Movement 1975–1980* (London, 1981).

Mitchell, J., *Woman's Estate* (Harmondsworth, 1971).

National Abortion Campaign, *Aims and Structures* (London, 1982).

NAC, 'NAC: The Case for Change: Two Views' in H. Kanter, S. Lefanu, S. Shah and C. Spedding (eds), *Sweeping Statements: Writings from the Women's Liberation Movement 1981–1983* (London, 1984).

Oakley, A., *Subject Women: A Powerful Analysis of Women's Experience in Society Today* (London, 1981).

Pizzey, E., *Scream Quietly or the Neighbours Will Hear* (Harmondsworth, 1974).

Redstockings, 'Manifesto' in R. Baxandall and L. Gordon (eds), *Dear Sisters: Dispatches from the Women's Liberation Movement* (New York, 2000).

Rowbotham, S., 'The Beginnings of Women's Liberation in Britain' in M. Wandor (ed.), *The Body Politic: Women's Liberation in Britain 1969–1972* (London, 1972).

Rowbotham, S., *Women's Consciousness, Man's World* (Harmondsworth, 1973).

Sarachild, K., 'Consciousness-raising: A Radical Weapon?' in Redstockings (ed.), *Feminist Revolution* (New York, 1975).

Scottish Women's Aid, *A Guide to the Matrimonial Homes (Family Protection) (Scotland) Act 1981* (Edinburgh, 1981).

Scottish Women's Aid, *Battered Women in Scotland – Your Rights and Where to Turn for Help* (Edinburgh, 1977).

Scottish Women's Aid, *The Herstory of Women's Aid – Scotland* (Edinburgh, 1984).

Sjoo, M., 'Abortion Accounts' in S. Allen, L. Sanders and J. Wallis (eds), *Conditions of Illusion: Papers from the Women's Movement* (Leeds, 1974).

The Soho Sixteen Support Sisterhood, 'The Soho Sixteen and Reclaim the Night' in Feminist Anthology Collective (eds), *No Turning Back: Writings from the Women's Liberation Movement 1975–1980* (London, 1981).

Wandor, M., *The Body Politic: Writings from the Women's Liberation Movement in Britain 1969–1972* (London, 1972).

Williamson, N., 'Ten Years After – The Revolutionary Left in Scotland' in H. M. Drucker and N. L. Drucker (eds), *The Scottish Government Yearbook 1979* (Edinburgh, 1978).

Journals and newspapers

Women's liberation newsletters and journals

Catcall
Edinburgh Women's Liberation Newsletter
Feminists Against Sexual Terrorism (F.A.S.T.)
MsPrint
Nessie
St Andrews Lesbian Feminist Newsletter
Scarlet Women
Scottish Women's Liberation Journal
Socialist Woman
Spare Rib
Tayside Women's Liberation Newsletter
The Revolutionary and Radical Feminist Newsletter
The Second Wave – A Magazine of New Feminism
Whatever Happened to the Scottish Women's Liberation Journal?
WIRES
Women's Report

Other political newsletters and journals

A Woman's Right to Choose: Newssheet of the West of Scotland NAC
IMG International Bulletin
National Abortion Campaign Newsletter
Outcome
The Leveller

Newspapers

AIEN
Annasach
Brig
Dundee Courier and Advertiser
Dundee Standard
Gaudie
Scottish Catholic Observer
The Citizen
The Evening Express
The Evening Telegraph
The Glasgow Herald
The Glasgow University Guardian.
The Guardian
The Observer
The Scotsman
The Strathclyde Telegraph
The Student
The Times

Secondary sources

Books

Abrams, L., *Oral History Theory* (London, 2010).
Alberti, J., *Beyond Suffrage: Feminists in War and Peace 1914–1928* (London, 1989).
Anderson, K. and Jack, D.C., 'Learning to Listen: Interview Techniques and Analyses' in S. Berger Gluck and D. Patai (eds), *Women's Words: The Feminist Practice of Oral History* (London, 1991).
Arnot, K., 'Leaving the Pain Behind – Women's Aid in Scotland', in S. Henderson and A. Mackay (eds), *Grit and Diamonds: Women in Scottish History 1980–1990* (Edinburgh, 1990).
Arshad, R., 'The Scottish Black Women's Group' in S. Henderson and A. Mackay (eds), *Grit and Diamonds: Women in Scotland Making History 1980–1990* (Edinburgh, 1990).
Banaszak, L., Beckwith, K. and Rucht, D., 'When Power Relocates: Interactive Changes in Women's Movements and States' in L. Banaszak, K. Beckwith and D. Rucht (eds), *Women's Movements Facing the Reconfigured State* (Cambridge, 2003).

Barrett, M., *Women's Oppression Today: The Marxist/Feminist Encounter* (London, 1998).

Basu, A. (ed.), *The Challenge of Local Feminisms: Women's Movements in Global Perspective* (Oxford, 1995).

Beckett, A., *When the Lights Went Out: Britain in the 1970s* (London, 2009).

Beddoe, D., *Out of the Shadows – A History of Women in Twentieth Century Wales* (Cardiff, 2000).

Black, L. and Pemberton, H., 'Introduction: The Benighted Decade? Reassessing the 1970s' in L. Black, H. Pemberton and P. Thane (eds), *Reassessing 1970s Britain* (Manchester, 2013).

Black, L., Pemberton, H. and Thane, P. (eds), *Reassessing 1970s Britain* (Manchester, 2013).

Bornat, J., 'Oral History as a Social Movement: Reminiscence and Older People' in R. Perks and A. Thomson (eds), *The Oral History Reader* (London, 1998).

Bouchier, D., *The Feminist Challenge: The Movement for Women's Liberation in Britain and the United States* (London, 1983).

Bourke, J., *Rape: A History from 1860 to the Present* (London, 2008).

Breitenbach, E., '"Sisters are doing it for themselves": The Women's Movement in Scotland' in A. Brown and R. Parry (eds), *The Scottish Government Yearbook 1990* (Edinburgh, 1990).

Breitenbach, E. and Mackay, F., 'Introduction' in E. Breitenbach and F. Mackay (eds), *Women and Contemporary Scottish Politics: An Anthology* (Edinburgh, 2001).

Breitenbach, E. and Mackay, F., 'Feminist Politics in Scotland from the 1970s to 2000s: Engaging with the State' in E. Breitenbach and P. Thane (eds), *Women and Citizenship in Britain and Ireland in the Twentieth Century: What Difference Did the Vote Make?* (London, 2010).

Brenner, J., 'The Best of Times, The Worst of Times: Feminism in the United States' in M. Threlfall (ed.), *Mapping the Women's Movement: Feminist Politics and Social Transformation in the North* (London, 1996).

Brown, C.G. 'Charting Everyday Experience' in L. Abrams and C.G. Brown (eds), *Everyday Life in Twentieth Century Scotland* (Edinburgh, 2012).

Brown, C.G., *Religion and Society in Twentieth-Century Britain* (Harlow, 2006).

Brown, C.G., McIvor, A.J. and Rafeek, N., *The University Experience 1945–1975 – An Oral History of the University of Strathclyde* (Edinburgh, 2004).

Browne, S.F., 'Women, Religion and the Turn to Feminism: Experiences of Women's Liberation Activists in Britain in the Seventies' in M. Gauverau and N. Christie (eds), *The 1960s and Beyond: Dechristianization as History in Britain, Canada, the United States and Western Europe* (Toronto, 2013).

Browne, S.F. and Tomlinson, J.D., 'A Women's Town: Dundee Women on the Public Stage' in J.D. Tomlinson and C.A. Whatley (eds), *Jute No More: Transforming Dundee* (Dundee, 2011).

Carter, A., *The Politics of Women's Rights* (London, 1988).

Christianson, A., 'Making Choices – Scotland and the Women's Movement' in A. Sebestyen (ed.), *'68, '78, '88: From Liberation to Feminism* (New York, 1989).

Christianson, A. and Greenan, L., 'Rape Crisis Movement in Scotland 1977–2000' in E. Breitenbach and F. Mackay (eds), *Women and Contemporary Scottish Politics – An Anthology* (Edinburgh, 2001).

Clark, A., *Women's Silence, Men's Violence: Sexual Assault in England 1770–1845* (London, 1987).

Cohan, A., 'Abortion as a Marginal Issue: The Use of Peripheral Mechanisms in Britain and the United States' in J. Lovenduski and J. Outshoorn (eds), *The New Politics of Abortion* (London, 1986).

Coote, A. and Campbell, B, *Sweet Freedom: The Struggle for Women's Liberation* (London, 1982).

Craig, C., *The Scots' Crisis of Confidence* (Glasgow, 2004).

Crossley, N., *Contesting Psychiatry: Social Movements in Mental Health* (Abingdon, 2006).

Cuthbert, J. and Irving, L., 'Women's Aid in Scotland: Purity versus Pragmatism?' in E. Breitenbach and F. Mackay (eds), *Women and Contemporary Scottish Politics: An Anthology* (Edinburgh, 2001).

Dahlerup, D., 'Introduction' in D. Dahlerup (ed.), *The New Women's Movement: Feminism and Political Power in Europe and the USA* (London, 1986).

Dahlerup, D., 'Is the New Women's Movement Dead? Decline or Change of the Danish Movement' in D. Dahlerup (ed.), *The New Women's Movement: Feminism and Political Power in Europe and the USA* (London, 1986).

Dean, J., *Rethinking Contemporary Feminist Politics* (Basingstoke, 2010).

Della Porta, D., 'The Women's Movement, the Left, and the State' in L.A. Banaszak, K. Beckwith and D. Rucht (eds), *Women's Movements Facing the Reconfigured State* (Cambridge, 2003).

Dempsey, B., *Thon Wey: Aspects of Scottish Lesbian and Gay Activism 1968–1992* (n.d.).

Dobash, R. Emerson and Dobash, R, *Women, Violence and Social Change* (London, 1992).

Dobrowsolsky, A., 'Shifting States: Women's Constitutional Organizing Across Time and Space' in L.A. Banaszak, K. Beckwith and D. Rucht (eds), *Women's Movements Facing the Reconfigured State* (Cambridge, 2003).

Donnelly, M., *1960s Britain: Culture, Society and Politics* (Harlow, 2005).

Evans, S.M., *Born for Liberty: A History of Women in America* (New York, 1997).

Ewan, E., Innes, S., Reyonlds, S. and Pipes, R. (eds), *The Biographical Dictionary of Scottish Women* (Edinburgh, 2006).

Fairbairns, Z., 'Saying What We Want: Women's Liberation and the Seven Demands' in Z. Fairbairns, H. Graham, A. Neilson, E. Robertson and A. Kaloski (eds), *Saying What We Want: Women's Demands in the Feminist 1970s and Now* (York, 2002).

Galford, E. and Wilson, K., *Rainbow City: Stories from Lesbian, Gay, Bisexual and Transgender Edinburgh* (Edinburgh, 2006).

Geiger, S., 'What's So Feminist About Doing Women's Oral History?' in C. Johnson-Odim and M. Strobel (eds), *Expanding the Boundaries of Women's History: Essays on Women in the Third World* (Bloomington, 1992).

Gelb, J., 'Feminism in Britain: Politics without Power?' in D. Dahlerup (ed.), *The New Women's Movement: Feminism and Political Power in Europe and the USA* (London, 1986).

German, L., *Material Girls: Women, Men and Work* (London, 2007).

Giardina, C., *Freedom for Women: Forging the Women's Liberation Movement, 1953–1970* (Gainesville, 2010).

Gilmore, S., *Groundswell: Grassroots Feminism in Postwar America* (New York, 2013).

Gleadle, K., *British Women in the Nineteenth Century* (Basingstoke, 2001).

Gordon, E., 'The Family' in L. Abrams, E. Gordon, D. Simonton and E.J. Yeo (eds), *Gender in Scottish History* (Edinburgh, 2006).

Green, A. and Troup, K., *The Houses of History: A Critical Reader in Twentieth-Century History and Theory* (Manchester, 1999).

Green, J., *All Dressed Up – The 1960s and the Counterculture* (London, 1998).

Greenan, L., Volpp, L. and Christianson, A., 'Still a Long Fight Ahead – Edinburgh Rape Crisis Centre' in S. Henderson and A. Mackay (eds), *Grit and Diamonds: Women in Scottish History 1980–1990* (Edinburgh, 1990).

Hamer, E., *Britannia's Glory: A History of Twentieth-Century Lesbians* (London, 1996).

Henderson, S and Mackay, A. (eds), *Grit and Diamonds: Women in Scotland Making History 1980–1990* (Edinburgh, 1990).

Heron, L., *Truth, Dare or Promise – Girls Growing Up in the Fifties* (London, 1985).

Hewitt, N.A., 'Introduction' in N.A. Hewitt (ed.), *No Permanent Waves: Recasting Histories of U.S. Feminism* (New Brunswick, 2010).

Hill, M. and Ward, M., 'Conflicting Rights: The Struggle for Female Citizenship in Northern Ireland' in E. Breitenbach and P. Thane (eds), *Women and Citizenship in Britain and Ireland in the Twentieth Century: What Difference Did the Vote Make?* (London, 2010).

Hobsbawm, E., *Age of Extremes: The Short Twentieth Century, 1914–1994* (London, 1994).

Holdsworth, A., *Out of the Doll's House: The Story of Women in the Twentieth Century* (London, 1988).

Hughes, A., *Gender and Political Identities in Scotland, 1919–1939* (Edinburgh, 2010).

King, E., 'Review of J.D. Young's *Women and Popular Struggles*' in S. Henderson and A. Mackay (eds), *Grit and Diamonds: Women in Scotland Making History 1980–1990* (Edinburgh, 1990).

Lent, A., *British Social Movements since 1945: Sex, Colour, Peace and Power* (Basingstoke, 2001).

Lewis, J., 'From Equality to Liberation: Contextualising the Emergence of the Women's Liberation Movement' in B. Moore-Gilbert and J. Seed (eds), *Cultural Revolution?: The Challenge of the Arts in the 1960s* (London, 1992).

Lewis, J., 'Marriage' in I. Zweiniger-Bargielowska (ed.), *Women in Twentieth Century Britain* (Harlow, 2001).

Lewis, J., *Women in England 1870–1950: Sexual Divisions and Social Change* (Brighton, 1984).

Lovenduski, J., 'Parliament, Pressure Groups, Networks and the Women's Movements: The Politics of Abortion Law Reform in Britain (1967–83)', in J. Lovenduski and J. Outshoorn (eds), *The New Politics of Abortion* (London, 1986).

Lovenduski, J. and Randall, V., *Contemporary Feminist Politics: Women and Power in Britain* (Oxford, 1993).

Mackay, F., 'The Case of Zero Tolerance: Women's Politics in Action?' in E. Breitenbach and F. Mackay (eds), *Women and Contemporary Scottish Politics: An Anthology* (Edinburgh, 2001).

Mackay, F., 'The State of Women's Movements in Britain: Ambiguity, Complexity and Challenges from the Periphery' in S. Grey and M. Sawer (eds), *Women's Movements: Flourishing or in Abeyance?* (London, 2008).

Macleod, J., Bell, P. and Forman, J., 'Bridging the Gap: Feminist Development Work in Glasgow' in E. Breitenbach and F. Mackay (eds), *Women and Contemporary Scottish Politics: An Anthology* (Edinburgh, 2001).

Maitland, E., *Woman to Woman: An Oral History of Rape Crisis in Scotland 1976–1991* (Glasgow, 2009).

Manon, E., 'Women's Rights and Catholicism in Ireland' in M. Threlfall (ed.), *Mapping the Women's Movement: Feminist Politics and Social Transformation in the North* (London, 1996).

Marwick, A., *British Society Since 1945* (London, 1990).

Marwick, A., *The 1960s – Cultural Revolution in Britain, France, Italy and the United States c.1958–c. 1974* (Oxford, 1998).

McChlery, A., 'Our Bodies, Our Lives, Our Right to Decide!' in A. Henderson and S. Mackay (eds), *Grit and Diamonds: Women in Scotland Making History 1980–1990* (Edinburgh, 1990).

McCrindle, J. and Rowbotham, S., *Dutiful Daughters: Women Talk about Their Lives* (Harmondsworth, 1983).

McGarvey, N. and Cairney, P., *Scottish Politics: An Introduction* (Basingstoke, 2008).

McLeod, H., *The Religious Crisis of the 1960s* (London, 2009).

McQuiston, L., *Suffragettes to She-Devils – Women's Liberation and Beyond* (London, 1997).

Meehan, E., 'British Feminism from the 1960s to the 1980s' in H.L. Smith (ed.), *British Feminism in the Twentieth Century* (Aldershot, 1990).

Merz, C., *After the Vote: The Story of the National Union of Townswomen's Guilds in the Year of Its Diamond Jubilee* (Norwich, 1988).

Myer, D.S., 'Restating the Woman Question – Women's Movements and State Restructing' in L.A. Banaszak, K. Beckwith and D. Rucht (eds), *Women's Movements Facing the Reconfigured State* (Cambridge, 2003).

Passerini, L., 'Work Ideology and Consensus under Italian Fascism' in R. Perks and A. Thomson (eds), *The Oral History Reader* (London, 1998).

Perks, R. and Thomson, A., 'Introduction' in R. Perks and A. Thomson (eds), *The Oral History Reader* (London, 1998).

Pilcher, J., *Women in Contemporary Britain – An Introduction* (London, 1999).

Pizzey, E., *This Way to the Revolution: A Memoir* (London, 2011).

Portelli, A, 'What Makes Oral History Different' in R. Perks and A. Thomson (eds), *The Oral History Reader* (London, 1998).

Pugh, M., *Women and the Women's Movement in Britain 1914–1999* (Basingstoke, 2000).

Rafeek, N.C., *Communist Women in Scotland – Red Clydeside from the Russian Revolution to the End of the Soviety Union* (London, 2008).

'Redstockings', 'Manifesto' in R. Baxandall and L. Gordon (eds), *Dear Sisters: Dispatches from the Women's Liberation Movement* (New York, 2000).

Roberts, M., *Paper Houses: A Memoir of the '70s and Beyond* (London, 2007).

Robinson, L., *Gay Men and the Left in Postwar Britain: How the Personal Got Political* (Manchester, 2007).

Roseneil, S., *Common Women, Uncommon Practices: The Queer Feminisms of Greenham* (London, 2000).

Rowbotham, S., *A Century of Women: The History of Women in Britain and the United States* (London, 1999).

Rowbotham, S., 'Introduction: Mapping the Women's Movement' in M. Threlfall (ed.), *Mapping the Women's Movement: Feminist Politics and Social Transformation in the North* (London, 1996).

Rowbotham, S., *Promise of a Dream: Remembering the 1960s* (London, 2001).

Rowbotham, S., *The Past Is Before Us: Feminism in Social Action since the 1960s* (London, 1990).

Rowbotham, S., *Women in Movement: Feminism and Social Action* (London, 1992).

Sandbrook, D., *Seasons in the Sun: The Battle for Britain 1974–1979* (London, 2012).

Sandbrook, D., *State of Emergency: The Way We Were: Britain 1970–1974* (London, 2010).

Sawer, M. and Grey, S., 'Introduction' in S. Grey and M. Sawer (eds), *Women's Movements: Flourishing or in Abeyance?* (London, 2008).

Segal, L., *Is the Future Female? Troubled Thoughts on Contemporary Feminism* (London, 1987).

Segal, L., *Why Feminism? Gender, Psychology, Politics* (Cambridge, 1999).

Sharpe, S., *Just Like a Girl – How Girls Learn to Be Women – From the 1970s to the Nineties* (London, 1994).

Sounes, H., *1970s: The Sights, Sounds and Ideas of a Brilliant Decade* (London, 2007).

Spender, D., *There's Always Been a Women's Movement This Century* (London, 1993).

Steedman, C., *Landscape for a Good Woman: A Story of Two Lives* (New Brunswick, 1987).

Summerfield, P., *Reconstructing Women's Wartime Lives: Discourse and Subjectivity in Oral Histories of the Second World War* (Manchester, 1998).

Summerfield, P., 'The Women's Movement in Britain from the 1860s to the 1980s' in T. Cosslett, A. Easton and P. Summerfield (eds), *Women, Power and Resistance: An Introduction to Women's Studies* (Buckingham, 1996).

Taylor, V. and Rupp, L.J., 'Preface' in S. Grey and M. Sawer (eds), *Women's Movement: Flourishing or in Abeyance?* (London, 2008).

Threlfall, M., 'Conclusion' in M. Threlfall (ed.), *Mapping the Women's Movement: Feminist Politics and Social Transformation in the North* (London, 1996).

Turner, M., *The Women's Century: A Celebration of Changing Roles* (Kew, 2003).

Wandor, M., *Once a Feminist: Stories of a Generation* (London, 1990).

Whelehan, I., *Modern Feminist Thought: From the Second Wave to 'Post-Feminism'* (Edinburgh, 1995).

Winterson, J., *Why Be Happy When You Could Be Normal?* (London, 2012).

Wolf, N., *Fire with Fire: The New Female Power and How It Will Change the Twenty-First Century* (London, 1994).

Wolfe, L. R. and Tucker, J., 'Feminism Lives: Building a Multicultural Women's Movement in the United States' in A. Basu (ed.), *The Challenge of Local Feminisms: Women's Movements in Global Perspective* (Oxford, 1995).

Young, J.D., *Women and Popular Struggles: A History of Scottish and English Working Class Women 1500–1984* (Edinburgh, 1985).

Journal articles

Abrams, L., '"There was nobody like my daddy": Fathers, the Family and the Marginalisation of Men in Modern Scotland', *The Scottish Historical Review*, LXXVIII, 2:206 (1999), pp. 219–42.

Beaumont, C., 'Citizens Not Feminists: The Boundary Negotiated between Citizenship and Feminism by Mainstream Women's Organisations in England, 1928–1939', *Women's History Review*, 9:2 (2000), pp. 411–29.

Breitenbach, E., 'Scottish Feminism in Print', *Cencrastis*, 21 (Summer 1985), pp. 45–7.

Browne, S., '"A Veritable Hotbed of Feminism": Women's Liberation in St Andrews, Scotland c.1968–c. 1979', *Twentieth Century British History*, 23:1 (2012), pp. 100–23.

Caine, B., 'Feminist Biography and Feminist History', *Women's History Review*, 3:2 (1994), pp. 247–61.

Hill, M., 'Lessons and Legacies: Feminist Activism in the North c.1970–2000', *Women's Studies Review*, 9 (2004).

Issac, J., 'The Politics of Morality in the UK', *Parliamentary Affairs*, 47:2 (1994), pp. 175–89.

Lockyer, B., 'An Irregular Period? Participation in the Bradford Women's Liberation Movement', *Women's History Review*, 22:4 (2013), pp. 643–57.

Millns, S. and Thompson, B., 'Constructing British Abortion Law: The Role of the Legislature, Judiciary and European Institutions', *Parliamentary Affairs*, 47:2 (1994), pp. 190–202.

Read, M.D., 'The Pro-Life Movement', *Parliamentary Affairs*, 51:3 (1998), pp. 445–57.

Rees, J., 'A Look Back At Anger: The Women's Liberation Movement in 1978', *Women's History Review*, 19:3 (2010), pp.337–56.

Rees, J., '"Are You a Lesbian?": Challenges in Recording and Analysing the

Women's Liberation Movement in England', *History Workshop Journal*, 69 (Spring 2010), pp. 177–87.

Sangster, J., 'Gendering Labour History Across Borders', *Labour History Review*, 75:2 (August 2010), pp. 143–61.

Sangster, J., 'Telling our Stories: Feminist Debates and the Use of Oral History', *Women's History Review*, 3:1 (1994), pp. 5–27.

Segal, L., 'Slow Change or No Change?: Feminism, Socialism and the Problem of Men', *Feminist Review*, 31 (Spring 1989), pp. 5–21.

Setch, E., 'The Face of Metropolitan Feminism: The London Women's Liberation Workshop, 1969–79', *Twentieth Century British History*, 13:2 (2002), pp. 171–90.

Summerfield, P., 'Culture and Composure: Creating Narratives of the Gendered Self in Oral History Interviews', *Cultural and Social History*, I (2004), pp. 65–93.

Thomlinson, N., 'The Colour of Feminism: White Feminists and Race in the Women's Liberation Movement', *History*, 97:237 (2012), pp. 453–75.

Thompson, B., 'Problems of Abortion in Britain – Aberdeen, a Case Study', *Population Studies*, 31:1 (March 1977), pp. 143–54.

Weir, A. and Wilson, E., 'The British Women's Movement', *New Left Review*, 148 (November–December 1984), pp. 74–103.

Unpublished secondary sources

Conference papers

Beaumont, C., 'The Personal Is Political: Voluntary Women's Organisations and Political Campaigning in the Postwar Years', 'Women in British Politics', University of Lincoln, 6–7 May 2011.

Breitenbach, E., 'Feminist Politics and Devolution in Scotland', Colloque Franco-Britannique, Lyon, March 2007.

Dissertations and theses

Bartie, A., 'Festival City: The Arts, Culture and Moral Conflict in Edinburgh 1947–1967' (unpublished PhD thesis, University of Dundee, 2006).

Browne, S.F. '"Dreary Committee Work": The Work of Established Women's Groups in the North East of Scotland, c.1960– c.1970' (unpublished MLitt thesis, University of Dundee, 2006).

Hogg, J.L., 'How Did the Church of Scotland React to the Change in Women's Rights in the 1950s and 1960s?' (unpublished MA dissertation, University of Dundee, 2009).

Rees, J., 'All the Rage: Revolutionary Feminism in England, 1977–1983' (unpublished PhD thesis, University of Western Australia, 2007).

Setch, E., 'The Women's Liberation Movement in Britain, 1969–79: Organisation, Creativity and Debate' (unpublished PhD thesis, University of London, Royal Holloway, 2000).

Wright., V. 'Women's Organisations and Feminism in Interwar Scotland' (unpublished PhD thesis, University of Glasgow, 2008).

Internet resources

www.abortionrights.org.uk
www.feministarchivenorth.org.uk/chronology/appendixi.htm
www.guardian.co.uk/society/2011/may/15/slutwalk-debate-sexual-discrimination
www.opsi.gov.uk/acts/acts1967/pdf/ukpga_19670087_en.pdf
www.rapecrisisscotland.org.uk/news.htm
www.rapecrisisscotland.org.uk/rcs.php?fileid=news_nov_2003.htm
www.sussex.ac.uk/clhlwr/research/sisterhoodafter

Index

Lightning Source UK Ltd.
Milton Keynes UK
UKOW03f1313240517

301903UK00002B/416/P